ACCOUNTING HANDBOOK AND STUDY GUIDE™

A Comprehensive Accounting Reference Book

Covers the Fundamentals of Accounting and Complements the Material in any Class Text

Grades 8 to 12 and Beyond

SIMEON MANTEL

FOREWORD

STUDENTS

The Accounting Handbook and Study Guide covers every aspect of the school Accounting curriculum for Grades 8–12. It is a comprehensive reference book that will accompany you throughout your High School years. This book should be used in conjunction with a grade-appropriate Accounting text book.

The presentation is simple, logical and colour-coded for easy understanding and recall. Through constant usage, the information will become familiar and will be retained, unlike photocopied notes, which are usually discarded at the end of each year.

TEACHERS

The Accounting Handbook and Study Guide will provide a ready-made, user-friendly scheme of work. It is not meant to be used in isolation, but rather in conjunction with regular lessons and grade-appropriate text books.

The fundamentals of Accounting do not change as Students progress through the High School curriculum, and they will be able to use this book as a constant source of reference. You will therefore be able to focus on teaching using practical examples, without having to stop for extensive revision, note-taking or lengthy explanations each time.

ABOUT THE AUTHOR

Simeon is passionate about Accounting and is a constant learner himself. He discovered his passion for teaching in Grade 8 and tutored students throughout High School. He went on to become a teaching assistant at University, where he taught Financial and Cost Accounting. Simeon completed a Bachelors Degree in Accounting at Northeastern State University in the US and a Masters Degree in Financial Economics at Erasmus University in Holland.

After graduating, he joined Deloitte & Touche in Holland. During his time there he was often required to present complex problems to his clients in an easy-to-understand manner. Simeon has applied this same approach to the writing of the Accounting Handbook and Study Guide.

More recently Simeon started Tutors24, which has provided online support to over 150 000 High School students. He also works closely with publishers to develop educational content.

Simeon has gained valuable Accounting knowledge over the years and works closely with Educators, Accountants and Professionals. With this book, Simeon aims to provide learners with an all-in-one guide that is an essential reference for Grades 8–12 and even for first year Tertiary students who have not studied Accounting at school.

Simeon has recently relocated to Cape Town and is enjoying discovering the city on his bicycle.

ACKNOWLEDGEMENTS

I would like to thank all the Students, Teachers and Professionals who provided me with continuous feedback during the writing of this book. A special thanks must be made to the following people: Christine A. Oosthuizen (NPDE (Wits)) and Anzel Harmse (B.Ed Hons Curriculum Studies (UJ)), who have decades of teaching experience between them, and who were rigorous in working through all our examples and making sure that the curriculum has been fully covered; Janice Kellman (BCom (Unisa)) who used her daily experience from tutoring students to highlight the areas that learners tend to struggle with, and who contributed helpful additions to the text; Lynne Owen-Smith (BSc Hons (Wits)), who I could bounce ideas off on a daily basis, and for language editing and support. Last but not least, many thanks must go to Beryl Lutrin (BA (Wits) H.Dip.Ed (JCE)) who played a key role in editing and proofreading, but who, above all, inspired my writing and made this book possible.

ACCOUNTING HANDBOOK AND STUDY GUIDE
SUMMARY OF CONTENTS

FOREWORD		2
A **INTRODUCTION**		4—7
B **FINANCIAL ACCOUNTING**		8—215
	1. Basic Concepts of Financial Accounting	8
	2. The Accounting Cycle	19
	3. Source Documents	25
	4. Journals	30
	5. Ledgers	55
	6. Trial Balance	83
	7. Financial Statements and Notes	86
	8. Analysis and Interpretation of Financial Statements [10]	105
	9. Year-End Procedures [10]	120
	10. Reconciliations [10]	134
	11. GAAP and IFRS [10]	152
	12. Inventory [10]	154
	13. Fixed Assets	166
	14. VAT [10]	175
	15. Partnerships [11]	182
	16. Non-Profit Companies (Clubs) [11]	190
	17. Closed Corporations [12]	200
	18. Companies [12]	203
	19. Analysis of Published Financial Statements [12]	212
C **MANAGERIAL ACCOUNTING**		216—256
	1. Ethics [10]	216
	2. Internal Control [10]	221
	3. Budgeting [10]	226
	4. Cost Accounting [11]	235
D **GLOSSARY OF ACCOUNTING TERMS**		256—262

INTRODUCTION
SUMMARY OF CONTENTS

A OVERVIEW OF FINANCIAL ACCOUNTING AND MANAGERIAL ACCOUNTING **5**

B A CLOSER LOOK AT BUSINESSES **6**

    1. Types of businesses **6**

        a. Service Business

        b. Trading Business

        c. Manufacturing Business

    2. Ownership of a business **6**

        a. Non-Profit Company (NPC)

        b. For-Profit Businesses

C OVERVIEW OF THE DIFFERENT FORMS OF FOR-PROFIT BUSINESSES **7**

INTRODUCTION

Accounting is known as the language of business.
Accounting allows us to **gather, record, summarise, analyse** and **report** all of the financial activities of a business.

A. OVERVIEW OF FINANCIAL ACCOUNTING AND MANAGERIAL ACCOUNTING

Accounting is separated into Financial Accounting and Managerial Accounting.

	FINANCIAL ACCOUNTING	MANAGERIAL ACCOUNTING
AIM	To prepare **Financial Statements** to accurately summarise the financial information of a business	To provide **useful information** that helps a business to plan and make decisions
USERS	**External**: Governments, Banks, Credit Lenders and Shareholders	**Internal**: Owners, Managers, Employees
PREPARATION	• Must comply with various standards • Prepared in accordance with **G**enerally **A**ccepted **A**ccounting **P**rinciples (**GAAP**) and **I**nternational **F**inancial **R**eporting **S**tandards (**IFRS**)	• No need to comply with standards • Prepared according to what managers request
DOCUMENTS	Financial Statements	Internal Reports
DETAILS	Summarised information	Detailed information
REPORTS	Prepared quarterly and annually	Prepared whenever requested, or on a monthly basis
FOCUS	All aspects of the business	Specific information requested by different departments of the business at different times
TIME PERIOD	Activities that have already taken place (in the past)	Activities that have already taken place (in the past), or that are expected to happen (in the future)

B. A CLOSER LOOK AT BUSINESSES

Businesses can be classified according to what they do and how they have been formed.

1. **TYPES OF BUSINESSES**
   Businesses can be classified into one of three different groups based on what they do.

   a. **Service Business**
      The business provides a service for a fee.
      i. Mark tutors Grade 10 learners in Life Sciences. He charges a fee of R180/hour for his services.
      ii. Deloitte Auditing Company charges companies a fee to audit their Accounts.

   b. **Trading Business** Also known as a Retail business.
      The business buys products and then sells them for a Profit.
      i. Thandi buys oranges from a farm close to her house and sells them at a higher price in her spaza shop.
      ii. Edgars buys clothes from suppliers and sells them in their stores across the country.

   c. **Manufacturing Business**
      The business produces and sells products.
      i. Thabo produces giraffes out of beads and metal and sells them to gift shops.
      ii. Apple manufactures Iphones and sells them to retail businesses.

    There are also businesses that fall into more than one category. E.g. a hairdresser cuts hair (Service Business) and sells hair products (Trading Business).

2. **OWNERSHIP OF A BUSINESS**
   The main aim of a business is either to benefit society (Non-Profit Company) or to make a Profit (For-Profit Business).

   a. **Non-Profit Company (NPC)**
      Non-Profit Companies are businesses formed to benefit society.
      Any Profit made is used to achieve the organisation's goals rather than being paid out to the Owners. One of the main benefits offered to NPCs is that they **do not** have to pay **Income Tax** or **VAT (Value-Added Tax)**.
      i. Doctors without Borders is an organisation that provides free medical assistance across the world.
      ii. The NSPCA is an organisation that takes care of abandoned animals.

   b. **For-Profit Businesses**
      Most businesses aim to make a Profit and will therefore fall under this category.
      There are **five forms of ownership** for businesses that aim to make a Profit.
      There are also other forms of ownership that are not covered in the school curriculum; e.g. Trusts.

C. OVERVIEW OF THE DIFFERENT FORMS OF FOR-PROFIT BUSINESSES

It is important to understand the advantages and disadvantages of each form of ownership when forming a business.

	SOLE TRADER [8][9][10]	PARTNERSHIP [11]	CLOSED CORPORATION [12]	PRIVATE COMPANY [12]	PUBLIC COMPANY [12]
NAME ENDING	--	--	CC	Proprietary Limited (Pty) Ltd	Limited (Ltd)
SET-UP	Easy	Easy	Easy – however the setting up of new CCs is no longer allowed	Expensive – requiring a Memorandum of Incorporation	Expensive – requiring a Memorandum of Incorporation
OWNERS	Only 1 Owner	2—20 Partners	1—10 Members	Limited to 50 Shareholders	7 to an unlimited number of Shareholders
LEGAL ENTITY	Not recognised as a separate legal entity – Owner's affairs combined with the business	Not recognised as a separate legal entity – Owners' affairs combined with the business	Recognised as a separate legal entity – Owners' affairs are separate	Recognised as a separate legal entity – Owners' affairs are separate	Recognised as a separate legal entity – Owners' affairs are separate
LIABILITY	Owner is liable for all the business's debts	Partners are liable for all the business's debts	Limited Liability – Members not liable for all the business's debts	Limited Liability – Shareholders not liable for all the business's debts	Limited Liability – Shareholders not liable for all the business's debts
CONTINUITY	No continuity – the business does not continue to exist if the Owner dies	No continuity – the business does not continue to exist if one Partner dies	Continuity – the business continues to exist if one Member dies	Continuity – the business continues to exist if one Shareholder dies	Continuity – the business continues to exist if one Shareholder dies
CONTROL OF BUSINESS	Decisions made by the Owner	Decisions made by all or some Partners	Decisions made by all or some Members	Decisions made by one or more Directors	Decisions made by three or more Directors
INCOME TAX	Owner pays Income Tax on the Profit received from the business	Partners pay Income Tax on the Profit received from the Partnership	• CC pays 28% Income Tax on Net Profit • Members pay 20% on Dividends received	• Company pays 28% Income Tax on Net Profit • Shareholders pay 20% on Dividends received	• Company pays 28% Income Tax on Net Profit • Shareholders pay 20% on Dividends received
CAPITAL Assets contributed to start the business	Only the Owner can contribute Capital	All Partners can contribute Capital	All Members can contribute Capital	Business issues Shares privately to raise Capital	Business issues Shares publicly to raise Capital
COMPLEXITY OF BOOKKEEPING	Low	Medium	Medium	High	High

© Berlut Books CC

FINANCIAL ACCOUNTING

BASIC CONCEPTS OF FINANCIAL ACCOUNTING
SUMMARY OF CONTENTS

A **FIVE BASIC ACCOUNT TYPES** .... 9—10
    1. Asset Accounts 9
        a. Current Asset Accounts
        b. Non-Current Asset Accounts
    2. Owner's Equity Accounts 9
    3. Liability Accounts 9
        a. Current Liability Accounts
        b. Non-Current Liability Accounts
    4. Income Accounts 9
    5. Expense Accounts .... 9—10

B **ACCOUNTING EQUATION** 11
    1. The Accounting Equation using T Accounts
    2. The effects of transactions on the Accounting Equation

C **DOUBLE-ENTRY SYSTEM** .... 12—14
    1. Increasing and decreasing the balance of an Account 12
    2. Recording a transaction using Debits and Credits 13
        a. General Steps to record a transaction
        b. Transactions that affect more than two Accounts .... 13—14

D **COMMON TRANSACTIONS** .... 14—18
    1. Transactions by an Owner 14
        a. Capital 14
        b. Drawings 15
    2. Paying cash for Expenses/Assets and receiving cash for Income earned 15
        a. Paying for Assets and Expenses with cash
        b. Receiving cash for Income earned 16
    3. Credit Transactions 16
        a. Selling Inventory on credit
        b. Purchasing items on credit 17

BASIC CONCEPTS OF FINANCIAL ACCOUNTING

Bookkeeping is the process of recording the financial information of a business.
Businesses classify and record financial information in a **standardised** way.
- **Five basic Account types** are used to classify financial information.
- The **Accounting Equation** shows the relationship between Assets, Liabilities and Owner's Equity. The Accounting Equation is the foundation on which Double-Entry Accounting is based.
- The **Double-Entry** Bookkeeping System is used by bookkeepers to record financial information.

A. FIVE BASIC ACCOUNT TYPES

Five basic Account types are used to classify financial information.

1. **ASSET ACCOUNTS**
   Asset Accounts show items that have value and are owned by the business.
   Asset Accounts can be further divided into Current Asset Accounts and Non-Current Asset Accounts.
   a. **Current Asset Accounts (< 1 year)**
      The business expects to receive cash for the Assets **within one year.**
      Bank Account, Trading Stock Account, Debtors Control Account
   b. **Non-Current Assets Accounts (> 1 year)**
      The business expects to keep the Assets for **longer than one year.**
      Equipment Account, Vehicles Account, Land and Buildings Account, Fixed Deposit Account
      Non-Current Assets can be further divided into Fixed Assets and Financial Assets.

2. **OWNER'S EQUITY ACCOUNTS**
   Owner's Equity Accounts show the value of the Assets that belong to the Owner(s) of the business.
   An Owner can increase Owner's Equity by contributing Assets to the business (this is known as **Capital**) and can decrease Owner's Equity by taking Assets out of the business (this is known as **Drawings**).
   Income increases Owner's Equity and Expenses decrease Owner's Equity.
   Owner's Equity = Assets — Liabilities

3. **LIABILITY ACCOUNTS**
   Liability Accounts show amounts the business must pay.
   Liability Accounts can be further divided into Current Liability Accounts and Non-Current Liability Accounts.
   a. **Current Liability Accounts (< 1 year)**
      The business has **less** than **one year** to pay the amount owed.
      Creditors Control Account
   b. **Non-Current Liability Accounts (> 1 year)**
      The business has **more** than **one year** to pay the amount owed.
      Loan Account, Mortgage Bond Account

4. **INCOME ACCOUNTS**
   Income Accounts show the amounts the business earns.
   - The main Income Account of a Service Business is the **Current Income Account**, which is used to record the amounts earned from services.
   - The main Income Account of a Trading Business is the **Sales Account**, which is used to record the amounts earned from Inventory sold.
      Sales Account, Current Income Account, Interest Income Account, Rent Income Account

5. **EXPENSE ACCOUNTS**
   Expense Accounts show the costs of running the business.
   Interest Expense Account, Salaries and Wages Account, Cost of Sales Account, Advertising Account

EXAMPLES OF COMMON ACCOUNTS USED

Account names are created under each of the five basic Account types, to explain the different Accounts that are affected.

 Make sure that you know all the Accounts. You can write a list of all the Accounts that you deal with and ask your teacher to check that you have included everything.

1. ASSET ACCOUNTS	EXPLANATION
Land and Buildings	Cost Price of the land and buildings owned
Vehicles	Cost Price of the vehicles owned
Equipment	Cost Price of the equipment owned
Accumulated Depreciation (Negative Asset Account)	Total Depreciation recorded for each different type of Fixed Asset – there is a separate Accumulated Depreciation Account for each Fixed Asset (e.g. Vehicles and Equipment)
Trading Stock	Cost Price of the Inventory available to sell
Debtors Control	Amount owed to the business by Debtors/customers
Bank	Balance of cash available in the bank account
Petty Cash	Amount of Petty Cash available
Fixed Deposit	Amount of Fixed Deposit invested

2. OWNER'S EQUITY	EXPLANATION
Capital	Total amount owned/contributed by the Owner(s)
Drawings	Total amount of Assets (taken out of the business) by the Owner

3. LIABILITIES	EXPLANATION
Loan	Balance of a Loan owed
Creditors Control	Amount owed to Creditors
Bank Overdraft	Amount owed to the bank (this happens if there is a negative bank balance)

4. INCOME	EXPLANATION
Current Income	Amount earned from services
Sales	Amount earned from Inventory sold
Rent Income	Amount earned from rent
Discount Received	Discounts received from Creditors
Interest Income	Amount earned from interest other than on Fixed Deposits
Interest on Fixed Deposit	Amount of interest earned on Fixed Deposits

5. EXPENSES	EXPLANATION
Cost of Sales	Cost of Inventory sold
Salaries and Wages	Costs incurred from Salaries and Wages
Advertising	Costs incurred from advertising
Water and Electricity	Costs incurred from water and electricity
Telephone	Costs incurred for the telephone
Stationery	Costs incurred from stationery purchased
Maintenance	Costs incurred for maintenance
Discount Allowed	Discounts given to Debtors
Repairs	Costs incurred for repairs
Donations	Costs incurred for donations made
Insurance	Costs incurred for insurance
Depreciation	Costs of Depreciation on Assets

B. ACCOUNTING EQUATION

 Make sure you memorise the Accounting Equation!

The Accounting Equation shows the relationship between Assets, Owner's Equity and Liabilities.
All Assets are purchased either with money that belongs to the Owners (Owner's Equity), or by borrowing money (Liabilities). The total value of the Assets is always equal to the total Owner's Equity plus the total Liabilities.
(Left hand side = Right hand side)

Assets	=	Owner's Equity	+	Liabilities
The Assets of the business	=	What the Owners own	+	What the business owes someone else

1. The Accounting Equation using T Accounts
The Accounting Equation can also be shown using T Accounts.

These will be used throughout the book to show how Accounts are affected.

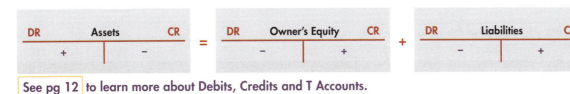

See pg 12 to learn more about Debits, Credits and T Accounts.

2. The effects of transactions on the Accounting Equation
The Accounting Equation can be used to show how transactions affect the Assets, Owner's Equity and Liability Accounts of a business.
The effects of Income and Expenses are shown under the Owner's Equity Account.
- Expense Accounts **decrease** Owner's Equity (on the Debit side).
- Income Accounts **increase** Owner's Equity (on the Credit side).

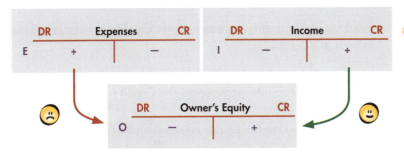

Notice that the effects of Expenses and Income are recorded under Owner's Equity in the Accounting Equation.

WEISS TRADERS purchases a new vehicle for R400 000 cash.
Always indicate no effect with a 0.

DEBIT	CREDIT	ASSETS	OWNER'S EQUITY	LIABILITIES
Vehicles Account	Bank Account	+ 400 000 − 400 000	0	0

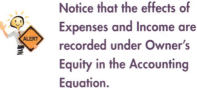

BICKSY PLUMBERS pays R800 for water and electricity.

DEBIT	CREDIT	ASSETS	OWNER'S EQUITY	LIABILITIES
Water and Electricity Account	Bank Account	− 800	− 800	0

C. DOUBLE-ENTRY SYSTEM

The **Double-Entry System** is used to record financial information.
The effects of a transaction are recorded by showing increases or decreases in the Accounts of the business.
This is called the **Double-Entry System** because a transaction always affects at least two Accounts in the business.
In Accounting, a transaction is anything that affects the Financial Position (wealth) of a business.

1. INCREASING AND DECREASING THE BALANCE OF AN ACCOUNT
Two columns are drawn under an Account to form a T.
The left hand side is known as the **Debit (DR)** side and the right hand side is known as the **Credit (CR)** side.
An amount is entered on either the **Debit (left)** side of an Account or the **Credit (right)** side of an Account, to increase or decrease the Account. Each Account increases or decreases on a specific side.

 Make sure you memorise the table below!

ACCOUNT	EXPLANATION
A — Assets: DR + / CR −	**A**sset Accounts **increase** on the **Debit** side and decrease on the Credit side.
O — Owner's Equity: DR − / CR +	**O**wner's Equity Accounts **increase** on the **Credit** side and decrease on the Debit side.
L — Liability: DR − / CR +	**L**iability Accounts **increase** on the **Credit** side and decrease on the Debit side.
I — Income: DR − / CR +	**I**ncome Accounts **increase** on the **Credit** side and decrease on the Debit side. Notice that Owner's Equity increases on the Credit side. Income makes the Owner happy.
E — Expense: DR + / CR −	**E**xpense Accounts **increase** on the **Debit** side and decrease on the Credit side. Notice that Owner's Equity decreases on the Debit side. Expenses make the Owner sad.

TIP TO REMEMBER ON WHICH SIDES TO INCREASE AND DECREASE ACCOUNTS

Make sure you know which sides are Debit and Credit and which sides to use to increase or decrease each Account.

You can use "**D**octor **C**rab" to remember which side is Debit (left) and which side is Credit (right):
- **D**ebit (Dr) is the left side and **C**redit (Cr) is the right side.

You can use **DAE COIL** to remember which side an Account increases on:
- **D**ebit **A**ssets and **E**xpenses to increase the Accounts.
- **C**redit **O**wner's Equity, **I**ncome and **L**iabilities to increase the Accounts.

2. RECORDING A TRANSACTION USING DEBITS AND CREDITS

Every transaction has at least one Debit and one Credit entry.  Never forget this!
The total amount of Debit entries must be equal to the total amount of Credit entries.

a. **General Steps to record a transaction**

ii. **Identify which Accounts are affected by the transaction.** See pg 10 for a list of common Accounts.
There are always at least two Accounts affected by a transaction.

iii. **Determine which basic Account each Account is classified under and on which sides (Debit or Credit) to record the amounts.** See pg 12 for the sides on which Accounts increase and decrease.
Each Account can be classified as an **A**sset, **O**wner's Equity, **L**iability, **I**ncome or **E**xpense Account.

Show the Accounts of BC COMPUTER SERVICES that are affected by the transactions below.

1. Received R4 000 cash for a computer service provided to the client

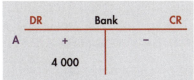

2. Paid R1 500 cash for the monthly Telephone Account

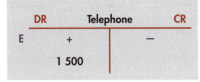

---

b. **Transactions that affect more than two Accounts**
Some transactions will affect more than two Accounts.
Remember that the total amount of the Debit entries recorded must always equal the total amount of the Credit entries recorded.

A common transaction that affects more than two Accounts:
More than two Accounts are affected when a Trading Business sells Inventory.
Inventory is the name given to the products that a business sells.
This is also known as **Trading Stock**, **Items**, **Goods** or **Stock**.
The Profit is the difference between the price that the Inventory is sold for and the cost of the Inventory.
Profit = Selling Price − Cost Price

A business adds a percentage to the cost of the Inventory to determine the Selling Price of the Inventory.
The percentage that is added to the Cost Price is known as the **Percentage Mark-Up**.
Selling Price = Cost Price ÷ 100 × (100 + mark-up)

Important Formulas Memorise these!

- **Profit = Selling Price − Cost Price**

- **Selling Price = Cost Price ÷ 100 × (100 + mark-up)** or **Selling Price = Cost Price × $\frac{100 + \text{mark-up}}{100}$**

- **Cost Price = Selling Price × 100 ÷ (100 + mark-up)** or **Cost Price = Selling Price × $\frac{100}{100 + \text{mark-up}}$**

BM STATIONERY sells 5 pens for R100 cash (each pen costs R20). The pens are marked up at 25%.

Accounts that are affected by this transaction
- The **Bank Account** records the amount of cash received.
- The **Sales Account** records the amount of Income earned from the sale of Inventory.
- The **Cost of Sales Account** records the Cost Price of the Inventory sold.
- The **Trading Stock Account** records the decrease in the balance of Inventory available to sell.

Cost Price of the Inventory sold
Cost Price = Selling Price × 100 ÷ (100 + mark-up)
Cost Price = 100 × 100 ÷ (100 + 25)
Cost Price = 100 × 100 ÷ (125)
Cost Price = 80

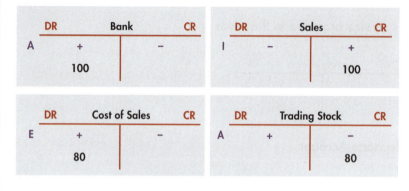

D. COMMON TRANSACTIONS

Certain transactions occur often.
The effect on the Accounts and on the Accounting Equation are shown for the most common transactions.

1. TRANSACTIONS BY AN OWNER
An Owner can invest Assets (Capital) into a business or take Assets (Drawings) out of a business.

a. Capital
An Owner can contribute Assets to the business. This is known as a **Capital** contribution.

LEBO contributes R20 000 cash to start her business.

DEBIT	CREDIT	ASSETS	OWNER'S EQUITY	LIABILITIES
Bank Account	Capital Account	+ 20 000	+ 20 000	0

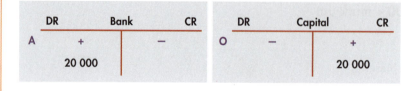

b. **Drawings**
   An Owner can take Assets out of the business. This is known as **Drawings**.

NTOMBI decides to take R2 000 cash out of her business.

DEBIT	CREDIT	ASSETS	OWNER'S EQUITY	LIABILITIES
Drawings Account	Bank Account	− 2 000	− 2 000	0

	DR	Drawings	CR		DR	Bank	CR
O	−		+	A	+		−
	2 000						2 000

---

2. PAYING CASH FOR EXPENSES/ASSETS AND RECEIVING CASH FROM INCOME EARNED
Paying and receiving cash are the most common transactions that are recorded by a business.
The Bank Account is used to show an increase (Debit side) or decrease (Credit side) in the cash available to the business.

a. **Paying for Assets and Expenses with cash**
   A business often pays for Assets and Expenses with cash.
   Paying with cash does not only refer to paying with physical cash (notes and coins).
   A Business can pay cash using Cheques, Debit Cards, Credit Cards or by transferring the cash online (EFT).
   In the school curriculum, the assumption is that most cash payments are made using **Cheques**.
   These days, most businesses do not use Cheques. Cash payments are usually made with **Debit Cards, Credit Cards or online transfers (EFTs)**. 💡

NABILA pays R5 000 at the end of the month for the rent of her shop.

DEBIT	CREDIT	ASSETS	OWNER'S EQUITY	LIABILITIES
Rent Expense Account	Bank Account	− 5 000	− 5 000	0

	DR	Rent Expense	CR		DR	Bank	CR
E	+		−	A	+		−
	5 000						5 000

TOM pays R3 000 cash for a new printer for his business.

DEBIT	CREDIT	ASSETS	OWNER'S EQUITY	LIABILITIES
Equipment Account	Bank Account	+ 3 000 − 3 000	0	0

	DR	Equipment	CR		DR	Bank	CR
A	+		−	A	+		−
	3 000						3 000

b. **Receiving cash for Income earned**
   A business can sell services or Inventory for cash.
   Receiving cash does not only refer to receiving physical cash (notes and coins).
   A Business can also receive cash when the customer pays with a Cheque, Debit Card, Credit Card or by transferring the cash online (EFT).

N&S ATTORNEYS receives R8 000 cash for services rendered.

DEBIT	CREDIT	ASSETS	OWNER'S EQUITY	LIABILITIES
Bank Account	Current Income Account	+ 8 000	+ 8 000	0

```
    DR      Bank      CR           DR   Current Income   CR
A    +        |        -        I    -        |        +
   8 000     |                              |      8 000
```

---

3. **CREDIT TRANSACTIONS**
   A business can purchase items and services on credit and can sell services or Inventory on credit.

   a. **Selling Inventory on credit**
      A person who receives Inventory on credit from a business is known as a Debtor.
      Debtors must pay the amount that they owe the business within a certain time period.
      The Debtors Control Account is used to show the amount of cash that Debtors owe the business.

RAF TRADERS sells a guitar for R2 000 on credit to Alice. The Cost Price of the guitar was R1 000.

DEBIT	CREDIT	ASSETS	OWNER'S EQUITY	LIABILITIES
Debtors Control Account	Sales Account	+ 2 000	+ 2 000	0
Cost of Sales Account	Trading Stock Account	− 1 000	− 1 000	0

```
    DR   Debtors Control   CR        DR       Sales       CR
A    +         |         -        I    -         |         +
    2 000     |                              |       2 000

    DR    Cost of Sales    CR        DR   Trading Stock   CR
E    +         |         -        A    +         |         -
    1 000     |                              |       1 000
```

Alice pays RAF TRADERS R2 000 to settle her outstanding balance within two months and receives a R100 discount.

DEBIT	CREDIT	ASSETS	OWNER'S EQUITY	LIABILITIES
Bank Account	Debtors Control Account	+ 1 900 − 1 900	0	0
Discount Allowed Account	Debtors Control Account	− 100	− 100	0

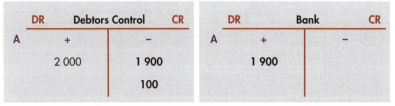

The 2 000 shows the balance of the Debtors Control Account (amount owed to the business) from the previous transaction.

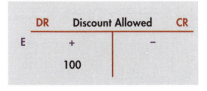

b. Purchasing items on credit
The supplier that a business owes for items purchased on credit is known as a Creditor.
The business must pay the amount that it owes a Creditor within a certain time period.
The **Creditors Control Account** is used to show the amount of cash that the business owes Creditors.

MT SPORTS purchases stationery for R400 on credit.

DEBIT	CREDIT	ASSETS	OWNER'S EQUITY	LIABILITIES
Stationery Account	Creditors Control Account	0	− 400	+ 400

MT SPORTS pays the outstanding amount that is owed and receives a R50 discount.

DEBIT	CREDIT	ASSETS	OWNER'S EQUITY	LIABILITIES
Creditors Control Account	Bank Account	− 350	0	− 350
Creditors Control Account	Discount Received Account	0	+ 50	− 50

DR	Creditors Control	CR
L	−	+
	350	400
	50	

DR	Bank	CR
A	+	−
		350

DR	Discount Received	CR
I	−	+
		50

The 400 shows the balance of the Creditors Control Account (amount owed by the business) from the previous transaction.

THE ACCOUNTING CYCLE
SUMMARY OF CONTENTS

A   OVERVIEW OF THE BASIC ACCOUNTING CYCLE **20**

B   STEPS IN THE BASIC ACCOUNTING CYCLE **21**

     1. Transactions ⎤
     2. Source Documents ⎬ **DAILY STEPS**
     3. Journals ⎦

     4. General Ledger ⎤
                           ⎬ **MONTHLY STEPS**
     5. Trial Balance ⎦

     6. Financial Statements — **AT THE END OF THE ACCOUNTING PERIOD** **22**

C   OVERVIEW OF THE FULL ACCOUNTING CYCLE **22**

D   STEPS IN THE FULL ACCOUNTING CYCLE **23–24**

     1. Transactions ⎤   **23**
     2. Source Documents ⎬ **DAILY STEPS**
     3. Journals ⎦

     4. Ledgers ⎤
     5. Reconciliations ⎬ **MONTHLY STEPS**
     6. Pre-Adjustment Trial Balance ⎦

     7. Adjustments ⎤   **24**
     8. Adjusted Trial Balance ⎥
     9. Final Accounts ⎥
     10. Post-Closing Trial Balance ⎬ **AT THE END OF THE ACCOUNTING PERIOD**
     11. Financial Statements ⎥
     12. Analysis of Financial Statements ⎥
     13. Reversals ⎦

THE ACCOUNTING CYCLE

 This chapter provides you with an overview of the steps in the Accounting Cycle. You should refer back to this chapter as a reference when working through the chapters that follow.

The Accounting Cycle is a representation of the different steps that a bookkeeper follows to record all the financial information of a business during the Accounting Period.
The **steps** of the Accounting Cycle are followed to make sure that all the **financial information** related to the business is **recorded** and is **accurate**.
The **Accounting Period** is the name given to the time period from when the Accounting Cycle starts to when it ends. The Accounting Period of a business is usually **quarterly** (once every four months) or **annually** (once a year).

A. OVERVIEW OF THE BASIC ACCOUNTING CYCLE

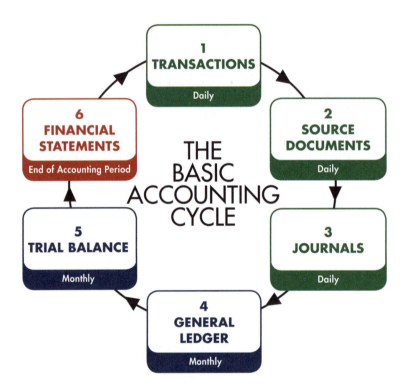

 The full Accounting Cycle covered in Grades 10—12 is on page 22.

B. STEPS IN THE BASIC ACCOUNTING CYCLE

DAILY STEPS
Transactions are recorded on a daily basis on Source Documents and in Journals.

1. **Transactions**
   A transaction is any event that affects the Financial Position (wealth) of a business.
   All transactions are recorded in the books of a business. Transactions can be classified into three categories:
   - **Cash Transactions**
     Transactions where cash is received or paid
     A business pays cash for Stationery.
   - **Credit Transactions**
     Transactions where Inventory or a service is purchased or sold on credit
     A business purchases a car on credit.
   - **Other Transactions**
     Transactions that do not involve cash or Credit
     A business records Depreciation on its Fixed Assets for the year.
     See pg 168 for more information about Depreciation.

2. **Source Documents** pg 26
   A Source Document is the first document used to record a transaction.
   Source Documents include all the important information about the transaction such as the name, date, document number, reason for the transaction and the amount. The buyer keeps the original Source Document and the seller keeps the duplicate Source Document for each transaction that takes place.
   Receipts, Deposit Slips, Cheques, Invoices, Payslips, Debit Notes, Credit Notes, etc.
   It is important that both the buyer and seller keep their Source Documents so that they have proof of the details of the transaction. Ask for the Receipt the next time you buy something at the shops.

3. **Journals** pg 30
   Journals are used to record transactions in a standardised format. They are the books of first entry.
   The transactions are recorded daily in the order in which they occur.

MONTHLY STEPS
The General Ledger and Trial Balance are prepared at the end of each month.

4. **General Ledger** pg 55
   The Journals are posted to the General Ledger. To post something means to transfer it.
   The General Ledger records all the effects of the Financial Activities of a business in the Asset, Liability, Owner's Equity, Expense and Income Accounts.

5. **Trial Balance** pg 83
   The names of the Accounts and their balances are listed to form the Trial Balance.
   This information is taken from the Accounts in the General Ledger. The purpose of the Trial Balance is to show an overview of the Accounts and their balances and to check that the total Debits are equal to the total Credits. Any errors picked up are adjusted in the General Journal.

AT THE END OF THE ACCOUNTING PERIOD

6. **Financial Statements** pg 86
   The Financial Statements are prepared at the **end** of the Accounting Period.
   The Financial Statements **summarise** all the important **financial information** of a business.

FINANCIAL STATEMENT	DETAILS
INCOME STATEMENT	Used to show the **Income** and **Expense** Accounts
BALANCE SHEET STATEMENT	Used to show the **Asset, Liability** and **Owner's Equity** Accounts
CASH FLOW STATEMENT	Used to show the changes in the **Cash** position of the business. Cash includes all the money of the business: bank notes, coins and any money in bank accounts.

C. OVERVIEW OF THE FULL ACCOUNTING CYCLE

There are more steps in the Full Accounting Cycle than there are in the Basic Accounting Cycle.

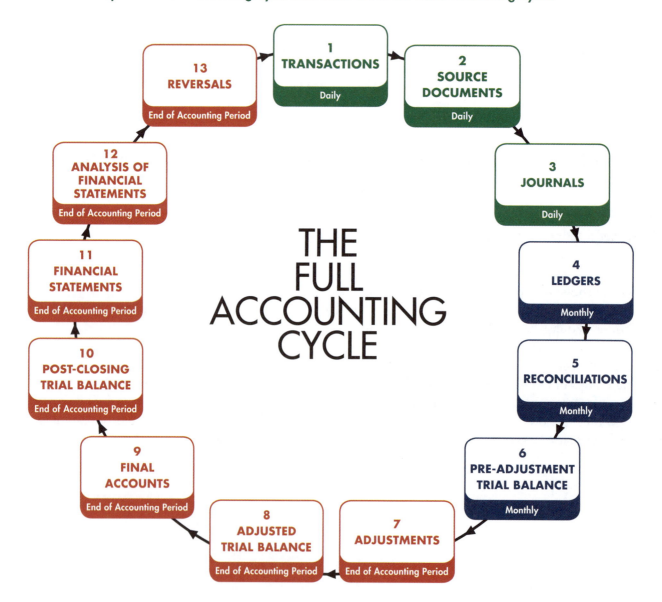

D. STEPS IN THE FULL ACCOUNTING CYCLE

DAILY STEPS The daily steps are the same as the daily steps in the Basic Accounting Cycle.
Transactions are recorded on a daily basis on Source Documents and in Journals.

1. **Transactions**
   A transaction is any event that affects the Financial Position (wealth) of a business.
   All transactions are recorded in the books of a business. Transactions can be classified into three categories:
   - **Cash Transactions**
     Transactions where **cash** is **received** or **paid**
     A business pays cash for Stationery.
   - **Credit Transactions**
     Transactions where **Inventory** or a **service** is **purchased** or **sold on credit**
     A business purchases a car on credit.
   - **Other Transactions**
     Transactions that do **not involve cash or Credit**
     A business records Depreciation on its Fixed Assets for the year.
     See pg 168 for more information about Depreciation.

2. **Source Documents** pg 26
   A Source Document is the **first document** used to record a transaction.
   Source Documents include all the important **information** about the **transaction** such as the name, date, document number, reason for the transaction and the amount. The **buyer keeps** the **original** Source Document and the **seller keeps** the **duplicate** Source Document for each transaction that takes place.
   Receipts, Deposit Slips, Cheques, Invoices, Payslips, Debit Notes, Credit Notes, etc.
   It is important that both the buyer and seller keep their Source Documents so that they have proof of the details of the transaction. Ask for the Receipt the next time you buy something at the shops.

3. **Journals** pg 30
   Journals are used to record transactions in a standardised format. They are the books of first entry.
   The transactions are recorded daily in the **order** in which they **occur**.

MONTHLY STEPS
The Ledgers, Unadjusted Trial Balance and Reconciliations are prepared at the end of each month.

4. **Ledgers** pg 55
   The Journals are posted to the General Ledger, Debtors Ledgers and Creditors Ledger.
   To post something means to transfer it.
   The **General Ledger** records all the effects of the Financial Activities of a business in the **Asset, Liability, Owner's Equity, Expense** and **Income Accounts**.
   - The **Debtors Ledger** records additional details about the Debtors Control Account in the General Ledger.
     It includes all the transactions with each Debtor.
   - The **Creditors Ledger** records additional details about the Creditors Control Account in the General Ledger.
     It includes all the transactions with each Creditor.

5. **Reconciliations** pg 134
   Reconciliation is the process of finding the differences between two financial Accounts and correcting these so that the records agree with each other.
   Reconciliations are an important part of the **Internal Control** process.

6. **Pre-Adjustment Trial Balance** pg 83
   The names and balances of the Accounts are listed to form the Pre-Adjustment Trial Balance.
   This **information** is **taken** from the Accounts in the **General Ledger**. The purpose of the Unadjusted Trial Balance is to show an **overview** of the Accounts and their balances and to **check** that the **total Debits** are **equal** to the **total Credits**. Any **errors** picked up are **adjusted**.

AT THE END OF THE ACCOUNTING PERIOD
There are a number of different tasks that need to be completed at the end of the Accounting Period.
This is the busiest time of the year for a bookkeeper!

7. **Adjustments** pg 122
   Adjustments are made to correct mistakes and update Account balances.
   All the Accounts should be **correct** and **up to date** after the Adjusting Entries have been made.

8. **Adjusted Trial Balance** pg 83   This is also called the Post-Adjustment Trial Balance.
   An Adjusted Trial Balance is drawn up from the adjusted balances in the General Ledger.
   The **purpose** of the Adjusted Trial Balance is to show an overview of the Accounts and their balances and to **check** that the **total Debits** are **equal** to the **total Credits** after Adjusting Entries have been made.

9. **Final Accounts** pg 129
   Closing transfers are recorded to close all the Income and Expense Accounts for the Accounting Period and to prepare the Final Accounts.
   Final Accounts are prepared to determine the **Profit or Loss** for the Accounting Period.
   All the Income and Expense Accounts have a zero balance at the beginning of the next Period.

10. **Post-Closing Trial Balance** pg 83
    A Post-Closing Trial Balance is drawn up once the Income and Expenses Accounts have been closed off at the end of the Accounting Period.
    The **purpose** of the Post-Closing Trial Balance is to show an **overview** of the Accounts and their balances and to **check** that the **total Debits** are **equal** to the **total Credits** after the Income and Expense Accounts have been closed off.
    All the Income and Expense Accounts are closed off in the Post-Closing Trial Balance.
    The Trial Balance only contains Asset, Liability and Owner's Equity Accounts.

11. **Financial Statements** pg 86
    The Financial Statements are prepared at the end of the Accounting Period.
    The Financial Statements **summarise** all the important **financial information** of a business. The Financial Statements are prepared **using** the **information** from the **Adjusted Trial Balance**.

FINANCIAL STATEMENT	DETAILS
INCOME STATEMENT (Statement of Comprehensive Income)	Used to show the Income and Expense Accounts
BALANCE SHEET STATEMENT (Statement of Financial Position)	Used to show the Asset, Liability and Owner's Equity Accounts
CASH FLOW STATEMENT	Used to show the changes in the Cash of the business

Cash includes all the money of the business: bank notes, coins and any money in bank accounts.

12. **Analysis of Financial Statements** pg 105
    Financial Statements are analysed to better understand the results of the business.
    This includes **how well** the business **performed** during the Accounting Period, and the **Financial Position** (wealth) of the business at the end of the Accounting Period.

13. **Reversals** pg 132
    Reversals are made to prepare the Accounting records for the next Accounting Period.
    Reversals are made **before** the **next Accounting Period** starts.

   You have now completed the Accounting Cycle – well done!

SOURCE DOCUMENTS
SUMMARY OF CONTENTS

A	**TABLE OF TRANSACTIONS AND SOURCE DOCUMENTS**	**26**
B	**LAYOUT OF COMMON SOURCE DOCUMENTS**	**27 – 28**
	1. Receipt	**27**
	2. Cheque and Cheque Counterfoil	
	3. Original Invoice and Duplicate Invoice	**28**
	4. Credit Note and Debit Note	**28 – 29**
	5. Petty Cash Voucher	**29**

SOURCE DOCUMENTS

A Source Document is the first document used to record a transaction.
Source Documents are an important tool for **Internal Control**. Each Source Document contains the **key information** about a transaction, such as the **name**, **date**, **document number**, the **reason** for the transaction and the **amount**. The **buyer keeps** the **original** Source Document and the **seller keeps** the **duplicate** Source Document for the transaction.
It is important that both the buyer and seller keep their Source Documents so that they have proof of the details of the transaction. Ask for a Receipt the next time you buy something at the shops.

A. TABLE OF TRANSACTIONS AND SOURCE DOCUMENTS

JOURNAL	TYPE OF TRANSACTION	SOURCE DOCUMENT
A	Cash received	Receipt, Deposit Slip, Duplicate Receipt, Cash Register Roll (CRR), Cash Invoice, Bank Statement (B/S), Cash Register Tape (CRT), Till Slip, proof of online payment (EFT)
B	Cash paid	Cheque, Cheque Counterfoil, Bank Statement (B/S), proof of online payment (EFT)
C	Petty Cash used	Petty Cash Voucher
D	Inventory sold on credit	Duplicate Invoice
E	Items purchased on credit	Original Invoice
F	Customers return items purchased on credit to the business	Credit Note (C/N)
G	Items purchased on credit by the business are returned to the suppliers	Debit Note (D/N)
H	Salaries of employees / Wages of employees	Payslip
I	Any other type of transaction that is recorded in the General Journal	Journal Voucher

B. LAYOUT OF COMMON SOURCE DOCUMENTS

Each business will have its own **unique layout** for Source Documents. The following information is usually included on a Source Document:
- The **name** of the business
- A **description** of the transaction
- The **date** of the transaction
- The **amount** of the transaction
- The **number** of the Source Document. Each Source Document has a unique number
- The **address** of the business/person involved in the transaction (if applicable)

> The layouts of the Source Documents below are covered in the curriculum. In Grade 8 and Grade 9, you need to make sure that you understand the information found on these Source Documents.

1. **RECEIPT**
   A business completes a Receipt for each **cash sale**.
   A Cash Register Roll (CRR) shows all the Receipts for cash received at the till.

   ```
   RECEIPT                                           No. 337

   Received from  B. Brown                    DATE: 09/04/2017
   CASH [X]  Cheque [ ]  EFT [ ]
   For  Accounting Handbook
        and Study Guides                      R    1 500,00
   The amount of  One thousand, five hundred rands
   Received by  J. Jones
   ```

2. **CHEQUE and CHEQUE COUNTERFOIL**
   A business can make a **payment** using a Cheque. A Cheque Counterfoil is completed to record the details of the transaction.

   The business **issues** the **Cheque** and **keeps** the Cheque **Counterfoil**. The business must make sure to cash any Cheques received before they **expire** (within 6 months).

   These days, most businesses do not use Cheques. Cash payments are usually made using Debit Cards, Credit Cards, or online transfers (EFTs).

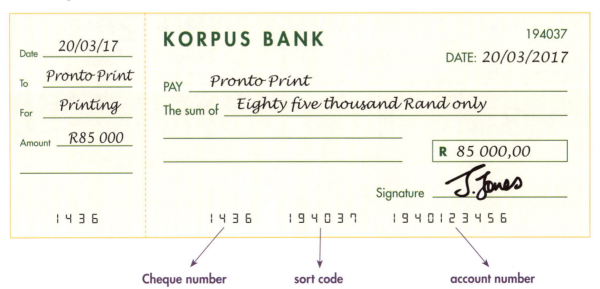

3. **ORIGINAL INVOICE and DUPLICATE INVOICE**
   A business keeps a duplicate Invoice when it sells Inventory on credit. The customer is given the original Invoice.
   The original Invoice and duplicate Invoice are exactly the same – the business may use carbon paper to create the duplicate copy.

   TAX INVOICE   No: 678

   TO: SCHOOL SUPPLIERS (PTY) LTD   ACCOUNTING INC
       54 Main Road   P.O. Box 07953
       Durban   Johannesburg
       4001   2000

   DATE: 09/04/2017

QUANTITY	DETAILS	PRICE PER UNIT	AMOUNT
20	Accounting Handbook & Study Guide	300,00	6 000,00
TERMS AND CONDITIONS:		VAT (incl.)	736,84
30 days from date of statement		TOTAL	6 000,00

   Signature: J. Jones

   E & O.E.

   You will learn more about VAT in Grade 10. See pg 175

4. **CREDIT NOTE and DEBIT NOTE**
   A business issues a Credit Note when items are returned by a Debtor.
   A business issues a Debit Note when it returns items to a Creditor.

   CREDIT NOTE   No: 275

   TO: SCHOOL SUPPLIERS (PTY) LTD   ACCOUNTING INC
       54 Main Road   P.O. Box 07953
       Durban   Johannesburg
       4001   2000

   DATE: 09/04/2017

QUANTITY	DETAILS	PRICE PER UNIT	AMOUNT
5	Accounting Books (Surplus Stock)	300,00	1 500,00
		VAT (incl.)	184,21
		TOTAL	1 500,00

   Signature: J. Jones

   You will learn more about VAT in Grade 10. See pg 175

   The Debit Note is shown on the next page.

DEBIT NOTE			No: 27
TO: STATIONERY STORES CC 25 Pine Road East London 5201		**ACCOUNTING INC** P.O. Box 07953 Johannesburg 2000	

DATE: 05/06/2017

QUANTITY	DETAILS	PRICE PER UNIT	AMOUNT
100	Ball point pens (damaged)	7,99	799,00
		TOTAL	799,00

Signature: *J. Jones*

5. PETTY CASH VOUCHER 🔟
A business fills in a Petty Cash Voucher when Petty Cash is spent.

PETTY CASH VOUCHER — No. 38
Accounting Inc

DATE: 3 March 2017

Required for	Office supplies	AMOUNT	
		R350	00

Signature: *J. Jones*   Authorised by: *T. Boss*

JOURNALS
SUMMARY OF CONTENTS

1 **DIFFERENT TYPES OF JOURNALS** **31**

2 **TABLE OF JOURNALS** **31**

    C. Cash Receipts Journal (CRJ) **32**

    D. Cash Payments Journal (CPJ) **34**

    E. Petty Cash Journal (PCJ) **36**

    F. Debtors Journal (DJ) **38**

    G. Creditors Journal (CJ) **40**

    H. Debtors Allowances Journal (DAJ) **42**

    I. Creditors Allowances Journal (CAJ) **44**

    J. Salaries Journal (SJ) and Wages Journal (WJ) **46**

    K. General Journal (GJ) **53**

JOURNALS

Journals are used to record transactions in a standardised format. They are the books of first entry.
All transactions are recorded on **Source Documents** and then transferred to the relevant **Journals** on a **daily** basis, in the **order** in which they **occur**. A bookkeeper records transactions in the Journals to capture all the information for each transaction. The Journals are then posted to the **General Ledger** at the end of the month to show how the transactions recorded affect the Accounts of the business.
Notice that the details of any transaction can be found in a Journal.

1. DIFFERENT TYPES OF JOURNALS

There are various types of Journals, which are used to record different types of transactions.
The different Journals make it easy to find and record transactions, by **grouping transactions** of the **same type** together. **Each Journal has specific columns** to record all the important information for a transaction.
The main **differences** between the layouts of the various Journals are the names of the columns used to record the effects of the transactions on the Accounts of the business. Each Journal has a unique code called a **Folio Reference (Fol)**. The Folio Reference makes it easy to find and to refer to a specific Journal.

2. TABLE OF JOURNALS

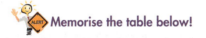 Memorise the table below!

	JOURNAL	TYPE OF TRANSACTION	SOURCE DOCUMENT
A	CASH RECEIPTS JOURNAL (CRJ)	Cash received	Receipt, Deposit Slip, Duplicate Receipt, Cash Register Roll (CRR), Cash Invoice, Bank Statement (B/S), Cash Register Tape (CRT), Till Slip, proof of online payment (EFT)
B	CASH PAYMENTS JOURNAL (CPJ)	Cash paid	Cheque, Cheque Counterfoil, Bank Statement (B/S), proof of online payment (EFT), stop orders, debit orders
C	PETTY CASH JOURNAL (PCJ) ⑩	Petty Cash used	Petty Cash Voucher
D	DEBTORS JOURNAL (DJ) ⑨	Inventory sold on credit	Duplicate Invoice
E	CREDITORS JOURNAL (CJ) ⑨	Items purchased on credit	Original Invoice
F	DEBTORS ALLOWANCES JOURNAL (DAJ) ⑨	Customers return items purchased on credit to the business	Credit Note (C/N)
G	CREDITORS ALLOWANCE JOURNAL (CAJ) ⑨	Items purchased on credit by the business are returned to the suppliers	Debit Note (D/N)
H	SALARIES JOURNAL (SJ) / WAGES JOURNAL (WJ) ⑩	Salaries of employees / Wages of employees	Payslip
I	GENERAL JOURNAL (GJ) ⑩	Any transaction that does not belong in one of the above Journals, is recorded in the General Journal.	Journal Voucher

Make sure you know the layout of each Journal and how to record a transaction in a Journal.

A. CASH RECEIPTS JOURNAL (CRJ)

The CRJ of a business is used to record all transactions where cash is received.

FORMAT OF THE CRJ
All transactions entered in the CRJ **increase** the Bank Account (Bank Column) and affect at least one other Account (Analysis Columns or Sundry Accounts Columns).

For every **Debit** there is a **Credit**.

Cash Receipts Journal of [Name of business] – [Month Year]   Each Journal has a unique Folio Reference → **CRJ [XX]**

				Physical cash collected		All amounts deposited in the bank account by the end of the day		Effect on the Current Income Account		Effect on the other Accounts		
1. Doc	2. Day	3. Details	4. Fol	5. Analysis of Receipts		6. Bank (Main Account)		7. Current Income (Analysis Column)		8. Sundry Accounts		
										Amount		Fol	Details
				R	c	R	c	R	c	R	c		

Balancing lines are drawn with the totals of the Bank Column, Analysis Columns and Sundry Accounts Column at the end of the month.

1. The **Doc** Column shows the details of the **Source Document** for the transaction.

2. The **Day** Column shows the **day** of the **month** on which the transaction takes place.

3. The **Details** Column shows the **name** of the **person/business** from whom cash is received.
   If no name is given, then 'Service fee'/'Services rendered'/'Customer'/'Cash' is written under the Details Column.

4. The **Fol** Column shows the **Folio Reference** of the **Debtor** in the Debtors Ledger.
   Each Debtor is assigned a unique code called a Folio Reference. This column is only used when a **Debtor pays** the business. The reference of a Debtor **starts with a D**. ⑨

5. The **Analysis of Receipts** Column is only used to record the amount of **cash collected.**
   All the notes, coins and Cheques received from each transaction are recorded in the Analysis of Receipts Column. At the end of the day, a line is drawn under the last amount and the total amount of cash collected for the day is recorded under the Bank Column. **This column is never posted to the General Ledger.**

6. The **Bank** Column shows the amount of **cash deposited** in the **bank account** of the business.
   The Bank Column includes the physical cash collected and deposited at the end of the day as well as any amounts that are directly deposited in the bank account of the business.

7. The **Current Income** Column (**Analysis Column**) shows the **amounts** that **affect** the **Current Income** Account.
   The Column is known as an Analysis Column. Analysis Columns makes it easy to record the amounts for Accounts that are used often. Each business will decide which Accounts to use as Analysis Columns.
   - A **Service Business** usually has an Analysis Column for **Current Income**.
   - A **Trading Business** usually has Analysis Columns for **Sales,** to record the Sales Price of Inventory sold, and for **Cost of Sales,** to record the Cost Price of Inventory sold.
   There can be more than one Analysis Column.

8. The **Sundry Accounts** Columns are used to fill in the **details** of the **other Accounts affected** that are not shown in Analysis Columns.
   - The **Amount** Column shows the **amount** by which the **Account** is **affected**.
   - The **Fol** Column shows the **Folio Reference** of the **Account** affected. Each Account is assigned a unique code called a Folio Reference. The Folio References either **start with a B** (Asset, Owner's Equity and Liability Accounts) **or an N** (Expense or Income Accounts).
   - The **Details** Column shows the **name** of the **Account affected**. Any Account name can be recorded. This allows the business to record the effect on any Accounts that are not shown in the Analysis Columns.

© Berlut Books CC

CARLY'S CLEVER TUTORS charges fees for tutoring services. Complete the **Cash Receipts Journal** for April.
This is an example of a CRJ of a Service Business.

Transactions during April 2018 for Carly's Clever Tutors.
5   The Owner, Carly, contributed R3 500 Capital by depositing it directly into the bank account.
    Received R2 000 cash from customers for Geography and Life Science tutoring (CRT 67 to 77).
9   Received R400 cash from N. Dube for Mathematics tutoring (Receipt 14).
30 J. Smith deposited his rent of R5 000 in the bank account of the business (Receipt 15).

Cash Receipts Journal of Carly's Clever Tutors - April 2018   CRJ 04

Doc	Day	Details	Fol	Analysis of Receipts		Bank		Current Income (Analysis Column)		Sundry Accounts			
										Amount		Fol	Details
				R	c	R	c	R	c	R	c		
BS	5	Carly				3 500	00			3 500	00		Capital
CRT 67—77		Customers		2 000	00	2 000	00	2 000	00				
Rec 14	9	N. Dube		400	00	400	00	400	00				
Rec 15	30	J. Smith				5 000	00			5 000	00		Rent Income
						10 900	00	2 400	00	8 500	00		

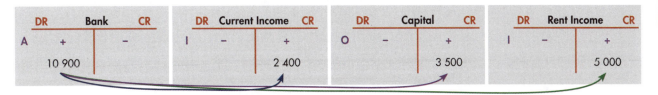

BENNY'S BICYCLES makes and sells bicycles. They mark up their Stock by 20% on cost. Complete the **Cash Receipts Journal**. This is an example of a CRJ of a Trading Business.

Transactions during June 2017
1   The Bank Statement reflected the R5 000 Loan received from Bizzy Bank.
4   Sold bicycles to customers for R24 000 cash (CRR 01 to 12).
19 Issued a Receipt (Rec. 02) to S. Bakone (D1) who paid his outstanding balance of R400.

Cash Receipts Journal of Benny's Bicycles – June 2017   These columns have been added.   CRJ 06

Doc	Day	Details	Fol	Analysis of Receipts		Bank (Main Account)		Sales (Analysis Column)		Cost of Sales (Analysis Column)		Sundry Accounts			
												Amount		Fol	Details
				R	c	R	c	R	c	R	c	R	c		
BS	1	Bizzy Bank				5 000	00					5 000	00		Loan: Bizzy Bank
CRR 01—12	4	Cash		24 000	00	24 000	00	24 000	00	20 000	00				
Rec. 02	19	S. Bakone	D1	400	00	400	00					400	00		Debtors Control
						29 400	00	24 000	00	20 000	00	5 400	00		

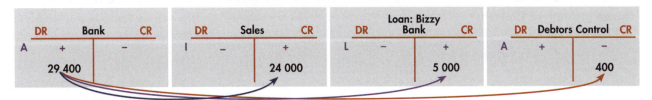

Cost of Sales does not affect the Bank Account. Cost of Sales shows the cost of Inventory sold.
The other Account affected is the Trading Stock Account.

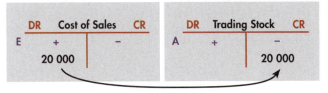

Cost Price = Selling Price × $\dfrac{100}{100 + \text{mark-up}}$

B. CASH PAYMENTS JOURNAL (CPJ)

The CPJ is used to record all transactions where cash is paid from the current bank account of the business.
A Business can pay cash using Cheques, Debit Cards, Credit Cards or by transferring the cash online (EFT).
In the school curriculum, the assumption is made that most cash payments are made using **Cheques**.
These days, most businesses do not use Cheques. Cash payments are usually made with Debit Cards, Credit Cards or online transfers (EFTs).

FORMAT OF THE CPJ
All transactions entered in the CPJ decrease the Bank Account (Bank Column) and affect at least one other Account (Analysis Columns or Sundry Accounts Columns).

For every Debit there is a Credit.

Cash Payments Journal of [Name of business] – [Month Year]

Each Journal has a unique Folio Reference → CPJ [XX]

All cash amounts paid by the business ↓ — column 5. Bank
Effect on the Equipment Account ↓ — column 6. Equipment
Effect on the other Accounts ↓ — column 7. Sundry Accounts

1. Doc	2. Day	3. Name of Payee	4. Fol	5. Bank (Main Account)		6. Equipment (Analysis Column)	7. Sundry Accounts		
				R	c		Amount	Fol	Details
							R	c	

Balancing lines are drawn with the totals of the Bank Column, Analysis Columns and Sundry Accounts Column at the end of the month.

1. The **Doc** Column shows the details of the **Source Document** for the transaction.

2. The **Day** Column shows the **day** of the **month** on which the transaction takes place.

3. The **Name of Payee** Column shows the **name** of the **person/business** that the business pays.
   If the details are not provided then 'Cash' is entered in this column.

4. The **Fol** Column shows the **Folio Reference** of the **Creditor** in the Creditors Ledger.
   Each Creditor is assigned a unique code called a Folio Reference which starts with a C.
   This column is only used when a **Creditor is paid**.

5. The **Bank** Column shows the amount of **cash paid** from the **bank account** of the business in the transaction.

6. The **Equipment** Column is an Analysis Column that shows the **amounts** that **affect** the **Equipment** Account.

7. The **Sundry Accounts** Columns are used to fill in the **details** of the **other Accounts affected** that are not shown in Analysis Columns.

CINDY'S PRINTS designs and sells posters. Complete the Cash Payments Journal for June. Include Analysis Columns for Salaries and Creditors Control.

Transactions during June 2016
- 2 Issued a Cheque (CC 21) to BN Stores for R100 to buy new stationery.
- 4 Paid J. Nkosi a monthly Salary of R12 500.
- 8 Bought a new computer for R6 000 from CC Computers.
- 24 Paid M. Molefe (C1) R5 000 to settle an Account.
- 30 Paid TN Mobile the Telephone Account of R990.

Cash Payments Journal of Cindy's Prints – June 2016   CPJ 06

Doc	Day	Name of payee	Fol	Bank (Main Account)		Salaries (Analysis Column)		Creditors Control (Analysis Column)		Sundry Accounts			
										Amount		Fol	Details
				R	c	R	c	R	c	R	c		
CC 21*	2	BN Stores		100	00					100	00		Stationery
CC 22	4	J. Nkosi		12 500	00	12 500	00						
CC 23	8	CC Computers		6 000	00					6 000	00		Equipment
CC 24	24	M. Molefe	C1	5 000	00			5 000	00				
CC 25	30	TN Mobile		990	00					990	00		Telephone
				24 590	00	12 500	00	5 000	00	7 090	00		

*If a document number is given in the first transaction, continue with this numbering.

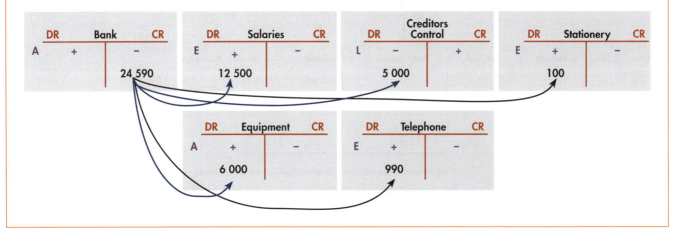

C. PETTY CASH JOURNAL (PCJ)

The PCJ is used to record all transactions where Petty Cash is used by the business to make payments.
Petty Cash is the physical cash (bank notes and coins) kept by the business to pay for small Expenses.
The business draws physical cash (bank notes) from the bank or an ATM to use as Petty Cash.
The transaction is recorded in the Cash Payments Journal to show the decrease of the Bank Account and the increase of the Petty Cash Account (physical cash available).

IMPREST SYSTEM
Some businesses use an **Imprest System** to ensure that the amount of Petty Cash available at the **end** of the month is the **same** as what was available at the **beginning** of the month. When using this system, the business looks at the total amount of Petty Cash spent at the end of each month and **replaces** this amount.

Steve Tyres uses an Imprest System. Each month the business should start with R1 000 Petty Cash.
The bookkeeper calculated that R800 Petty Cash was spent during May. The bookkeeper will therefore replace the R800 at the end of May, so that June starts with R1 000 Petty Cash.

FORMAT OF THE PCJ
All transactions entered in the PCJ decrease the Petty Cash Account (Petty Cash Column) and affect at least one other Account (Analysis Columns or Sundry Accounts Columns).
The **difference** between the **PCJ** and the **CPJ** (Cash Payments Journal) is the main Account which is affected.
In the **PCJ** the main Account is the **Petty Cash Account** and in the **CPJ** the main Account is the **Bank Account**.

Petty Cash Journal of [Name of business] – [Month, year]   Each Journal has a unique Folio Reference → PCJ [XX]

Column descriptions:
- 5. Petty Cash (Main Account): All Petty Cash amounts paid by the business
- 6. Stationery (Analysis Column): Effect on the Stationery Account
- 7. Sundry Accounts: Effect on the other Accounts

1. Doc	2. Day	3. Details	4. Fol	5. Petty Cash (Main Account)		6. Stationery (Analysis Column)		7. Sundry Accounts			
								Amount		Fol	Details
				R	c	R	c	R	c		

Balancing lines are drawn with the totals of the Bank Column, Analysis Columns and Sundry Accounts Column at the end of the month.

1. The **Doc** Column shows the details of the **Source Document** for the transaction. The Source Document used is a Petty Cash Voucher.

2. The **Day** Column shows the **day** of the **month** on which the transaction takes place.

3. The **Details** Column shows the **name** of the **person/business** that the business pays.

4. The **Fol** Column shows the **Folio Reference** of the **Creditor** in the Creditors Ledger.
   Each Creditor is assigned a unique code called a Folio Reference, which **starts with a C**.
   This column is only used when a Creditor is paid.

5. The **Petty Cash** Column shows the amount of **Petty Cash paid** by the business in the transaction.

6. The **Stationery** Column is an Analysis Column used to record the **amounts** that **affect** the **Stationery** Account.

7. The **Sundry Accounts** Columns are used to fill in the **details** of the **other Accounts affected** that are not shown in Analysis Columns.

RR SPORTS sells sports equipment. Complete the **Petty Cash Journal**.
Include Analysis Columns for Stationery and Repairs.

Transactions during September 2017

- **2** Donated R120 from Petty Cash to CVC charity. Petty Cash Voucher 105.
- **12** The Owner, Mark, took R65 from Petty Cash for personal use.
- **19** Paid S. Ndlovu R180 from Petty Cash for repairs done to the window.
- **22** Paid R320 from the Petty Cash for stationery bought from KL Stores.

Petty Cash Journal of RR Sports – September 2017   PCJ 09

Doc	Day	Details	Fol	Petty Cash (Main Account)		Stationery (Analysis Column)		Repairs (Analysis Column)		Sundry Accounts			
										Amount		Fol	Details
				R	c	R	c	R	c	R	c		
105	2	CVC charity		120	00					120	00		Donations Paid
106	12	Mark		65	00					65	00		Drawings
107	19	S. Ndlovu		180	00			180	00				
108	22	KL Stores		320	00	320	00						
				685	00	320	00	180	00	185	00		

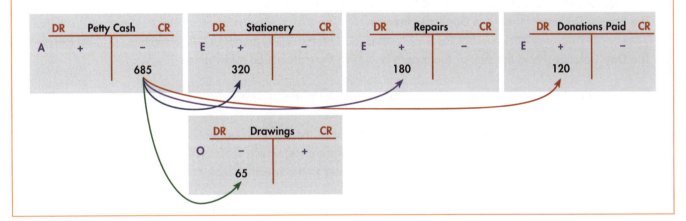

D. DEBTORS JOURNAL (DJ)

The DJ is used to record all transactions where Inventory is sold on credit.

FORMAT OF THE DJ
The Sales Column and Cost of Sales Column are used to record all transactions in the DJ.

Debtors Journal of [Name of business] – [Month, year]   Each Journal has a unique Folio Reference → DJ [XX]

Sales Column: **Sales Price of Inventory sold on credit**
Cost of Sales Column: **Cost Price of Inventory sold on credit**

1. Doc	2. Day	3. Debtor	4. Fol	5. Sales		6. Cost of Sales	
				R	c	R	c

Balancing lines are drawn with the totals of the Sales Column and Cost of Sales Column.

1. The **Doc** Column shows the details of the **Source Document** for the transaction.
   The Source Document used is a **Duplicate Invoice**.

2. The **Day** Column shows the **day** of the **month** on which the transaction takes place.

3. The **Debtor** Column shows the **name** of the **Debtor** that the business sells items on credit to.

4. The **Fol** Column shows the **Folio Reference** of the **Debtor** in the Debtors Ledger.
   Each Debtor is assigned a unique code called a Folio Reference, which starts with a D.
   The same Folio Reference is used in every Journal to refer to the specific Debtor.

5. The **Sales** Column shows the **Selling Price** of the Inventory sold on credit. The Debtor owes the business this amount and must pay it within a certain period of time.

6. The **Cost of Sales** Column shows the **Cost Price** of the Inventory sold on credit.

 Make sure you can calculate the Selling Price and Cost Price using the formulas below:

- **Selling Price = Cost Price ÷ 100 × (100 + mark-up)** or **Selling Price = Cost Price × $\dfrac{100 + \text{mark-up}}{100}$**

- **Cost Price = Selling Price × 100 ÷ (100 + mark-up)** or **Cost Price = Selling Price × $\dfrac{100}{100 + \text{mark-up}}$**

NELI RINGS sells wedding rings. The business sells goods using a 20% mark-up on cost. Complete the Debtors Journal. Note that the reference number for each Debtor is provided in brackets next to their name.

Transactions during December, 2017
9   Issued an Invoice (no. 109) to M. Mandla (D3) for R20 000 for a ring purchased on credit.
24 Sold merchandise to S. Richards (D1) for R25 000 on account.
27 Sold a ring on credit to N. Govind (D5) for R6 000.

Debtors Journal of Neli Rings – December 2017   DJ 12

Doc	Day	Debtor	Fol	Sales		Cost of Sales	
				R	c	R	c
109	9	M. Mandla	D3	20 000	00	16 666	67
110	24	S. Richards	D1	25 000	00	20 833	33
111	27	N. Govind	D5	6 000	00	5 000	00
				51 000	00	42 500	00

Notice that Cost of Sales = Sales × $\dfrac{100}{100 + \text{mark-up}}$ = 51 000 × $\dfrac{100}{120}$ = 42 500

The total of the Sales Column is posted to the Sales Account and the Debtors Control Account:

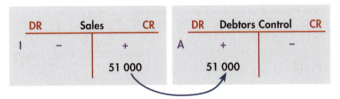

The total of the Cost of Sales Column is posted to the Cost of Sales Account and the Trading Stock Account:

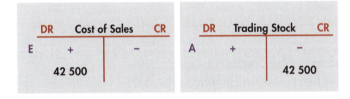

E. CREDITORS JOURNAL (CJ)

The CJ is used to record transactions where the business makes Purchases on credit.

FORMAT OF THE CJ
All transactions entered in the CJ increase the Creditors Control Account (Creditors Control Column) and affect at least one other Account (Analysis Columns or Sundry Accounts Columns).

The main difference between the CJ and the CPJ (Cash Payments Journal) is the main Account that is affected. In the **CJ** the main Account affected is the **Creditors Control Account** to show that Purchases are made on credit and in the **CPJ** the main Account affected is the **Bank Account** to show that Purchases are made using cash.

Creditors Journal of [Name of business] – [Month, year]   Each Journal has a unique Folio Reference → CJ [XX]

- All amounts for Purchases on credit → **5. Creditors Control**
- Effect on the Trading Stock Account → **6. Trading Stock (Analysis Column)**
- Effect on the other Accounts → **7. Sundry Accounts**

1. Doc	2. Day	3. Creditor	4. Fol	5. Creditors Control (Main Account)		6. Trading Stock (Analysis Column)		7. Sundry Accounts			
								Amount		Fol	Details
				R	c	R	c	R	c		

Balancing lines are drawn with the totals of the Creditors Control Column, Analysis Columns and Sundry Accounts Column at the end of the month.

1. The **Doc** Column shows the details of the **Source Document** for the transaction.
   The Source Document used is an **Original Invoice**.

2. The **Day** Column shows the **day** of the **month** on which the transaction takes place.

3. The **Creditor** Column shows the **name** of the **Creditor** that the business makes the Purchase on credit from.

4. The **Fol** Column shows the **Folio Reference** of the **Creditor** in the Creditors Ledger.
   Each Creditor is assigned a unique code called a Folio Reference, which **starts with a C**.
   The same Folio Reference is used in every Journal to refer to the specific Creditor.

5. The **Creditors Control** Column shows the amount **purchased on credit.**
   The business owes the Creditor this amount and must pay it within a certain period of time.

6. The **Trading Stock** Column is an Analysis Column that is used to record the **amounts** that **affect** the **Trading Stock** Account.

7. The **Sundry Accounts** Columns are used to fill in the **details** of the **other Accounts affected** that are not shown in Analysis Columns.

JJ PAINTINGS sells modern paintings and frames. Complete the **Creditors Journal**. Note that the reference number for each Creditor is provided in brackets next to its name.

Transactions during December 2016

- **2** Received Invoice 602 from DC Suppliers (C1) for Trading Stock, which cost R1 200.
- **19** Purchased a new machine to make frames for R15 000 from MCM (C2) on credit. Invoice 909.
- **22** Received Invoice 321 for the purchases of stationery for R250 and Trading Stock for R1 800 from AZ Dealers (C4) on credit.
- **23** Invoice 201 for R82 000 was received from MM Motors (C3) for a new delivery van purchased.

Creditors Journal of JJ Paintings – December 2016   CJ12

Doc	Day	Creditor	Fol	Creditors Control		Trading Stock (Analysis Column)		Equipment (Analysis Column)		Sundry Accounts			
										Amount		Fol	Details
				R	c	R	c	R	c	R	c		
602	2	DC Suppliers	C1	1 200	00	1 200	00						
909	19	MCM	C2	15 000	00			15 000	00				
321	22	AZ Dealers	C4	2 050	00	1 800	00			250	00		Stationery
201	23	MM Motors	C3	82 000	00					82 000	00		Vehicles
				100 250	00	3 000	00	15 000	00	82 250	00		

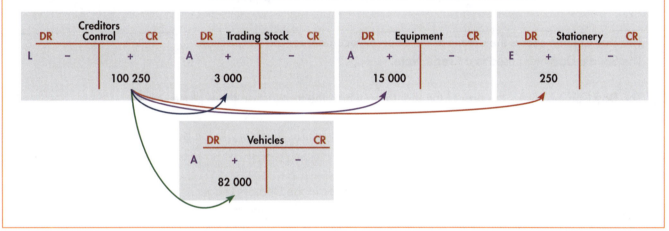

F. DEBTORS ALLOWANCES JOURNAL (DAJ)

The DAJ is used to record all transactions where:
- Inventory, sold on credit, is returned to the business
- the business gives a Debtor a discount on the amount owed.

FORMAT OF THE DAJ
All transactions are recorded in the **Debtors Allowances Column**. The **Cost of Sales Column** is also used only if Inventory is **returned** to the business.

Debtors Allowances Journal of [Name of business] – [Month, year]   Each Journal has a unique Folio Reference → **DAJ [XX]**

Discount given or value of items returned ↓ (column 5)
Cost Price of items returned ↓ (column 6)

1. Doc	2. Day	3. Debtor	4. Fol	5. Debtors Allowances		6. Cost of Sales	
				R	c	R	c

Balancing lines are drawn with the totals of the Debtors Allowances Column and Cost of Sales Column.

1. The **Doc** Column shows the details of the **Source Document** for the transaction.
   The Source Document used is a **Credit Note**.

2. The **Day** Column shows the **day** of the **month** on which the transaction takes place.

3. The **Debtor** Column shows the **name** of the **Debtor** that returns Inventory to the business, or the Debtor that receives a discount from the business.

4. The **Fol** Column shows the **Folio Reference** of the **Debtor** in the Debtors Ledger.
   Each Debtor is assigned a unique code, called a Folio Reference, which **starts with a D**.
   The same Folio Reference is used in every Journal to refer to the specific Debtor.

5. The **Debtors Allowances** Column shows the **Selling Price** of the **returned Inventory** that was sold on credit, or the **discount** given to the Debtor.

6. The **Cost of Sales** Column shows the **Cost Price** of the returned **Inventory** that was sold on credit.

MINDA'S CAR PARTS sells different types of car parts for a range of cars. The business uses a mark-up of 50% on cost. Complete the **Debtors Allowances Journal**. Note that the reference number for each Debtor is provided in brackets next to the Debtor's name.

Transactions during March 2018

- **6** Mr Khan (D2) asked for a discount for a cracked exhaust pipe purchased on credit. Credit Note no. 34 for R400 was issued to him.
- **12** G. Lohrman (D1) returned break pads. The Cost Price of the break pads returned was R2 200.
- **20** T. Lukhele (D4) returned damaged stock. A Credit Note for R8 250 was issued.
- **30** A Credit Note for R20 000 was issued to M. Mckenzie (D5) for returning an engine that was not functioning properly.

Debtors Allowances Journal of Minda's Car Parts – March 2018   DAJ 03

Doc	Day	Debtor	Fol	Debtors Allowances		Cost of Sales	
				R	c	R	c
34	6	Mr Khan	D2	400	00		
35	12	G. Lohrman	D1	3 300	00	2 200	00
36	20	T. Lukhele	D4	8 250	00	5 500	00
37	30	M. Mckenzie	D5	20 000	00	13 333	33
				31 950	00	21 033	33

 If no Inventory is returned (see 06 March above) then nothing is entered under the Cost of Sales Column.

Calculations

The Selling Price (Sales) and Cost Price (Cost of Sales) only need to be recorded if items are returned.

Cost Price = Selling Price × $\frac{100}{100 + \text{mark-up}}$

- $8\ 250 \times \frac{100}{150} = 5\ 500$
- $20\ 000 \times \frac{100}{150} = 13\ 333{,}33$

Selling Price = Cost Price × $\frac{100 + \text{mark-up}}{100}$

- $2\ 200 \times \frac{150}{100} = 3\ 300$

The total of the Debtors Allowances Column is posted to the Debtors Allowances Account and the Debtors Control Account:

The total of the Cost of Sales Column is posted to the Cost of Sales Account and the Trading Stock Account:

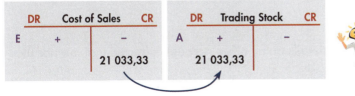

Trading Stock is increasing because Inventory is returned.

G. CREDITORS ALLOWANCES JOURNAL (CAJ)

The CAJ is used to record all transactions where:
- the business returns an item that was purchased on credit.
- the business receives a discount on the amount it owes a Creditor.

The CAJ is used to decrease the amounts recorded in the CJ.
- The **CJ** (Creditors Journal) is used to record **Purchases on credit** to show an **increase** in the **Creditors Control** Account.
- The **CAJ** is used to record the **return** of **items purchased on credit** or **discounts received** from a Creditor, to show a **decrease** in the **Creditors Control** Account.

FORMAT OF THE CAJ

All transactions entered in the CAJ decrease the **Creditors Control Account** (Creditors Control Column) and affect at least one other Account (Analysis Columns or Sundry Accounts Columns).

Creditors Allowances Journal of [Name of business] – [Month, year]

Each Journal has a unique Folio Reference → CAJ [XX]

- Column 5: Price of items returned or amount of discount received
- Column 6: Effect on the Trading Stock Account
- Column 7: Effect on the other Accounts

1. Doc	2. Day	3. Creditor	4. Fol	5. Creditors Control (Main Account)		6. Trading Stock (Analysis Column)		7. Sundry Accounts			
								Amount		Fol	Details
				R	c	R	c	R	c		

Balancing lines are drawn with the totals of the Creditors Control Column, Analysis Columns and Sundry Accounts Column at the end of the month.

1. The **Doc** Column shows the details of the **Source Document** for the transaction.
   The Source Document used is a **Debit Note**.

2. The **Day** Column shows the **day** of the **month** on which the transaction takes place.

3. The **Creditor** Column shows the **name** of the **Creditor** that the business is returning the items purchased on credit to, or the name of the Creditor that gives the business a discount on the outstanding amount owed.

4. The **Fol** Column shows the **Folio Reference** of the **Creditor** in the Creditors Ledger.
   Each Creditor is assigned a unique code called a Folio Reference, which **starts with a C**.
   The same Folio Reference is used in every Journal to refer to the specific Creditor.

5. The **Creditors Control** Column shows the **cost** of the **returned Asset** purchased on credit, **or** the **discount** received. The balance that the business owes the Creditor decreases by this amount.

6. The **Trading Stock** Column is an Analysis Column used to record the **amounts** that **affect** the **Trading Stock** Account.

7. The **Sundry Accounts** Columns are used to fill in the **details** of the **other Accounts affected** that are not shown in Analysis Columns.

© Berlut Books CC

T&T TABLES sells kitchen tables and living room tables. Use the following information to complete the Creditors Allowances Journal. Note that the reference number for each Creditor is provided in brackets next to the Creditor's name.

Transactions during January 2017
2   Damaged Trading Stock for R3 800 was returned to NC Suppliers (C2). Issued debit note 23.
18 T&T Tables returned a machine bought on credit for R28 000 to BC Machinery (C4).
26 AG Wood (C1) overcharged T&T Tables R100 on Trading Stock purchased on account.
31 Issued a debit note to SS Stationery Suppliers (C3) for R300. The stationery delivered to T&T Tables was not correct.

Creditors Allowances Journal of T&T Tables – January 2017   CAJ 01

Doc	Day	Creditor	Fol	Creditors Control		Trading Stock		Equipment		Sundry Accounts			
										Amount		Fol	Details
				R	c	R	c	R	c	R	c		
23	2	NC Suppliers	C2	3 800	00	3 800	00						
24	18	BC Machinery	C4	28 000	00			28 000	00				
25	26	AG Wood	C1	100	00	100	00						
26	31	SS Stationery	C3	300	00					300	00		Stationery
				32 200	00	3 900	00	28 000	00	300	00		

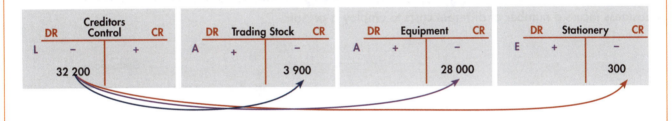

H. SALARIES JOURNAL (SJ) AND WAGES JOURNAL (WJ)

The Salaries Journal is used to record the Salaries of employees.
The Wages Journal is used to record the Wages of employees.
Businesses have employees who are either paid Salaries or Wages.

 The employee is the person who receives the Wage/Salary.
The employer is the person who pays the Wage/Salary to the employee.

DIFFERENCES BETWEEN SALARIES AND WAGES

	SALARIES	WAGES
BASIC AMOUNT PAID	**Fixed** amount	Amount paid depends on the **number of hours** worked
WHEN PAID	Monthly	Weekly
OVERTIME	No overtime	Paid for overtime hours worked
BONUS	May receive a bonus	No bonus

OVERVIEW OF THE AMOUNTS RECORDED IN THE SALARIES JOURNAL AND THE WAGES JOURNAL
A business incurs a number of different costs to employ a person.

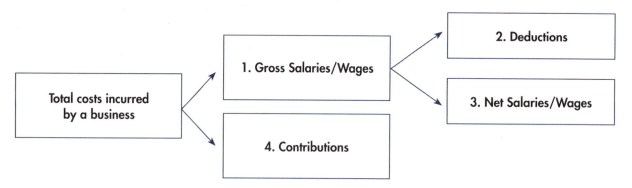

1. **GROSS SALARIES/WAGES**
   The total Salary or Wage that an employee earns before Deductions is known as the Gross Salary or Gross Wage.
   The employer subtracts Deductions from the Gross Salary/Wage before paying the employee his or her **Net Salary/Wage**.

2. **DEDUCTIONS**
   Deductions are amounts that the business subtracts from the employee's Gross Salary/Wage.
   The amounts are paid by the business to various organisations.

   a. If an employee belongs to a **Pension Fund**, then the business can deduct an amount from the employee's Gross Salary/Wage and pay the amount to the Pension Fund. The Pension Fund is paid an amount usually equal to a percentage of the employee's Gross Salary/Wage.

b. If an employee belongs to a **Medical Aid Fund**, then the business can deduct an amount from the employee's Gross Salary/Wage and pay the amount to the Medical Aid Fund.

c. Income Tax (**PAYE**) is deducted from the Gross Salary/Wage of the employee and paid to SARS (South African Revenue Services). PAYE stands for **P**ay **A**s **Y**ou **E**arn.   **This is mandatory.**

d. If an employee belongs to a **Trade Union**, then the business can deduct an amount from the employee's Gross Salary/Wage and pay the amount to the Trade Union.

e. 1% of the employee's Gross Salary/Wage is deducted and the amount is paid to the Department of Labour for **UIF** (**U**nemployment **I**nsurance **F**und). The amount paid for UIF is limited to a maximum of R148,72. **This is mandatory.**
If 1% of the employees' Net Salary/Wage comes to more than R148,72 then only R148,72 is paid for UIF.

3. NET SALARIES/WAGES

The amount that an employee earns after Deductions is known as the Net Salary or Net Wage.
Net Salary = Gross Salary — Deductions
Net Wage = Gross Wage — Deductions
The employer pays the employee his or her Net Salary/Wage.

4. CONTRIBUTIONS

The employer can also make contributions on behalf of the employee.
- Contributions to **Medical Aid** and a **Pension Fund** are **optional**.
- Contributions to **UIF** and **SDL** (if applicable) are **mandatory**.

The contributions are **not deducted** from the Gross Salary/Wage. The contributions are an additional **Expense** to the business.

a. The employer can decide to pay an additional contribution to the employee's **Pension Fund.**

b. The employer can decide to pay an additional contribution to the employee's **Medical Aid Fund**.

c. The employer must contribute 1% of the Gross Salary/Wage of the employee to **UIF (Unemployment Insurance Fund)**. The amount paid to UIF is limited to a maximum of R148,72.

d. Employers who pay a total of R500 000 or more on Salaries/Wages every year must contribute 1% of the annual Salary/Wage to **SDL (Skills Development Levy)**. The Skills Development Levy is a fund that has been set up by the government to develop and improve the skills of employees.

FORMAT OF THE SJ

Salaries Journal of [Name of business] – [Month, year]

Each Journal has a unique Folio Reference → SJ [XX]

1. Employees	2. Basic Salary	3. Bonus	4. Gross Salary	5. Deductions						6. Net Salary	7. Cheque no.	8. Employer's Contribution				
				Pension fund	Medical Aid Fund	PAYE	Union fees	UIF	Total			Pension Fund	Medical Aid Fund	UIF	SDL	Total

1. The **Employees** Column shows the **name** of the **employee.**
2. The **Basic Salary** Column shows the **Basic Salary** (bonus not included) of the employee.
3. The **Bonus** Column shows the **bonus** earned by the employee.
4. The **Gross Salary** Column shows the **sum** of the **Basic Salary** and **bonus** (Basic Salary + Bonus).
5. The **Deductions** Columns show **all** the **Deductions** that are **subtracted** from the **Gross Salary** of the employee.

   The employer owes the various organisations the Deductions made:
   - The **Pension Fund** Column shows the amount **deducted** from the Gross Salary for the **Pension Fund**.
   - The **Medical Aid Fund** Column shows the amount **deducted** from the Gross Salary for the **Medical Aid Fund**.
   - The **PAYE** Column shows the amount **deducted** from the Gross Salary for **Income Tax**.
   - The **Union Fees** Column shows the amount **deducted** from the Gross Salary for **Union Fees**.
   - The **UIF** Column shows the **1% of Gross Salary deducted** from the Gross Salary for the **UIF (Unemployment Insurance Fund)**.
   - The **Total** Column shows the **sum** of all the **Deductions** (Pension Fund + Medical Aid Fund + PAYE + Union Fees + UIF).

6. The **Net Salary** Column shows the difference between the **Gross Salary and Deductions** (Gross Salary – Deductions). **This is the amount the employee receives.**
7. The **Cheque no.** Column shows the **number** of the **Cheque** that will be used to **pay** the Salary of the employee. A Cheque is written to each employee to pay his or her Wages. These days, Cheques are rarely used and most payments are made using online transfers (EFTs) or cash..
8. The **Employer's Contribution** Columns show all the different **Contributions** made by the business.

   The employer owes the different organisations the Contributions that have been made.
   - The **Pension Fund** Column shows the **Contribution** made by the business to the **Pension Fund** of the employee.
   - The **Medical Aid Fund** Column shows the **Contribution** made by the business to the **Medical Aid Fund** of the employee.
   - The **UIF** Column shows the **Contribution** made (**1% of Gross Salary** of the employee) by the business to **UIF**.
   - The **SDL** Column shows the **Contribution** made by the business to SARS for the **Skills Development** of employees.
   - The **Total** Column shows the **sum** of all **Contributions** (Pension Fund + Medical Aid Fund + UIF + SDL).

Make sure you know all the headings and what to record under each heading!

FORMAT OF THE WJ

Wages Journal of [Name of business] – [Month, year]

Each Journal has a unique Folio Reference → WJ [XX]

1. Employees	2. Basic Wage	3. Overtime			4. Gross Wage	5. Deductions					6. Net Wage	7. Cheque no.	8. Employer's Contribution				
		Hours	Rate	Amount		Pension Fund	Medical Aid Fund	PAYE	Union fees	UIF	Total			Pension Fund	Medical Aid Fund	UIF	SDL	Total

1. The **Employees** Column shows the **name** of the **employee.**
2. The **Basic Wage** Column shows the **Basic Wage** (no overtime included) of the employee.
3. The **Overtime** Column shows the amount of **overtime worked** by the employee.
   - The **Hours** Column shows the number of **overtime hours** worked.
   - The **Rate** Column shows the **hourly rate** paid for overtime worked.
   - The **Amount** Column shows the **total overtime** paid (Hours × Rate).
4. The **Gross Wage** Column shows the **sum** of the **Basic Wage and overtime** (Basic Wage + Overtime).
5. The **Deductions** Columns show **all the Deductions** that are **subtracted** from the **Gross Wage** of the employee.

   The employer owes the different organisations the Deductions made:
   - The **Pension Fund** Column shows the amount **deducted** from the Gross Wage for the **Pension Fund.**
   - The **Medical Aid Fund** Column shows the amount **deducted** from the Gross Wage for the **Medical Aid Fund.**
   - The **PAYE** Column shows the amount **deducted** from the Gross Wage for **Income Tax.**
   - The **Union Fees** Column shows the amount **deducted** from the Gross Wage for **Union Fees.**
   - The **UIF** Column shows the **1% of Gross Wage deducted** from the Gross Wage for the **UIF.**
   - The **Total** Column shows the **sum** of all the **Deductions** (Pension Fund + Medical Aid Fund + PAYE + Union Fees + UIF).
6. The **Net Wage** Column shows the difference between the Gross Wage and Deductions (Gross Wage − Deductions). This is the amount the employee receives.
7. The **Cheque no.** Column shows the number of the **Cheque** that will be used to **pay** the Wage of the employee. A Cheque is written to each employee to pay his or her Wages. These days, Cheques are rarely used and most payments are made using online transfers (EFTs) or cash.
8. The **Employer's Contribution** Columns show all the different **Contributions** made by the business.

   The employer owes the different organisations the Contributions that have been made.
   - The **Pension Fund** Column shows the **Contribution** made by the business to the **Pension Fund** of the employee.
   - The **Medical Aid Fund** Column shows the **Contribution** made by the business to the **Medical Aid Fund** of the employee.
   - The **UIF** Column shows the **Contribution** made (1% of Gross Wage of the employee) by the business to **UIF.**
   - The **SDL** Column shows the **Contribution** made by the business to SARS for the **skills development** of employees.
   - The **Total** Column shows the **sum** of all **Contributions** (Pension Fund + Medical Aid Fund + UIF + SDL).

Make sure you know all the headings and what to record under each heading!

WIZZY WOOD makes and sells furniture. They have six employees who either work part-time or full-time. Use the following information to prepare the **Salaries Journal and Wages Journal**.

Information on the employees of Wizzy Wood for December 2016:
The business has three employees who earn a monthly **Salary**. Use the information below to prepare the Salaries Journal.

Employee	Gross Salary (monthly)	Bonus	Medical aid	PAYE
S. Khala	R5 500	R500	R300	R400
N. du Plessis	R4 200	R200	R300	R380
Y. Qwabaza	R6 000	R300	R300	R450

- UIF is calculated at 1% of Gross Salary.
- Employer contributes 10% and employee contributes 5% of the Basic Salary to the Pension Fund.
- Employer contributes R2 for every R1 contribution by the employee to the Medical Aid Fund.
- 1% of the Gross Salary is contributed to SDL.

The business has three employees who earn **Wages** each month. Use the information below to prepare the Wages Journal for the week ended 07 December 2016.

Employee	Hours	Rate per hour	Overtime	PAYE	Medical aid	NN Union
A. Hussein	40	R50	4	40	100	25
L. Krom	40	R20	10	30	50	25
C. Theron	35	R40	0	36	100	25

- Overtime is paid at one and a half times the normal rate.
- UIF is calculated at 1% of Gross Wage.
- No contributions are made towards the Pension Fund.
- The employer contributes the same amount as the employee towards the Medical Aid Fund.
- 1% of the Gross Wage is contributed to SDL.

See solutions on next 2 pages.

Salaries Journal of Wizzy Wood – December 2016

Employees	Basic Salary	Bonus	Gross Salary	Deductions					Net Salary	Cheque no.	Employer's contribution				
				Pension Fund	Medical Aid Fund	PAYE	Union fees	UIF	Total			Pension Fund	Medical Aid Fund	UIF	SDL	Total
S. Khala	5 500	500	6 000	275	300	400	0	60	1085	4 965		550	600	60	60	1 205
N. du Plessis	4 200	200	4 400	210	300	380	0	44	934	3 466		420	600	44	44	1 062
Y. Qwabaza	6 000	300	6 300	300	300	450	0	63	1 113	5 187		600	600	63	65	1 260
	15 700	1 000	16 700	785	900	1 230	0	167	3 082	13 618		1 570	1 800	167	167	3 527

Wizzy Wood owes money to the employees and the different organisations:

The following Expenses are recorded:

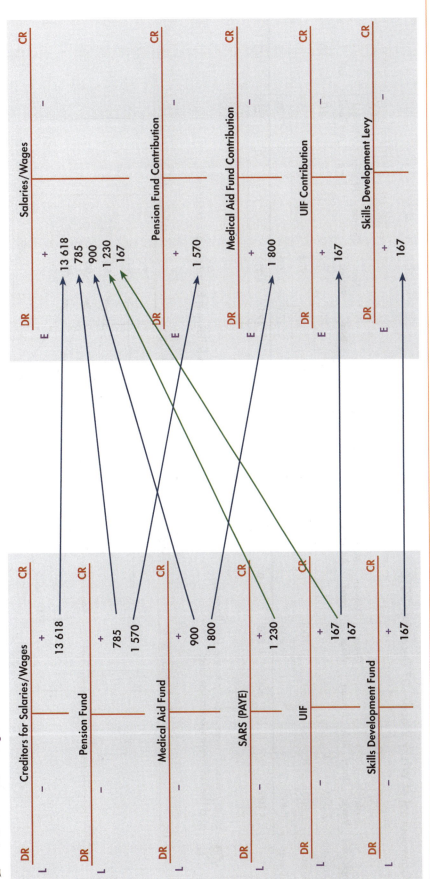

Wages Journal of Wizzy Wood – 07 December 2016

Employees	Basic Wage	Overtime			Gross Wage	Deductions						Net Wages	Cheque no.	Employer's contribution				Total
		Hours	Rate	Amount		Pension Fund	Medical Aid Fund	PAYE	Union fees	UIF	Total			Pension Fund	Medical Aid Fund	UIF	SDL	
A. Hussein	2 000	4	75	300	2 300		100	40	25	23	188	2 112			100	23		123
L. Krom	800	10	30	300	1 100		50	30	25	11	116	984			50	11		61
C. Theron	1 400				1 400		100	36	25	14	175	1 225			100	14		114
	4 200			600	4 800	0	250	106	75	48	479	4 321		0	250	48	0	298

💡 Wizzy Wood owes money to the employees and the different organisations:

The following Expenses are recorded:

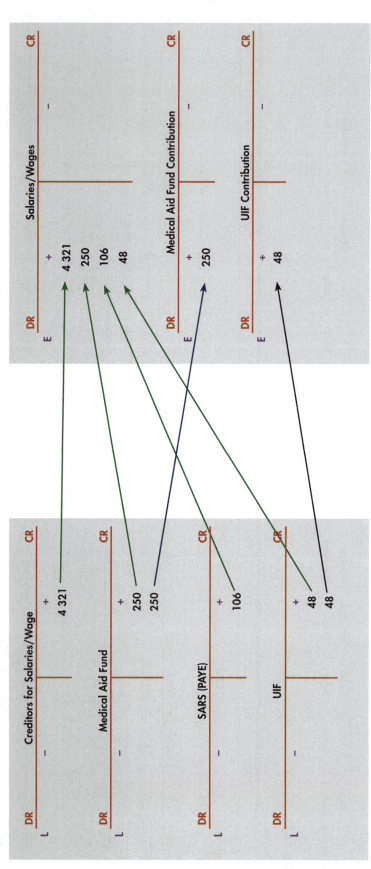

I. GENERAL JOURNAL (GJ)

The GJ is used to record all transactions that do not belong in any of the other Journals.
Some of the **common transactions** recorded in the General Journal include **Year-End Adjustments, Reversals, Depreciation** and the **Correction of Errors**.

Format of the GJ
The format of the GJ is designed to record any transaction.

General Journal of [Name of business] – [Month, year]   Each Journal has a unique Folio Reference ➜ GJ [XX]

1. Date	2. Details	3. Fol	4. General Ledger		5. Debtors Control		6. Creditors Control	
			Debit	Credit	Debit	Credit	Debit	Credit
	Account to debit							
	Account to credit							
	Narration							

1. The **Date** Column shows the **day** of the **month** on which the transaction takes place.

2. The **Details** Column shows the **Account** to be **debited** and the **Account** to be **credited** and **explains** the **transaction** that is recorded.
    a. The Account to be **debited** is recorded **first.**
    b. The Account to be **credited** is recorded **below** the Account to be debited. The Account to be credited is **slightly indented** (slightly more to the right than the Account to be debited).
    c. A **narration** (a **brief explanation** that explains the transaction) is recorded below the Accounts.
       Since the General Journal is used to record different types of transactions, the narration is important to explain the transaction recorded.

3. The **Fol** Column shows the **Folio Reference** of the **Account affected**. Each Account is assigned a unique code called a Folio Reference thats **starts with a B** (Assets, Liability or Owner's Equity Accounts) **or an N** (Income and Expense Accounts).

4. The **General Ledger** Column shows the **Debit amount** and the **Credit amount** of the transaction.

5. The **Debtors Control** Column shows any **amounts** that **affect** the **Debtors Control Account**.

6. The **Creditors Control** Column shows any **amounts** that **affect** the **Creditors Control** Account.

> The following General Journal entries are often asked in a test:
> - Bad Debts
> - Owner takes Inventory for personal use
> - Interest charged to Debtors on overdue Accounts
> - Discount cancelled on dishonoured Cheques
> - Correction of errors
> - Year-End Adjustments see pg 120

D&G PETS sells all different types of cat and dog food. Use the following information to complete the General Journal.

Transactions during December 2017
5   The Owner took dog food to the value of R500 for his dogs.
17 The bookkeeper entered R830 for Stationery paid by Cheque. However, the transaction was for Repairs.
20 Depreciation on vehicles for the year amounted to R18 000.

General Journal of D&G Pets – December 2017   GJ 12

Date	Details	Fol	General Ledger Debit	General Ledger Credit	Debtors Control Debit	Debtors Control Credit	Creditors Control Debit	Creditors Control Credit
5	Drawings		500					
	Trading Stock *Note that the Account to be credited is indented.*			500				
	Owner took Trading Stock for personal use							
17	Repairs		830					
	Stationery			830				
	Correct the Incorrect entry							
20	Depreciation		18 000					
	Accumulated Depreciation on Vehicles			18 000				
	Record Depreciation on Vehicles for the year							

Each transaction recorded is posted separately to the Accounts affected.

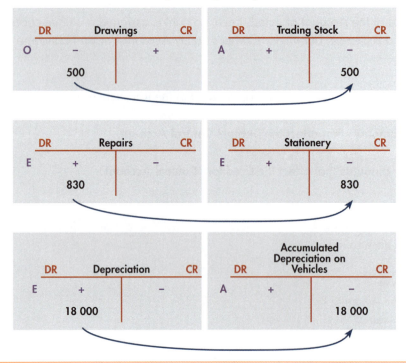

That's the end of Journals – phew!

LEDGERS
SUMMARY OF CONTENTS

GENERAL LEDGER (GL)   56—82

    1. Overview of the Journals posted to the General Ledger   56

    2. Overview of the layout of the General Ledger   57

    3. Layout of the Accounts in the General Ledger

    4. Opening and closing Accounts in the General Ledger   58

A POSTING THE CASH RECEIPTS JOURNAL (CRJ) TO THE GENERAL LEDGER   59

B POSTING THE CASH PAYMENTS JOURNAL (CPJ) TO THE GENERAL LEDGER   62

C POSTING THE PETTY CASH JOURNAL (PCJ) TO THE GENERAL LEDGER   64

D POSTING THE DEBTORS JOURNAL (DJ) TO THE GENERAL LEDGER   66

E POSTING THE CREDITORS JOURNAL (CJ) TO THE GENERAL LEDGER   68

F POSTING THE DEBTORS ALLOWANCES JOURNAL (DAJ) TO THE GENERAL LEDGER   70

G POSTING THE CREDITORS ALLOWANCES JOURNAL (CAJ) TO THE GENERAL LEDGER   72

H POSTING THE SALARIES JOURNAL (SJ) AND WAGES JOURNAL (WJ)

TO THE GENERAL LEDGER   74

I POSTING THE GENERAL JOURNAL (GJ) TO THE GENERAL LEDGER   77

SUBSIDIARY LEDGERS   79

    1. Debtors Ledger

    2. Creditors Ledger   81

LEDGERS

The **General Ledger** contains the **Asset, Liability, Owner's Equity, Income** and **Expense** Accounts to show all the Financial Activities of a business. This information is posted from the various Journals at the end of each month. The **Subsidiary Ledgers** record **additional details** from specific Control Accounts in the General Ledger. See pg 79 for more information on the Subsidiary Ledgers.

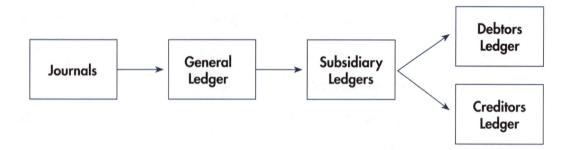

GENERAL LEDGER (GL)

All the Journals are posted to the General Ledger at the **end** of each month to show the effect of the transactions recorded on the Asset, Owner's Equity, Liability, Income and Expense Accounts.

1. **OVERVIEW OF THE JOURNALS POSTED TO THE GENERAL LEDGER**  Memorise the table below!

	JOURNAL	ACCOUNTS TO BE DEBITED	ACCOUNTS TO BE CREDITED
A	CASH RECEIPTS JOURNAL (CRJ)	Bank Account	Various Accounts Exception – Cost of Sales Exception – Discount Allowed
B	CASH PAYMENTS JOURNAL (CPJ)	Various Accounts Exception – Discount Received	Bank Account
C	PETTY CASH JOURNAL (PCJ)	Various Accounts	Petty Cash Account
D	DEBTORS JOURNAL (DJ)	Debtors Control Account Cost of Sales Account	Sales Account Trading Stock Account
E	CREDITORS JOURNAL (CJ)	Various Accounts	Creditors Control Account
F	DEBTORS ALLOWANCES JOURNAL (DAJ)	Debtors Allowances Account Trading Stock Account	Debtors Control Account Cost of Sales Account
G	CREDITORS ALLOWANCES JOURNAL (CAJ)	Creditors Control Account	Various Accounts
H	SALARIES JOURNAL (SJ)/ WAGES JOURNAL (WJ)	Salaries/Wages Account All Contribution Expense Accounts	Creditors for Salaries/Wages Accounts All deductions from Gross Salaries/Wages Accounts
I	GENERAL JOURNAL (GJ)	Depends on entries	Depends on entries

Make sure that you know how to post each Journal to the General Ledger.

2. **OVERVIEW OF THE LAYOUT OF THE GENERAL LEDGER**
   The General Ledger is divided into the Balance Sheet Accounts Section and the Nominal Sheet Accounts Section.
   The names and details of the Accounts are listed under the relevant sections.
   - The Folio References of all the Accounts under the **B**alance sheet Accounts Section start with a **B**.
   - The Folio References of all the Accounts under the **N**ominal sheet Accounts Section start with an **N**.

   > **GENERAL LEDGER OF [NAME OF BUSINESS]**
   > **Balance Sheet Accounts Section**
   > **Asset** Accounts
   > **Owner's Equity** Accounts
   > **Liability** Accounts
   > **Nominal Accounts Section**
   > **Income** Accounts
   > **Expense** Accounts

3. **LAYOUT OF THE ACCOUNTS IN THE GENERAL LEDGER**
   The Accounts in the General Ledger are in the form of T Accounts.

   The Debit (left) side for each Account has the same columns as the Credit (right) side has.

DR				1. Name of Account		2. Folio		CR
3. Date	4. Details	5. Fol	6. Amount	3. Date	4. Details	5. Fol	6. Amount
	All the entries that affect the Account on the Debit side are entered here.				All the entries that affect the Account on the Credit side are entered here.		

   1. **Name of Account:** The name of the Account is shown at the top.

   2. **Folio:** Each Account has a unique code called a **Folio Reference**.
      The Folio Reference makes it easy to refer to the Account without having to write out the full name of the Account in the Journals.

   3. **Date:** The **month** and **day** on which the business records the entry in the Account.

   4. **Details:** The **other Account affected** is recorded under the Details Column. This Account is known as the **Contra Account**. **Each entry** posted from the Journal affects **at least two Accounts** in the **General Ledger**. The first Account is shown by its name and the other Accounts are shown under this column.

   5. **Fol:** The **Folio Reference** of the **Journal** from which the amount is posted is recorded under the Fol Column. Each Journal has a unique code called a Folio Reference. The Folio Reference makes it easy to refer to the Journal without having to write out the full name of the Journal.

   6. **Amount:** The amount by which the Account increases or decreases is recorded under the Amount Column.

   > It is important to know on which sides Accounts increase and decrease when posting Journals to the General Ledger. See pg 12

4. OPENING AND CLOSING ACCOUNTS IN THE GENERAL LEDGER

Each Account in the General Ledger is opened at the **beginning** of the month with the opening balance and closed at the **end** of the month with the closing balance.

Steps to open and close Accounts in the General Ledger See below for an example.

a. **Open the Account with the opening balance** brought down (b/d) from the previous month.
The side that the balance is on depends on the type of Account.

- Asset Accounts have a Debit balance.
- Liability and Owner's Equity Accounts have Credit balances.

b. **Balancing lines are drawn on the Debit and Credit sides.** The lines are drawn two spaces below the last amount in the Account. Add up all the Debit amounts and Credit amounts to determine which side has the highest total. The **highest total** is recorded in the **balancing lines**.

c. **The new balance is worked out and recorded (above the balancing lines) on the side with the lower total.** The new balance is equal to the difference between the Debit and Credit sides.
- If the **Debit (left)** side has the **highest total**, then the **Balance (c/d)** is recorded on the **Credit (right)** side to balance the Account. This is usually the case for Asset Accounts.
- If the **Credit (right)** side has the **highest total**, then the **Balance (c/d)** is recorded on the **Debit (left)** side to balance the Account. This is usually the case for Liability and Owner's Equity Accounts.

d. **On the first day of the new month, the Account is opened with the new balance (b/d) for the Account.**
The opening balance (Balance b/d) of the Account at the beginning of the month is equal to the amount used to balance (Balance c/d) the Account at the end of the previous month.

Expense and Income Accounts often only have entries on one side of the Account.
These Accounts do not need to be balanced. A line is drawn under the last entry and the total is recorded at the end of the month.

Examples of General Ledger Accounts in the books of PNC PANCAKES

DR — Equipment — **B1** — **CR**

Date		Details	Fol	Amount		Date		Details	Fol	Amount	
2019 Jan.	01	Balance	b/d	20 000	00	2019 Jan.	05	Creditors Control	CPJ	5 000	00
	18	Creditors Control	CJ	10 000	00						
							30	Balance 30 000 − 5 000	c/d	25 000	00
				30 000	00					30 000	00
2019 Feb.	01	Balance	b/d	25 000	00						

DR — Stationery — **N1** — **CR**

Date		Details	Fol	Amount		Date		Details	Fol	Amount	
2019 Jan.	01	Total	b/d	300	00						
	09	Bank	CAJ	200	00						
	26	Creditors Control	CJ	600	00						
				1 100	00						

There are only Debit entries, so a line is drawn under the last amount and the total is added up.

A. POSTING THE CASH RECEIPTS JOURNAL (CRJ) TO THE GENERAL LEDGER

The CRJ is posted to the General Ledger at the end of each month to record the effect of all the transactions in the CRJ on the Accounts of the business.

 The total of the Bank Column in the CRJ shows the total amount of cash received for the month.
The total of the Analysis Columns and the entries under the Sundry Accounts Column in the CRJ shows what the cash was received for. See pg 32

OVERVIEW OF POSTING THE COLUMNS OF THE CRJ TO THE GENERAL LEDGER

BANK COLUMN	ANALYSIS COLUMNS	SUNDRY ACCOUNTS COLUMNS
The total of the Bank Column is posted to the **Debit** side of the **Bank Account**. • **Total Receipts** is written under the **Details** Column. • The date on which the **Journal** is **posted** (last day of the month) is written under the **Date** Column.	The total of each Analysis Column is posted to the **Credit** side of the **Account affected**. **Except for Cost of Sales and Discount Allowed** • **Bank** is written under the **Details** Column. • The date on which the **Journal** is **posted** (last day of the month) is written under the **Date** Column.	Each entry in the Sundry Accounts Column is posted to the **Credit** side of the **Account affected**. **Except for Cost of Sales and Discount Allowed** • **Bank** is written under the **Details** Column. • The date on which the **transaction** was **recorded** is written under the **Date** Column.

DIFFERENT STEPS ARE FOLLOWED TO POST COST OF SALES AND DISCOUNT ALLOWED

Cost of Sales and Discount Allowed do not affect the amount of cash available to the business.
The steps below show how to post the amounts for these Accounts in the CRJ to the General Ledger.

COST OF SALES	DISCOUNT ALLOWED
Cost of Sales is posted to: a. The **Debit** side of the **Cost of Sales** Account • **Trading Stock** is written under the **Details** Column. b. The **Credit** side of the **Trading Stock** Account • **Cost of Sales** is written under the **Details** Column. See pg 13 to learn more about Cost of Sales.	Discount Allowed is posted to: a. The **Debit** side of the **Discount Allowed** Account • **Debtors Control** is written under the **Details** Column. b. The **Credit** side of the **Debtors Control** Account • **Discount Allowed** is written under the **Details** Column. See pg 17 to learn more about Discount Allowed.

Required: Post the Cash Receipts Journal of **CARLY'S CLEVER TUTORS** to the General Ledger.

CASH RECEIPTS JOURNAL of CARLY'S CLEVER TUTORS – April 2018   CRJ 04

Doc	Day	Details	Fol	Analysis of Receipts		Bank		Current Income (Analysis Column)		Sundry Accounts			
										Amount		Fol	Details
				R	c	R	c	R	c	R	c		
BS	5	Carly				3 500	00			3 500	00	B2	Capital
CRT 67–77		Customers		2 000	00	2 000	00	2 000	00				
CRT 78	9	N. Dube		400	00	400	00	400	00				
Rec 15	30	J. Smith				5 000	00			5 000	00	N2	Rent Income
						10 900	00	2 400	00	8 500	00		
						B1		N1					

The references B1, N1, B2, N2 show the Folio References of the Accounts in the General Ledger to which the amounts are posted. If they are not provided then make up your own unique Folio References.

GENERAL LEDGER of CARLY'S CLEVER TUTORS

Balance Sheet Section

DR   **Bank**   **B1**   **CR**

Date		Details	Fol	Amount		Date	Details	Fol	Amount
2018 April	30	Total Receipts	CRJ04	10 900	00				

DR   **Capital**   **B2**   **CR**

Date	Details	Fol	Amount	Date		Details	Fol	Amount	
				2018 April	5	Bank	CRJ04	3 500	00

Take note of date

Nominal Accounts Section

DR   **Current Income**   **N1**   **CR**

Date	Details	Fol	Amount	Date		Details	Fol	Amount	
				2018 April	30	Bank	CRJ04	2 400	00

DR   **Rent Income**   **N2**   **CR**

Date	Details	Fol	Amount	Date		Details	Fol	Amount	
				2018 April	30	Bank	CRJ04	5 000	00

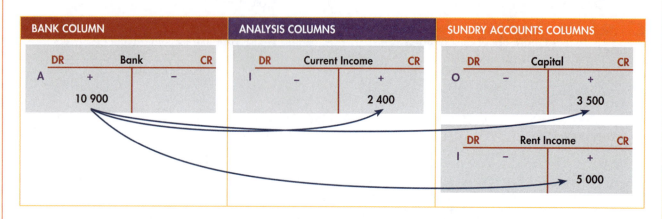

⚠ Dates are very important when posting from Sundry Accounts. Marks are deducted for incorrect dates.

Required: Post the Cash Receipts Journal of **BENNY'S BICYCLES** to the General Ledger.

CASH RECEIPTS JOURNAL of BENNY'S BICYCLES – June 2017 — CRJ 06

Doc	Day	Details	Fol	Analysis of Receipts		Bank		Sales (Analysis Column)		Cost of Sales (Analysis Column)		Sundry Accounts			
												Amount		Fol	Details
				R	c	R	c	R	c	R	c	R	c		
BS	1	Bizzy Bank				5 000	00					5 000	00	B4	Loan: Bizzy Bank
CRR 01–12	4	Cash		24 000	00	24 000	00	24 000	00	20 000	00				
Rec. 02	19	S. Bakone	D1	400	00	400	00					400	00	B2	Debtors Control
						29 400	00	24 000	00	20 000	00	5 400	00		
						B1		N1		N2					

GENERAL LEDGER of BENNY'S BICYCLES
Balance Sheet Section

DR — Bank — **B1** — **CR**

Date	Details	Fol	Amount	Date	Details	Fol	Amount
2017 June 30	Total Receipts	CRJ06	29 400 00				

DR — Debtors Control — **B2** — **CR**

Date	Details	Fol	Amount	Date	Details	Fol	Amount
				2017 June 19	Bank	CRJ06	400 00

Take note of date

DR — Trading Stock — **B3** — **CR**

Date	Details	Fol	Amount	Date	Details	Fol	Amount
				2017 June 30	Cost of Sales	CRJ06	20 000 00

DR — Loan: Bizzy Bank — **B4** — **CR**

Date	Details	Fol	Amount	Date	Details	Fol	Amount
				2017 June 1	Bank	CRJ06	5 000 00

Take note of date

Nominal Accounts Section

DR — Sales — **N1** — **CR**

Date	Details	Fol	Amount	Date	Details	Fol	Amount
				2017 June 30	Bank	CRJ06	24 000 00

DR — Cost of Sales — **N2** — **CR**

Date	Details	Fol	Amount	Date	Details	Fol	Amount
2017 June 30	Trading Stock	CRJ06	20 000 00				

BANK COLUMN

DR	Bank	CR
A	+	–
	29 400	

ANALYSIS COLUMNS

DR	Sales	CR
I	–	+
		24 000

SUNDRY ACCOUNTS COLUMNS

DR	Loan: Bizzy Bank	CR
L	–	+
		5 000

DR	Debtors Control	CR
A	+	–
		400

COST OF SALES (Exception — the Bank Account is not affected)

DR	Cost of Sales	CR
E	+	–
	20 000	

DR	Trading Stock	CR
A	+	–
		20 000

B. POSTING THE CASH PAYMENTS JOURNAL (CPJ) TO THE GENERAL LEDGER

The CPJ is posted to the General Ledger at the end of each month to record the effect of all the transactions in the CPJ on the Accounts of the business.

The total of the Bank Column in the CPJ shows the total amount of cash paid for the month.
The total of the Analysis Columns and the entries under the Sundry Accounts Column in the CPJ show what the cash was spent on. See pg 34

OVERVIEW OF POSTING THE COLUMNS OF THE CPJ TO THE GENERAL LEDGER

BANK COLUMN	ANALYSIS COLUMNS	SUNDRY ACCOUNTS COLUMNS
The total of the Bank Column is posted to the Credit side of the Bank Account. • Total Payments is written under the Details Column. • The date on which the Journal is posted (last day of the month) is written under the Date Column.	The total of each Analysis Column is posted to the Debit side of the Account affected. Except Discount Received • Bank is written under the Details Column. • The date on which the Journal is posted (last day of the month) is written under the Date Column.	Each entry in the Sundry Accounts Column is posted to the Debit side of the Account affected. Except Discount Received • Bank is written under the Details Column. • The date on which the transaction was recorded is written under the Date Column.

DIFFERENT STEPS ARE FOLLOWED TO POST DISCOUNT RECEIVED

Discount Received does not affect the amount of cash available to the business.
The steps below show how to post amounts for Discount Received in the CRJ to the General Ledger.

DISCOUNT RECEIVED

The total of Discount Received is posted to the following Accounts:
a. The Debit side of the Creditors Control Account
   • Discount Received is written under the Details Column.
b. The Credit side of the Discount Received Account
   • Creditors Control is written under the Details Column.

See pg 44 to learn more about Discount Received.

Required: Post the Cash Payments Journal of CINDY'S PRINTS to the General Ledger.

CASH PAYMENTS JOURNAL of CINDY'S PRINTS – June 2016   CPJ 06

Doc	Day	Name of payee	Fol	Bank		Salaries (Analysis Column)		Creditors Control (Analysis Column)		Sundry Accounts			
										Amount		Fol	Details
				R	c	R	c	R	c	R	c		
CC 21	2	BN Stores		100	00					100	00	N2	Stationery
CC 22	4	J. Nkosi		12 500	00	12 500	00						
CC 23	8	CC Computers		6 000	00					6 000	00	B2	Equipment
CC 24	24	M. Molefe	C1	5 000	00			5 000	00				
CC 25	30	TN Mobile		990	00					990	00	N3	Telephone
				24 590	00	12 500	00	5 000	00	7 090	00		
				B1		N1		B3					

GENERAL LEDGER of CINDY'S PRINTS
Balance Sheet Section

DR — Bank — B1 — **CR**

Date	Details	Fol	Amount	Date	Details	Fol	Amount
				2016 June 30	Total Payments	CPJ06	24 590 00

DR — Equipment — B2 — **CR**

Date	Details	Fol	Amount	Date	Details	Fol	Amount
2016 June 08	Bank	CPJ06	6 000 00				

DR — Creditors Control — B3 — **CR**

Date	Details	Fol	Amount	Date	Details	Fol	Amount
2016 June 30	Bank	CPJ06	5 000 00				

Nominal Accounts Section

DR — Salaries — N1 — **CR**

Date	Details	Fol	Amount	Date	Details	Fol	Amount
2016 June 30	Bank	CPJ06	12 500 00				

DR — Stationery — N2 — **CR**

Date	Details	Fol	Amount	Date	Details	Fol	Amount
2016 June 2	Bank	CPJ06	100 00				

DR — Telephone — N3 — **CR**

Date	Details	Fol	Amount	Date	Details	Fol	Amount
2016 June 30	Bank	CPJ06	990 00				

Dates are very important when posting from Sundry Accounts. Marks are deducted for incorrect dates.

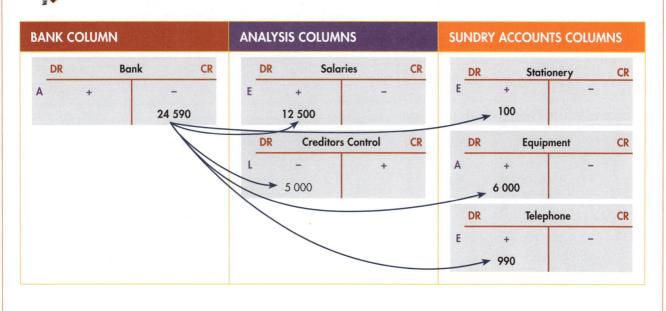

C. POSTING THE PETTY CASH JOURNAL (PCJ) TO THE GENERAL LEDGER

The PCJ is posted to the General Ledger at the end of each month to record the effect of all the transactions in the PCJ on the Accounts of the business.

 The total of the Petty Cash Column in the PCJ shows the total amount of Petty Cash paid for the month. The total of the Analysis Columns and the entries under the Sundry Accounts Column in the PCJ show what the Petty Cash was spent on. See pg 36

OVERVIEW OF POSTING THE COLUMNS OF THE PCJ TO THE GENERAL LEDGER

PETTY CASH COLUMN	ANALYSIS COLUMNS	SUNDRY ACCOUNTS COLUMNS
The total of the Petty Cash Column is posted to the **Credit** side of the **Petty Cash** Account. • **Total Payments** is written under the **Details** Column. • The date on which the **Journal** is **posted** (last day of the month) is written under the **Date** Column.	The total of each Analysis Column is posted to the **Debit** side of the **Account affected**. • **Petty Cash** is written under the **Details** Column. • The date on which the **Journal** is **posted** (last day of the month) is written under the **Date** Column.	Each entry in the Sundry Accounts Column is posted to the **Debit** side of the **Account affected**. • **Petty Cash** is written under the **Details** Column. • The date on which the **transaction** was **recorded** is written under the **Date** Column.

Required: Post the Petty Cash Journal of RR SPORTS to the General Ledger.

PETTY CASH JOURNAL of RR SPORTS – September 2017 PCJ 09

Doc	Day	Details	Fol	Petty Cash		Stationery (Analysis Column)		Repairs (Analysis Column)		Sundry Accounts			
										Amount		Fol	Details
				R	c	R	c	R	c	R	c		
105	2	CVC charity		120	00					120	00	N3	Donations
106	12	Mark		65	00					65	00	B2	Drawings
107	19	S. Ndlovu		180	00			180	00				
108	22	KL Stores		320	00	320	00						
				685	00	320	00	180	00	185	00		
				B1		N1		N2					

GENERAL LEDGER of RR SPORTS
Balance Sheet Section

DR							Petty Cash		B1		CR
Date		Details	Fol	Amount		Date		Details	Fol	Amount	
						2017 Sept.	30	Total Payments	PCJ09	685	00

DR							Drawings		B2		CR
Date		Details	Fol	Amount		Date		Details	Fol	Amount	
2017 Sept.	12	Petty Cash	PCJ09	65	00						

Nominal Accounts Section

DR							Stationery		N1		CR
Date		Details	Fol	Amount		Date		Details	Fol	Amount	
2017 Sept.	30	Petty Cash	PCJ09	320	00						

DR							Repairs		N2		CR
Date		Details	Fol	Amount		Date		Details	Fol	Amount	
2017 Sept.	30	Petty Cash	PCJ09	180	00						

DR							Donations Paid		N3		CR
Date		Details	Fol	Amount		Date		Details	Fol	Amount	
2017 Sept.	2	Petty Cash	PCJ09	120	00						

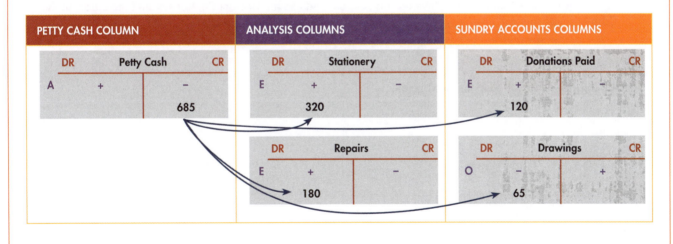

D. POSTING THE DEBTORS JOURNAL (DJ) TO THE GENERAL LEDGER

The DJ is posted to the General Ledger at the end of each month to record the effect of all the transactions in the DJ on the Accounts of the business.

 All transactions recorded in the DJ affect the Sales Account and the Cost of Sales Account. pg 38

OVERVIEW OF POSTING THE COLUMNS OF THE DJ TO THE GENERAL LEDGER

SALES COLUMN	COST OF SALES COLUMN
The total of the Sales Column is posted to: a. The Credit side of the Sales Account • Debtors Control is recorded under the Details Column. b. The Debit side of the Debtors Control Account • Sales is recorded under the Details Column. The date on which the Journal is posted (last day of the month) is written under the Date Column.	The total of the Cost of Sales Column is posted to: c. The Debit side of the Cost of Sales Account • Trading Stock is recorded under the Details Column. d. The Credit side of the Trading Stock Account • Cost of Sales is recorded under the Details Column. The date on which the Journal is posted (last day of the month) is written under the Date Column.

 The entries for posting Inventory sold in the Debtors Journal are similar to the entries for posting Inventory sold in the Cash Receipts Journal. The only difference is the Account used to record how the customer purchases the Inventory. In the Debtors Journal, Inventory is sold on credit so the Debtors Control Account increases. In the Cash Receipts Journal, Inventory is sold for cash so the Bank Account increases.

 See example NELI RINGS on next page.

Required: Post the Debtors Journal of NELI RINGS to the General Ledger.

DEBTORS JOURNAL of NELI RINGS – December 2017   DJ 12

Doc	Day	Debtor	Fol	Sales R	c	Cost of Sales R	c
109	9	M. Mandla	D3	20 000	00	16 666	67
110	24	S. Richards	D1	25 000	00	20 833	33
111	27	N. Govind	D5	6 000	00	5 000	00
				51 000	00	42 500	00
				N1		N2	

NELI RINGS uses a 20% mark-up.

GENERAL LEDGER of NELI RINGS
Balance Sheet Section

DR   **Debtors Control**   **B1**   **CR**

Date	Details	Fol	Amount	Date	Details	Fol	Amount
2017 Dec. 31	Sales	DJ12	51 000 00				

DR   **Trading Stock**   **B2**   **CR**

Date	Details	Fol	Amount	Date	Details	Fol	Amount
				2017 Dec. 31	Cost of Sales	DJ12	42 500 00

Nominal Accounts Section

DR   **Sales**   **N1**   **CR**

Date	Details	Fol	Amount	Date	Details	Fol	Amount
				2017 Dec. 31	Debtors Control	DJ12	51 000 00

DR   **Cost of Sales**   **N2**   **CR**

Date	Details	Fol	Amount	Date	Details	Fol	Amount
2017 Dec. 31	Trading Stock	DJ12	42 500 00				

SALES COLUMN

DR	Sales	CR
I −		+
		51 000

DR	Debtors Control	CR
A +		−
51 000		

COST OF SALES COLUMN

DR	Cost of Sales	CR
E +		−
42 500		

DR	Trading Stock	CR
A +		−
		42 500

- Selling Price = Cost Price ÷ 100 × (100 + mark-up) or Selling Price = Cost Price × $\dfrac{100 + \text{mark-up}}{100}$

- Cost Price = Selling Price × 100 ÷ (100 + mark-up) or Cost Price = Selling Price × $\dfrac{100}{100 + \text{mark-up}}$

E. POSTING THE CREDITORS JOURNAL (CJ) TO THE GENERAL LEDGER

The CJ is posted to the General Ledger at the end of each month to record the effect of all the transactions in the CJ on the Accounts of the business.

 The total of the Creditors Column in the CJ shows the increase in the total amount owed to Creditors during the month. The total of the Analysis Columns and the entries under the Sundry Accounts Column in the CJ show what the amounts are owed for (Assets or Expenses purchased on credit). See pg 40

OVERVIEW OF POSTING THE COLUMNS OF THE CJ TO THE GENERAL LEDGER

CREDITORS CONTROL COLUMN	ANALYSIS COLUMN	SUNDRY ACCOUNTS COLUMNS
The total of the Creditors Control Column is posted to the Credit side of the Creditors Control Account. • **Total Purchases** is written under the **Details** Column. • The date on which the **Journal** is **posted** (last day of the month) is written under the **Date** Column.	The total of each Analysis Column is posted to the Debit side of the Account affected. • **Creditors Control** is written under the **Details** Column. • The date on which the **Journal** is **posted** (last day of the month) is written under the **Date** Column.	Each entry in the Sundry Accounts Column is posted to the Debit side of the Account affected. • **Creditors Control** is written under the **Details** Column. • The date on which the **transaction** was **recorded** is written under the **Date** Column.

 See example **JJ PAINTINGS** on next page.

Required: Post the Creditors Journal of **JJ PAINTINGS** to the General Ledger.

CREDITORS JOURNAL of JJ PAINTINGS – December 2016   CJ12

Doc	Day	Creditor	Fol	Creditors Control		Trading Stock (Analysis Column)		Equipment (Analysis Column)		Sundry Accounts			
										Amount		Fol	Details
				R	c	R	c	R	c	R	c		
602	2	DC Suppliers	C1	1 200	00	1 200	00						
909	19	MCM	C2	15 000	00			15 000	00				
321	22	AZ Dealers	C4	2 050	00	1 800	00			250	00	N1	Stationery
201	23	MM Motors	C3	82 000	00					82 000	00	B3	Vehicle
				100 250	00	3 000	00	15 000	00	82 250	00		
				B4		B2		B1					

GENERAL LEDGER of JJ PAINTINGS
Balance Sheet Section

DR   Equipment   **B1**   **CR**

Date	Details	Fol	Amount		Date	Details	Fol	Amount	
2016 Dec. 31	Creditors Control	CJ12	15 000	00					

DR   Trading Stock   **B2**   **CR**

Date	Details	Fol	Amount		Date	Details	Fol	Amount	
2016 Dec. 31	Creditors Control	CJ12	3 000	00					

DR   Vehicles   **B3**   **CR**

Date	Details	Fol	Amount		Date	Details	Fol	Amount	
2016 Dec. 23	Creditors Control	CJ12	82 000	00					

DR   Creditors Control   **B4**   **CR**

Date	Details	Fol	Amount		Date	Details	Fol	Amount	
					2016 Dec. 31	Total Purchases	CJ12	100 250	00

Nominal Accounts Section

DR   Stationery   **N1**   **CR**

Date	Details	Fol	Amount		Date	Details	Fol	Amount	
2016 Dec. 22	Creditors Control	CJ12	250	00					

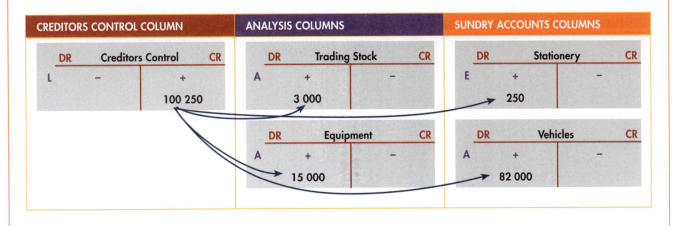

F. POSTING THE DEBTORS ALLOWANCES JOURNAL (DAJ) TO THE GENERAL LEDGER

The DAJ is posted to the General Ledger at the end of each month to record the effect of all the transactions in the DAJ on the Accounts of the business.

 The DAJ is used to record all transactions where:
- Inventory, sold on credit, is returned to the business
- The business gives Debtors a discount on the outstanding amount that they owe See pg 42

OVERVIEW OF POSTING THE COLUMNS OF THE DAJ TO THE GENERAL LEDGER

DEBTORS ALLOWANCES COLUMN	COST OF SALES COLUMN
The total of the Debtors Allowances Column is posted to the following Accounts: a. The **Debit** side of the **Debtors Allowances** Account • **Debtors Control** is recorded under the **Details** Column. b. The **Credit** side of the **Debtors Control** Account • **Debtors Allowances** is recorded under the **Details** Column. The date on which the **Journal** is **posted** (last day of the month) is written under the **Date** Column.	The total of the Cost of Sales Column is posted to the following Accounts: a. The **Debit** side of the **Trading Stock** Account • **Cost of Sales** is recorded under the **Details** Column. b. The **Credit** side of the **Cost of Sales** Account • **Trading Stock** is recorded under the **Details** Column. The date on which the **Journal** is **posted** (last day of the month) is written under the **Date** Column.

 See example **MINDA'S CAR PARTS** on next page.

Required: Post the Debtors Allowances Journal of **MINDA'S CAR PARTS** to the General Ledger.

DEBTORS ALLOWANCES JOURNAL of MINDA'S CAR PARTS – March 2018   DAJ 03

Doc	Day	Debtor	Fol	Debtors Allowances		Cost of Sales	
				R	c	R	c
34	6	Mr Khan	D1	400	00		
35	12	G. Lohrman	D3	3 300	00	2 200	00
36	20	T. Lukhele	D4	8 250	00	5 500	00
37	30	M. Mckenzie	D2	20 000	00	13 333	33
				31 950	00	21 033	33
				N1		N2	

GENERAL LEDGER of MINDA'S CAR PARTS
Balance Sheet Section

DR   **Debtors Control**   **B1**   **CR**

Date	Details	Fol	Amount	Date	Details	Fol	Amount
				2018 March 31	Debtors Allowances	DAJ03	31 950 00

DR   **Trading Stock**   **B2**   **CR**

Date	Details	Fol	Amount	Date	Details	Fol	Amount
2018 March 31	Cost of Sales	DAJ03	21 033 33				

Nominal Accounts Section

DR   **Debtors Allowances**   **N1**   **CR**

Date	Details	Fol	Amount	Date	Details	Fol	Amount
2018 March 31	Debtors Control	DAJ03	31 950 00				

DR   **Cost of Sales**   **N2**   **CR**

Date	Details	Fol	Amount	Date	Details	Fol	Amount
				2018 March 31	Trading Stock	DAJ03	21 033 33

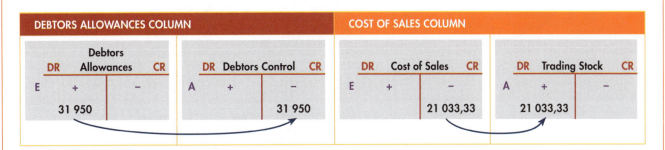

G. POSTING THE CREDITORS ALLOWANCES JOURNAL (CAJ) TO THE GENERAL LEDGER

The CAJ is posted to the General Ledger at the end of each month to record the effect of all the transactions in the CAJ on the Accounts of the business.

 The total of the Creditors Column in the CAJ shows the decrease in the total amount owed to Creditors during the month. The total of the Analysis Columns and the entries under the Sundry Accounts Column in the CAJ show the other Accounts affected. See pg 44

OVERVIEW OF POSTING THE COLUMNS OF THE CAJ TO THE GENERAL LEDGER

CREDITORS CONTROL COLUMN	ANALYSIS COLUMNS	SUNDRY ACCOUNTS COLUMNS
The total of the Creditors Control Column in the CAJ is posted to the **Debit** side of the **Creditors Control Account**. • **Total Returns** is written under the **Details** Column. • The date on which the **Journal** is **posted** (last day of the month) is written under the **Date** Column.	The total of each Analysis Column is posted to the **Credit** side of the **Account affected**. • **Creditors Control** is written under the **Details** Column. • The date on which the **Journal** is **posted** (last day of the month) is written under the **Date** Column.	Each entry in the Sundry Accounts Column is posted to the **Credit** side of the **Account affected**. • **Creditors Control** is written under the **Details** Column. • The date on which the **transaction** was **recorded** is written under the **Date** Column.

 See example **T&T TABLES** on next page.

Required: Post the Creditors Allowances Journal of T&T TABLES to the General Ledger.

CREDITORS ALLOWANCES JOURNAL of T&T TABLES – January 2017   CAJ 01

Doc	Day	Creditor	Fol	Creditors Control		Trading Stock		Equipment		Sundry Accounts			
										Amount		Fol	Details
				R	c	R	c	R	c	R	c		
23	2	NC Suppliers	C2	3 800	00	3 800	00						
24	18	BC Machinery	C4	28 000	00			28 000	00				
25	26	AG Wood	C1	100	00	100	00						
26	31	SS Stationery	C3	300	00					300	00	N1	Stationery
				32 200	00	3 900	00	28 000	00	300	00		
				B3		B1		B2					

GENERAL LEDGER of T&T TABLES
Balance Sheet Section

DR   Trading Stock   **B1**   **CR**

Date	Details	Fol	Amount	Date		Details	Fol	Amount	
				2017 Jan.	31	Creditors Control	CAJ01	3 900	00

DR   Equipment   **B2**   **CR**

Date	Details	Fol	Amount	Date		Details	Fol	Amount	
				2017 Jan.	31	Creditors Control	CAJ01	28 000	00

DR   Creditors Control   **B3**   **CR**

Date		Details	Fol	Amount		Date	Details	Fol	Amount
2017 Jan.	31	Total Returns	CAJ01	32 200	00				

Nominal Accounts Section

DR   Stationery   **N1**   **CR**

Date	Details	Fol	Amount	Date		Details	Fol	Amount	
				2017 Jan.	31	Creditors Control	CAJ01	300	00

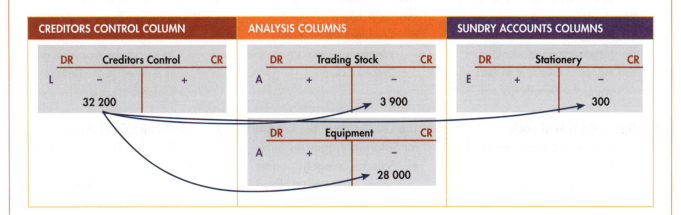

H. POSTING THE SALARIES JOURNAL (SJ) AND WAGES JOURNAL (WJ) TO THE GENERAL LEDGER

The SJ and WJ are posted to the General Ledger at the end of each month to record the effect of all the transactions in the SJ and WJ on the Accounts of the business.

The different costs to employ a person are recorded in the SJ/WJ.
The costs are **posted** to the **relevant Expense Accounts** to show the costs incurred and to the **relevant Liability Accounts** to show the amounts owed.

- The **Net Wages/Salaries** is **posted** to the **Wages/Salaries** Account and to the **Creditors for Wages/Salaries** Account that shows the total amount owed to the employees.

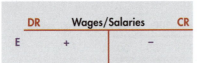
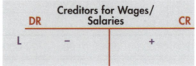

- The **Deduction**s are **posted** to the **Wages/Salaries** Account and to the relevant **Liability Accounts** that show the organisations to whom money is owed.

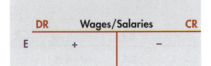
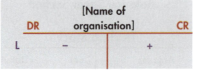

- The **Contributions** are additional Expenses which are **posted** to the relevant **Contribution Expense Accounts** and to the relevant **Liability Accounts** that show the organisations to whom money is owed.

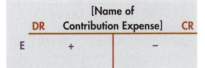
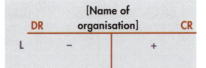

The same organisation can be owed money for both Deductions and Contributions.

OVERVIEW OF POSTING THE COLUMNS OF THE SJ/WJ TO THE GENERAL LEDGER

DEDUCTIONS COLUMNS				NET SALARY/WAGES COLUMN	EMPLOYER'S CONTRIBUTION COLUMNS			
PENSION FUND	MEDICAL AID FUND	PAYE	UIF		PENSION FUND	MEDICAL AID FUND	UIF	SDL
The total of each Deduction Column is posted to: a. **The Debit side of the Salaries/Wages Account** • The **name** of the **Column** (organisation to whom money is owed) is written under the **Details** Column. b. **The Credit side of each organisation to whom money is owed** • **Salaries/Wages** is written under the **Details** Column. The date on which the **Journal** is **posted** is written under the **Date** Column.				The total of the Net Salaries/Wages Column is posted to: a. **The Debit side of the Salaries/Wages Account** • **Creditors for Salaries/Wages** is written under the **Details** Column. b. **The Credit side of the Creditors for Salaries/Wages Account** • **Salaries/Wages** is written under the **Details** Column. The date on which the **Journal** is **posted** is written under the **Date** Column.	The total of each Employer's Contribution Column is posted to: a. **The Debit side of each Contribution Expense Account** • The **name** of the organisation to whom the money is **owed** is entered in the **Details** Column. b. **The Credit side of the organisation to whom money is owed** • The **name** of each **Contribution Account** is written under the **Details** Column. The date on which the **Journal** is **posted** is written under the **Date** Column.			

Required: Post the following Salaries Journal of **WIZZY WOOD** to the General Ledger.

SALARIES JOURNAL of WIZZY WOOD – December 2016   SJ 12

Employees	Basic Salary	Bonus	Gross Salary	Deductions					Net Salary	Employer's contribution				
				Pension Fund	Medical Aid Fund	PAYE	UIF	Total		Pension Fund	Medical Aid Fund	UIF	SDL	Total
S. Khala	5 500	500	6 000	275	300	400	60	1 035	4 965	550	600	60	60	1 205
N. du Plessis	4 200	200	4 400	210	300	380	44	934	3 466	420	600	44	44	1 062
Y. Qwabaza	6 000	300	6 300	300	300	450	63	1 113	5 187	600	600	63	63	1 260
	15 700	1 000	16 700	785	900	1 230	167	3 082	13 618	1 570	1 800	167	167	3 527
				N1	B2	B3	B4	B5	B1	N3/B2	N2/B3	N4/B5		

GENERAL LEDGER of WIZZY WOOD
Balance Sheet Section

DR   Creditors for Salaries   **B1**   **CR**

Date	Details	Fol	Amount	Date		Details	Fol	Amount	
				2016 Dec.	31	Salaries	SJ12	13 618	00

DR   Pension Fund   **B2**   **CR**

Date	Details	Fol	Amount	Date		Details	Fol	Amount	
				2016 Dec.	31	Salaries	SJ12	785	00
						Pension Fund contribution	SJ12	1 570	00

DR   Medical Aid Fund   **B3**   **CR**

Date	Details	Fol	Amount	Date		Details	Fol	Amount	
				2016 Dec.	31	Salaries	SJ12	900	00
						Medical Aid contribution	SJ12	1 800	00

DR   SARS (PAYE)   **B4**   **CR**

Date	Details	Fol	Amount	Date		Details	Fol	Amount	
				2016 Dec.	31	Salaries	SJ12	1 230	00

DR   UIF   **B5**   **CR**

Date	Details	Fol	Amount	Date		Details	Fol	Amount	
				2016 Dec.	31	Salaries	SJ12	167	00
						UIF contribution	SJ12	167	00

DR   SDL Fund   **B6**   **CR**

Date	Details	Fol	Amount	Date		Details	Fol	Amount	
				2016 Dec.	31	Salaries	SJ12	167	00

Nominal Accounts Section

DR   **Salaries**   **N1**   **CR**

Date		Details	Fol	Amount		Date	Details	Fol	Amount	
2016 Dec.	31	Creditors for Salaries	SJ12	13 628	00					
		Pension Fund	SJ12	785	00					
		Medical Aid Fund	SJ12	900	00					
		SARS (PAYE)	SJ12	1 230	00					
		UIF	SJ12	167	00					

DR   **Medical Aid contribution**   **N2**   **CR**

Date		Details	Fol	Amount		Date	Details	Fol	Amount	
2016 Dec.	31	Medical Aid Fund	SJ12	1 800	00					

DR   **Pension Fund contribution**   **N3**   **CR**

Date		Details	Fol	Amount		Date	Details	Fol	Amount	
2016 Dec.	31	Pension Fund	SJ12	1 570	00					

DR   **UIF contribution**   **N4**   **CR**

Date		Details	Fol	Amount		Date	Details	Fol	Amount	
2016 Dec.	31	UIF	SJ12	167	00					

DR   **SDL contribution**   **N4**   **CR**

Date		Details	Fol	Amount		Date	Details	Fol	Amount	
2016 Dec.	31	UIF	SJ12	167	00					

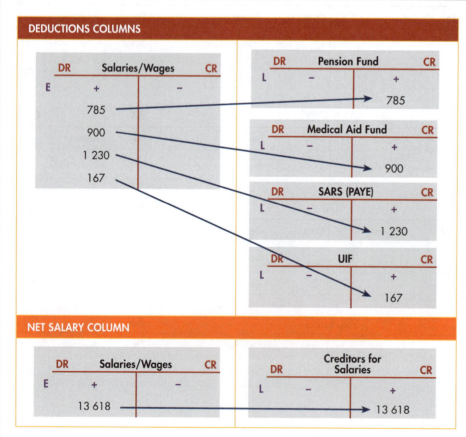

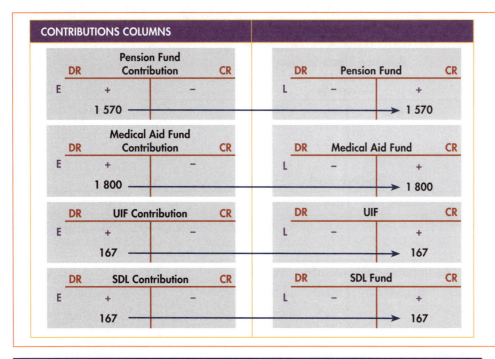

I. POSTING THE GENERAL JOURNAL (GJ) TO THE GENERAL LEDGER

The GJ is posted to the General Ledger to record the effect of all the transactions in the GJ on the Accounts of the business. There are no columns for specific Accounts affected in the General Ledger.
The names of the Accounts affected are written out for each transaction in the General Journal.

STEPS TO POST AMOUNTS FROM THE GJ TO THE GENERAL LEDGER
Each transaction is posted separately to the Accounts in the General Ledger.
The Account to be debited and the Account to be credited are written out in the **Details** Column of the General Journal. The date on which the **transaction** was **recorded** is written under the **Date** Column.

1. **Debit: First Account.** In the GJ, the **first** Account name recorded for the transaction is the Account to be **debited**. The amount is recorded on the Debit side of the Account and the name of the Account that is credited is written under the Details.

2. **Credit: Second Account.** In the GJ, the Account name that is **indented** (below the Account to be debited) is the Account to be **credited**. The amount is recorded on the Credit side of the Account and the name of the Account that is debited is written under the Details Column.

Required: Post the General Journal of D&G PETS to the General Ledger.
GENERAL JOURNAL of D&G PETS – December 2017   GJ 12

Date	Details	Fol	General Ledger		Debtors Control		Creditors Control	
			Debit	Credit	Debit	Credit	Debit	Credit
5	Drawings	B1	500					
	Trading Stock	B2		500				
	Owner took Trading Stock for personal use							
17	Repairs	N1	830					
	Stationery	N2		830				
	Correct the incorrect entry							
20	Depreciation	N3	18 000					
	Accumulated Depreciation on Vehicles	B3		18 000				
	Record Depreciation on vehicles for the year							

GENERAL LEDGER of D&G PETS
Balance Sheet Section

DR   Drawings   B1   **CR**

Date		Details	Fol	Amount		Date	Details	Fol	Amount
2017 Dec.	05	Trading Stock	GJ12	500	00				

DR   Trading Stock   B2   **Cr**

Date	Details	Fol	Amount	Date		Details	Fol	Amount	
				2017 Dec.	05	Drawings	GJ12	500	00

DR   Accumulated Depreciation: Vehicles   B2   **CR**

Date	Details	Fol	Amount	Date		Details	Fol	Amount	
				2017 Dec.	20	Depreciation	GJ12	18 000	00

Nominal Sheet Section

DR   Repairs   N1   **CR**

Date		Details	Fol	Amount	Date	Details	Fol	Amount
2017 Dec.	17	Stationery	GJ12	830				

DR   Stationery   N1   **CR**

Date	Details	Fol	Amount	Date		Details	Fol	Amount	
				2017 Dec.	17	Repairs	GJ12	830	00

DR   Depreciation   N1   **CR**

Date		Details	Fol	Amount		Date	Details	Fol	Amount
2017 Dec.	20	Accumulated Depreciation: Vehicles	GJ12	18 000	00				

Each transaction recorded is posted separately to the Accounts affected.

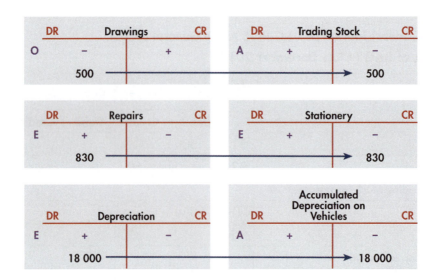

SUBSIDIARY LEDGERS

Subsidiary Ledgers provide additional details about specific Accounts in the General Ledger.
The **Debtors Ledger** and **Creditors Ledger** are the two most important Subsidiary Ledgers.

1. DEBTORS LEDGER

The Debtors Ledger shows additional details about the Debtors Control Account in the General Ledger.
The Debtors Ledger contains all the details of the individual Debtors.

All the Journal entries that affect the **Debtors Control Account** are also posted to the Debtors Ledger.
At the end of each month, the business checks that the total amount owed to the Debtors is the same in the **Debtors Control Account** in both the **General Ledger** and the **Debtors Ledger**.

 The Debtors Control Account is an Asset Account, so it increases on the Debit side and decreases on the Credit side.

a. Layout of the Debtors Ledger

Debtors Ledger of [Name of business]

1. [Name of Debtor]   **2. D [XX]**

3. Date	4. Details	5. Fol	6. Debit		7. Credit		8. Balance	
			R	c	R	c	R	c

1. The **Name** of the Debtor is shown at the top of the Debtor's Account.

2. Each Debtor has a unique **Folio Reference** starting with a **D**. The Folio Reference is a unique code that is given to each Debtor. The Folio References are used to refer to the Debtors.

3. The **Date** Column shows the **date** on which the transaction takes place.

4. The **Details** Column shows the **Source Document** name and number for the transaction.

5. The **Fol** Column shows the **Folio Reference** of the Journal from which the transaction is posted. Each Journal has a **unique code** called a Folio Reference that is used to refer to the Journal.

6. The **Debit** Column shows all entries that **increase** the Debtor's **balance**.

7. The **Credit** Column shows all the entries that **decrease** the Debtor's **balance**.

8. The **Balance** Column shows the **total** outstanding **amount** that the **Debtor owes** the business. The balance owed is the difference between the Debit amounts and the Credit amounts.

b. **Steps to post the Journals to the Debtors Ledger**
All the entries in the Journals that affect the Debtors Control Account are also posted to the individual Debtor's Accounts in the Debtors Ledger.

1. **On the first day of the month, the balance is brought down (b/d)** to show the amount owed by the Debtor at the beginning of the month. This amount is recorded under the Balance Column.
2. **The transactions from the Journals are posted** to each Debtor's Account in the order in which they occur. The details of the Source Document are recorded under the Details Column. The four possible entries are:
   a. **When Inventory is sold on credit, the transaction is recorded in the Debtors Journal.**
      An entry posted from the Debtors Journal **increases** the **balance** owed by the Debtor.
      The amount is recorded under the **Debit** Column of the Debtor's Account in the Debtors Ledger.
   b. **When a Debtor pays** an outstanding amount, the transaction is recorded in the Cash Receipts Journal. An entry posted from the Cash Receipts Journal **decreases** the **balance** owed by the Debtor. The amount is recorded under the **Credit** Column of the Debtor's Account in the Debtors Ledger.
   c. **When Inventory sold on credit is returned** to the business or a **discount** is given to the Debtor, the transaction is recorded in the Debtors Allowances Journal. An entry posted from the Debtors Allowances Journal **decreases** the **balance** owed by the Debtor. The amount is recorded under the **Credit Column** of the Debtor's Account in the Debtors Ledger.
   d. **When transactions do not belong in one of the specific Journals, they are recorded in the General Journal.** The transactions in the GJ can **either increase (Debit) or decrease (Credit)** the **balance** owed by the Debtor.

    Make sure you know how to record each transaction!

3. **After each transaction is recorded, the new outstanding balance is calculated and entered under the Balance Column.** A **Debit** amount **increases** the balance and a **Credit** amount **decreases** the balance.

Example of a Debtor's Account in the DEBTORS LEDGER of QQ FOODS

X. ZAMA   D 1

Date		Details	Fol	Debit		Credit		Balance	
				R	c	R	c	R	c
2018 May	01	Balance	b/d					2 000	00
	05	Duplicate Invoice 22	DJ	5 000	00			7 000	00
	17	Duplicate Receipt 23	CRJ			4 000	00	3 000	00
	22	Credit Note 19	DAJ			1 000	00	2 000	00
	31	Journal Voucher 6	GJ	500	00			2 500	00

 Explanation of the entries
- X. Zama owed QQ FOODS R2 000 on the **first day** of May 2018.
- An entry in the **DJ** was recorded for Inventory sold on credit to X. Zama for R5 000 (Inv. 22).
- An entry in the **CRJ** was recorded for R4 000 received from X. Zama (Rec. 23).
- An entry in the **DAJ** was recorded for R1 000 for Inventory returned by X. Zama (C/N 19).
- An entry in the **General Journal** was recorded for R500 to **correct an error**.
  The bookkeeper recorded R500 in the CRJ. However, the R500 was for items sold on credit to X. Zama (Journal Voucher 6).

2. CREDITORS LEDGER

The Creditors Ledger shows additional details about the Creditors Control Account in the General Ledger. The Creditors Ledger contains all the details of the individual Creditors.

All the Journal entries that affect the **Creditors Control Account** are also posted to the Creditors Ledger.
At the end of each month, the business checks that the total amount owed to the Creditors is the same in the **Creditors Control Account** in both the **General Ledger** and the **Creditors Ledger**.

 The Creditors Control Account is a Liability Account, so it decreases on the Debit side and increases on the Credit side.

Creditors Ledger of [Name of business]

1. [Name of Creditor]   2. C [XX]

3. Date	4. Details	5. Fol	6. Debit		7. Credit		8. Balance	
			R	c	R	c	R	c

1. **The Name** of the Creditor is shown at the top of the Creditor's Account.

2. Each Creditor has a unique **Folio Reference** starting with a **C**. The Folio Reference is a unique code that is given to each Creditor.

3. The **Date** Column shows the **date** on which the transaction takes place.

4. The **Details** Column shows the **Source Document** name and number for the transaction.

5. The **Fol** Column shows the **Folio Reference** of the Journal from which the transaction is posted. Each Journal has a **unique code** called a Folio Reference that is used to refer to the Journal.

6. The **Debit** Column shows all entries that **decrease** the amount that the business owes the Creditor.

7. The **Credit** Column shows all entries that **increase** the amount that the business owes the Creditor.

8. The **Balance** Column shows the **total** outstanding **amount** that the **business owes** the Creditor. The balance owed is the difference between the Credit amounts and the Debit amounts.

b. **Steps to post the Journals to the Creditors Ledger**
All the entries in the Journals that affect the Creditors Control Account in the General Ledger are also posted to the individual Creditor's Accounts in the Creditors Ledger.

1. On the first day of the month the balance is brought down (b/d) to show the amount owed to the Creditor. This amount is recorded under the Balance Column.
2. The transactions from the Journals are posted to each Creditor's Account in the order in which they occur. The four possible entries are:
   a. When items are purchased on credit, the transaction is recorded in the Creditors Journal. Each entry posted from the Creditors Journal increases the balance owed to the Creditor. The amount is recorded under the Credit Column of the Creditor's Account.
   b. When the business pays the Creditor the outstanding amount, the transaction is recorded in the Cash Payments Journal. Each entry posted from the Cash Payments Journal decreases the balance owed to the Creditor. The amount is recorded under the Debit Column of the Creditor's Account.
   c. When items bought on credit are returned to the supplier or a discount is received, the transaction is recorded in the Creditors Allowances Journal. Each entry posted from the Creditors Allowances Journal decreases the balance owed to the Creditor. The amount is recorded under the Debit Column of the Creditor's Account.
   d. When transactions do not belong in one of the specific Journals, they are recorded in the General Journal. The transactions in the GJ can either decrease (Debit) or increase (Credit) the Creditor's Account.

   Make sure you know how to record each transaction!
3. After each transaction is recorded, the new outstanding balance is calculated and entered under the Balance Column. A Debit amount decreases the balance and a Credit amount increases the balance.

Example of a Creditor's Account in the CREDITORS LEDGER of CT CAMERAS

ST SUPPLIERS   C 1

Date		Details	Fol	Debit		Credit		Balance	
				R	c	R	c	R	c
2017 Feb.	01	Balance	b/d					500	00
	07	Original Invoice 16	CJ			300	00	800	00
	17	Cheque Counterfoil 23	CPJ	400	00			400	00
	22	Debit Note 5	CAJ	200				200	00
	28	Journal Voucher 9	GJ			50	00	250	00

 Explanation of the entries
- CT CAMERAS owed ST SUPPLIERS R500 on the **first day** of February 2017.
- An entry in the **CJ** was recorded for stationery purchased on credit for R300 from ST SUPPLIERS (INV. 16).
- An entry in the **CPJ** was recorded for R400 cash paid to ST SUPPLIERS (Cheque 23).
- An entry in the **CAJ** was recorded for R200 worth of stationery returned to ST SUPPLIERS (D/N 5).
- An entry in the **General Journal** was recorded for R50 to **correct an error**. The bookkeeper recorded R50 in the CPJ. However, the stationery was purchased on credit for R50 from ST SUPPLIERS (Journal Voucher 9).

 That's the end of Ledgers – finally!

TRIAL BALANCE
SUMMARY OF CONTENTS

A	FORMAT OF THE TRIAL BALANCE	**84**
B	CHECKING THE TOTALS OF THE TRIAL BALANCE	**85**
C	DIFFERENT TRIAL BALANCES	**85**

TRIAL BALANCE

A Trial Balance is prepared to show an overview of the Account names and their balances in the General Ledger.

The balances of the Accounts are used to **check** that the sum of all the Debit amounts is equal to the sum of all the Credit amounts. The bookkeeper knows that a mistake has been made if the sums are not equal.

 There is a Debit amount for every Credit amount, so the total Debits should always be equal to the total Credits.

A. FORMAT OF THE TRIAL BALANCE

Trial Balance of [Name of business] on [month, year]

The heading of the Trial Balance shows the month and year in which it is prepared.

	3. Fol	4. Debit		5. Credit	
1. Balance Sheet Accounts Section					
Capital	B1			120 000	00
Drawings	B2	30 000	00		
Land and Buildings	B3	250 000	00		
Equipment	B4	200 000	00		
Vehicles	B5	250 000	00		
Bank	B6	35 000	00		
Loan: AZ Bank	B7			80 000	00
2. Nominal Sheet Accounts Section					
Current Income	N1			850 000	00
Rent Income	N2			150 000	00
Telephone	N3	3 000	00		
Stationery	N4	2 000	00		
Water and Electricity	N5	30 000	00		
Salaries	N6	400 000	00		
		1 200 000	00	1 200 000	00

The list of the Accounts will be different for each business.

Balancing lines are drawn with the sums of the Debit Column and the Credit Column.

1. All the **Asset**, **Liability** and **Owner's Equity** Account names and their balances are listed under the heading **Balance Sheet Accounts Section**.

2. All the names of the **Income Accounts** and **Expense Accounts** and their balances are listed under the heading **Nominal Sheet Accounts Section**.

3. The **Folio Reference** of each **Account** is entered under the **Fol** Column. Each Account in the General Ledger has a unique code that is called a Folio Reference. The Folio References for the Accounts in the **Balance Sheet Accounts section** all start with a **B**. The Folio References for the Accounts in the **Nominal Sheet Accounts section** all start with an **N**.

4. The **Debit balances** are recorded under the **Debit** Column.

5. The **Credit balances** are recorded under the **Credit** Column.

 If your Trial Balance does not balance, then make sure that you have calculated the amounts correctly and that you have recorded the balance on the correct side (Debit or Credit). E.g. Drawings, Assets and Expenses on the Debit side and Capital, Liabilities and Income on the Credit side.

B. CHECKING THE TOTALS OF THE TRIAL BALANCE

There are **two possible results** when we **compare** the **sum** of the **Debit** Column with the **sum** of the **Credit** Column in the Trial Balance.

1. **The sum of the Debit Column is not equal to the sum of the Credit Column**
   This shows that there is an error in the books of the business.
   The bookkeeper must find and correct the error.

2. **The sum of the Debit Column is equal to the sum of the Credit Column**
   This implies that the Double-Entry Principle has been followed correctly.
   However, be aware that it is possible that mistakes have been made even when the balances are equal in the Trial Balance.

   If the bookkeeper leaves out a transaction then the Accounts will still be in balance, even though there is a mistake.

C. DIFFERENT TRIAL BALANCES

There are a number of different Trial Balances listed in the Full Accounting Cycle.
Each Trial Balance provides a list of the names of the Accounts and their balances from the General Ledger.
The **purpose** of each Trial Balance is to **check** that the Accounts are in **balance** during the different stages of the Accounting Cycle.

TRIAL BALANCE	WHEN PREPARED	DETAILS
Pre-Adjustment Trial Balance	The first Trial Balance is prepared at the end of the month, **before adjusting entries** have been made.	All Balance Sheet Accounts All Nominal Sheet Accounts
Adjusted Trial Balance Also called Post-Adjustment Trial Balance	The Trial Balance is prepared **after adjusting entries** have been made.	All Balance Sheet Accounts All Nominal Sheet Accounts
Post-Closing Trial Balance	The Trial Balance is prepared **after closing entries** have been made. All Nominal Sheet Accounts are closed off to the Balance Sheet Accounts at the end of the Accounting Cycle.	All Balance Sheet Accounts Except for the Drawings Account which is closed off to the Capital Account.

FINANCIAL STATEMENTS AND NOTES
SUMMARY OF CONTENTS

	OVERVIEW OF THE DIFFERENT FINANCIAL STATEMENTS AND NOTES	87
A	INCOME STATEMENT	88
B	BALANCE SHEET STATEMENT	91
C	NOTES TO THE INCOME STATEMENT AND BALANCE SHEET STATEMENT	95
D	CASH FLOW STATEMENT	101
E	NOTES TO THE CASH FLOW STATEMENT	103

FINANCIAL STATEMENTS AND NOTES

Financial Statements summarise all the important financial information of a business.
Notes are used to show additional details of specific balances on the Financial Statements.
There are a number of different people and organisations that are interested in the Financial Statements of a business:

Investors, Lenders, Competitors, Creditors, Government, Employees, Managers and Owners

 Notes are also used to explain how amounts were calculated and what Accounting Procedures were used. This is not covered in the school curriculum.

OVERVIEW OF THE DIFFERENT FINANCIAL STATEMENTS AND NOTES

 Make sure that you know the format and purpose of all the Financial Statements and the Notes.

	STATEMENTS	INFORMATION	PURPOSE
A	**INCOME STATEMENT** (Statement of Comprehensive Income)	All the **Income** and **Expense** Accounts	Shows the Financial Performance of a business for a specific Accounting Period • Net Profit or Loss for the Accounting Period **Net Profit or Loss = Total Income – Total Expenses**
B	**BALANCE SHEET STATEMENT** (Statement of Financial Position)	All the **Asset**, **Liability** and **Owner's Equity** Accounts	Shows the Financial Position of a business on a specific date at the end of the Accounting Period: • What a business owns (**Assets**) • What the business owes (**Liabilities**) • What the Owners own (**Equity**)
C	**NOTES** to the **INCOME STATEMENT** and **BALANCE SHEET STATEMENT**	Additional details for specific balances on the Income Statement and Balance Sheet Statement	Shows additional details of important balances on the Income Statement and Balance Sheet Statement to better understand the balances
D	**CASH FLOW STATEMENT** (Statement of Cash Flows)	Details about cash received and cash paid	Shows the cash inflow and cash outflow of a business for a specific Accounting Period: • Where the cash came from • What the cash was spent on • How the cash balance changes
E	**NOTES** to the **CASH FLOW STATEMENT**	Additional details for specific balances on the Cash Flow Statement	Shows additional details of important balances on the Cash Flow Statement to better understand the balances

In a test, make sure you show all your calculations in brackets when working with Financial Statements and Notes – you will get marks for this.

A. INCOME STATEMENT

The Income Statement shows all the Income Accounts and Expense Accounts of a business.
The Income Statement is **prepared** for a **specific period**. The Income Statement is used to analyse the **Financial Performance** (Profitability) of a business.

LAYOUT OF THE INCOME STATEMENT OF A TRADING BUSINESS AND PARTNERSHIP
An Income Statement has a unique layout that makes it easy to understand the Financial Performance of a business. The headings of an Income Statement of a Sole Trader and the headings of an Income Statement of a Partnership are the same. Businesses in the same industry will have similar Income Accounts and Expense Accounts on their Income Statements.
- **Service** Businesses have a **Current Income Account** to record the Income received for services.
- **Trading** Businesses have a **Sales Account** and a **Cost of Sales Account** to record the Sales Prices and Cost Prices of Inventory sold.

The headings of the Income Statement of a Company are slightly different to that of a Sole Trader and a Partnership. The differences are found at the bottom of the Income Statement. A **Company** pays Income Tax, so there is an **additional row** for **Income Tax** on the Income Statement of a Company.

HEADINGS	EXPLANATION
Sales	**Sales** is one of the most important Accounts of a Trading Business and is listed right at the top of the Statement.
(Cost of Sales)	**Cost of Sales** shows the cost of Inventory sold.
Gross Profit	The **difference** between Sales and Cost of Sales. **Sales – Cost of Sales**
Other Operating Income	**Other Income** the business earned during the Accounting Period from operations. Interest Income is not included because it is not an Operating Income.
Gross Operating Income	The total amount of **Income** available from **operations**. **Gross Profit + Other Operating Income**
(Operating Expenses)	All the **Expenses** incurred from **operations**. Interest Expense is not included because it is not an Operating Expense.
Operating Profit	**Total Profit** from the business's **operations**. It is also known as **EBIT** (**E**arnings **B**efore **I**nterest and **T**axes) **Gross Operating Income – Operating Expenses**
Interest Income	The total **Interest earned** during the Accounting Period.
Profit (Loss) before Interest Expense	**Operating Profit + Interest Income**
(Interest Expense)	The total **Interest accrued** during the Accounting Period.
Net Profit (Loss) for the year See Below for a Company	This is the last line on the Income Statement of a **Sole Trader** and a **Partnership**: • The amount is transferred to the **Capital Account** of a Sole Trader. • The amount is transferred to the **Current Accounts** of a Partnership. **Profit (Loss) before Interest Expense – Interest Expense**
Profit (Loss) before Tax Company	For a Company, **Income Tax** is first **deducted** to determine the Profit/Loss. **Profit (Loss) before Interest Expense — Interest Expense**
(Tax) Company	The total **Income Tax** for the Accounting Period.
Profit (Loss) after Tax Company	The **Profit (Loss) after Tax** for the Accounting Period. The amount is transferred to the **Retained Income Account**. **Profit (Loss) before Tax – Tax**

 In Accounting, all negative numbers are put in brackets.

EXAMPLE OF AN INCOME STATEMENT OF A SOLE TRADER OR PARTNERSHIP

The layouts of an Income Statement of a Sole Trader and Partnership are the same.

PALETTE PAINTS
Income Statement for the year ended 31 December 2017

	Note	Amount
SALES This is the **Net Sales** amount. Remember to subtract Debtors Allowances from Sales to find this amount.		5 400 000
COST OF SALES Cost of Sales shows the **cost** of **Inventory sold**.		(3 600 000)
GROSS PROFIT Sales – Cost of Sales		1 800 000
OTHER OPERATING INCOME **All** the other **Income Accounts** (**except** for the **Interest Income** Account) are listed here with their balances.		270 000
Rent Income		180 000
Profit on Sale of Asset		80 000
Discounts Received		7 000
Bad Debts Recovered		3 000
GROSS OPERATING INCOME Gross Profit + Other Operating Income		2 070 000
OPERATING EXPENSES **All** the other **Expense Accounts** (**except** for the **Interest Expense** Account) are listed here with their balances.		(700 000)
Salaries and Wages		350 000
Bad Debts		4 000
Repairs		7 000
Water and Electricity		15 000
Stationery		4 000
Advertising		220 000
Depreciation		100 000
OPERATING PROFIT (LOSS) Gross Operating Income – Operating Expense It is also known as EBIT (Earnings Before Interest and Taxes)		1 370 000
INTEREST INCOME Total **Interest Income** earned by the business during the Accounting Period; see **Note #1** on pg 96 for details.	1	70 000
PROFIT (LOSS) BEFORE INTEREST EXPENSE Operating Profit/Loss + Interest Income		1 440 000
INTEREST EXPENSE Total **Interest Expense** the business accrued during the Accounting Period; see **Note #2** on pg 96 for details.	2	(120 000)
Profit (Loss) for the year Profit (Loss) before Interest Expense – Interest Expense		1 320 000

EXAMPLE OF AN INCOME STATEMENT OF A COMPANY

NPT LIMITED
Income Statement for the year ended 31 December 2017

	Note	Amount
SALES This is the **Net Sales** amount. Remember to subtract Debtors Allowances from Sales to find the Net Sales amount.		8 000 000
COST OF SALES Cost of Sales shows the **cost** of **Inventory sold**.		(5 000 000)
GROSS PROFIT Sales – Cost of Sales		3 000 000
OTHER OPERATING INCOME **All** the other **Income Accounts** (**except** for the **Interest Income Account**) are listed here with their balances.		500 000
Rent Income		300 000
Profit on Sale of Asset		150 000
Discount Received		30 000
Bad Debts Recovered		20 000
GROSS OPERATING INCOME Gross Profit + Other Operating Income		3 500 000
OPERATING EXPENSES **All** the other **Expense Accounts** (**except** for the **Interest Expense Account**) are listed here with their balances.		(2 300 000)
Salaries and Wages		1 000 000
Audit Fees		200 000
Directors Fees		300 000
Water and Electricity		100 000
Stationery		50 000
Advertising		400 000
Depreciation		250 000
OPERATING PROFIT (LOSS) Gross Operating Income – Operating Expense It is also known as EBIT (Earnings Before Interest and Taxes)		1 200 000
INTEREST INCOME Total **Interest Income** earned by the business during the Accounting Period; see **Note #1** on pg 96 for details.	1	70 000
PROFIT (LOSS) BEFORE INTEREST EXPENSE Operating Profit/Loss + Interest Income		1 270 000
INTEREST EXPENSE Total **Interest Expense** the business accrued during the Accounting Period; see **Note #2** on pg 96 for details.	2	(120 000)
PROFIT (LOSS) BEFORE TAX		1 150 000
INCOME TAX The Income Tax rate is 28% but 30% is usually used in school tests and exams.		(322 000)
Net Profit (Loss) after Tax Profit (Loss) before Tax – Tax		828 000

Alert: The Dividends on Ordinary Shares Account is not shown on the Income Statement.

Notice that there is an entry for Income Tax for a Company.

© Berlut Books CC

B. BALANCE SHEET STATEMENT

The Balance Sheet Statement shows balances of the Asset, Liability and Equity Accounts of a business on a specific date at the end of a period.
The Balance Sheet Statement is used to analyse the Financial Position of a business.
The **Accounting Equation** (Assets = Owner's Equity + Liabilities) must be in balance at the end of the Accounting Period.

LAYOUT OF THE BALANCE SHEET STATEMENT
A Balance Sheet Statement has a unique layout that makes it easy to understand the Financial Position of a business. The layout of the Balance Sheet Statement is **similar** for a **Sole Trader, Partnership and Company**.
The only Accounts that are different are the Equity Accounts which show the amounts that belong to the Owner(s).

SOLE TRADER pg 92	PARTNERSHIP pg 93	COMPANY pg 94
ASSETS	**ASSETS**	**ASSETS**
Non-Current Assets	Non-Current Assets	Non-Current Assets
• Fixed/Tangible Assets	• Fixed/Tangible Assets	• Fixed/Tangible Assets
• Financial Assets	• Financial Assets	• Financial Assets
Current Assets	Current Assets	Current Assets
• Inventories	• Inventories	• Inventories
• Trade and Other Receivables	• Trade and Other Receivables	• Trade and Other Receivables
• Cash and Cash Equivalents	• Cash and Cash Equivalents	• Cash and Cash Equivalents
TOTAL ASSETS	**TOTAL ASSETS**	**TOTAL ASSETS**
EQUITY AND LIABILITIES	**EQUITY AND LIABILITIES**	**EQUITY AND LIABILITIES**
Owner's Equity	Owners' Equity	Shareholders' Equity
• Capital	• Capital	• Share Capital
	• Current Accounts	• Retained Income
Non-Current Liabilities	Non-Current Liabilities	Non-Current Liabilities
• Loan from XX Bank	• Loan from XX Bank	• Loan from XX Bank
Current Liabilities	Current Liabilities	Current Liabilities
• Trade and Other Payables	• Trade and Other Payables	• Trade and Other Payables
• Bank Overdraft	• Bank Overdraft	• Bank Overdraft
• Current portion of Loan	• Current portion of Loan	• Current portion of Loan
TOTAL EQUITY AND LIABILITIES	**TOTAL EQUITY AND LIABILITIES**	**TOTAL EQUITY AND LIABILITIES**

EXAMPLE OF A BALANCE SHEET STATEMENT OF A SOLE TRADER

JEFF'S PAINTING STORE
Balance Sheet on 31 December 2016

	Note	Amount
ASSETS		
NON-CURRENT ASSETS		2 680 000
Fixed/Tangible Assets Total **Carrying Value** of all the **Vehicles, Equipment** and **Land and Buildings** See **Note #3** on pg 97 for details.	3	2 230 000
Financial Assets Value of the **Financial Assets**		450 000
CURRENT ASSETS		320 000
Inventories Balance of the **Trading Stock Account** and the **Consumable Stores on Hand Account** on the last day of the Accounting Period See **Note #4** on pg 97 for details.	4	20 000
Trade and Other Receivables Total of all the amounts the business **expects** to **receive within 12 months** See **Note #5** on pg 98 for details.	5	185 000
Cash and Cash Equivalents Total of all the **Cash and Cash Equivalent** amounts See **Note #6** on pg 98 for details.	6	115 000
TOTAL ASSETS		**3 000 000**
EQUITY AND LIABILITIES		
OWNER'S EQUITY		1 840 000
Capital Total amount that **belongs** to the **Owner** See **Note #7** on pg 98 for details.	7	1 840 000
NON-CURRENT LIABILITIES		1 000 000
Loan from MONT Bank List of the Loans that the business needs to **pay back** in **more** than **12 months**		1 000 000
CURRENT LIABILITIES		160 000
Trade and Other Payables Total of all the amounts the business must **pay back within 12 months** See **Note #8** on pg 101 for details.	8	150 000
Bank overdraft Amount the **business owes** the **bank** if the business has a **negative bank balance**		0
Current portion of Loan Parts of the **Loans** the business must **pay back within 12 months**		10 000
TOTAL EQUITY AND LIABILITIES		**3 000 000**

 Total Assets must equal Total Owner's Equity and Liabilities: A = O + L

EXAMPLE OF A BALANCE SHEET STATEMENT OF A PARTNERSHIP ⑪

FRED AND FRANK PARTNERS
Balance Sheet on 31 December 2016

ASSETS	Note	Amount
NON-CURRENT ASSETS		3 130 000
Fixed/Tangible Assets Total **Carrying Value** of all the **Vehicles**, **Equipment** and **Land and Buildings** See **Note #3** on pg 97 for details.	3	2 230 000
Financial Assets Value of the **Financial Assets**		900 000
CURRENT ASSETS		320 000
Inventories Balance of the **Trading Stock Account** and the **Consumable Stores on Hand Account** on the last day of the Accounting Period See Note **#4** on pg 97 for details.	4	20 000
Trade and Other Receivables Total of all the amounts the business **expects** to **receive within 12 months** See **Note #5** on pg 98 for details.	5	185 000
Cash and Cash Equivalents Total of all the **Cash and Cash Equivalent** amounts See **Note #6** on pg 98 for details.	6	115 000
TOTAL ASSETS		3 450 000
EQUITY AND LIABILITIES		
OWNERS' EQUITY		1 680 000
Capital Total **Capital contributed** by the Partners See **Note #7** on pg 99 for details.	7	680 000
Current Accounts Total amount that **belongs** to the **Partners** See **Note #8** on pg 99 for details.	8	1 000 000
NON-CURRENT LIABILITIES		1 500 000
Loan from MENZ Bank List of the **Loans** that the business needs to **pay back** in **more** than 12 months		1 500 000
CURRENT LIABILITIES		270 000
Trade and Other Payables Total of all the amounts the business must **pay back within** 12 months See **Note #9** on pg 101 for details.	9	150 000
Bank overdraft Amount the business **owes** the bank if the business has a **negative bank balance**		20 000
Current portion of Loan Parts of the **Loans** the business must pay **back within** 12 months		100 000
TOTAL EQUITY AND LIABILITIES		3 450 000

Total Assets must equal Total Owners' Equity and Liabilities: A = O + L

EXAMPLE OF A BALANCE SHEET STATEMENT OF A COMPANY

TS LIMITED STORE
Balance Sheet on 31 December 2016

ASSETS	Note	Amount
NON-CURRENT ASSETS		6 130 000
Fixed/Tangible Assets Total **Carrying Value** of all the **Vehicles**, **Equipment** and **Land and Buildings** See **Note #3** on pg 97 for details.	3	2 230 000
Financial Assets Value of the **Financial Assets**.		3 900 000
CURRENT ASSETS		320 000
Inventories Balance of the **Trading Stock Account** and the **Consumable Stores on Hand Account** on the last day of the Accounting Period See **Note #4** on pg 97 for details.	4	20 000
Trade and Other Receivables Total of all the amounts the business **expects** to **receive within 12 months** See **Note #5** on pg 98 for details.	5	185 000
Cash and Cash Equivalents Total of all the **Cash and Cash Equivalent** amounts See **Note #6** on pg 98 for details.	6	115 000
TOTAL ASSETS		6 450 000

EQUITY AND LIABILITIES	Note	Amount
Notice that the headings under Equity are different for a Company.		4 350 000
Share Capital Total **value** of the **Shares owned** by the Shareholders See **Note #7** on pg 100 for details.	7	3 867 800
Retained Income Total **Profit kept** by the **Company** See **Note #8** on pg 100 for details.	8	482 200
NON-CURRENT LIABILITIES		1 800 000
Loan from ABP Bank List of the **Loans** that the business needs to pay back in **more** than 12 months		2 000 000
CURRENT LIABILITIES		300 000
Trade and Other Payables Total of all the amounts the business must **pay back within** 12 months See **Note #9** on pg 101 for details.	9	150 000
Bank overdraft Amount the business **owes** the bank if the business has a **negative bank balance**		50 000
Current portion of Loan Parts of the **Loans** the business must **pay back within** 12 months		100 000
TOTAL EQUITY AND LIABILITIES		6 450 000

Total Assets must equal Total Owners' Equity and Liabilities: A = O + L

C. NOTES TO THE INCOME STATEMENT AND BALANCE SHEET STATEMENT

The Notes to the Income Statement and Balance Sheet Statement provide additional details about the balances shown on the Income Statement and the Balance Sheet Statement.

HEADINGS OF THE NOTES
The Notes are listed in the same order in which they are found on the Income Statement and on the Balance Sheet Statement. The Notes are **similar** for a **Sole Trader, Partnership** and **Company**. The first six notes are exactly the same. The **difference** lies in the **Notes** that show the details of the **Equity Accounts** for each form of Ownership.

For a **Partnership:** Owners' Equity = Capital Account + Current Accounts
For a **Company:** Owners' Equity = Share Capital Account + Retained Income Account

NOTE	HEADING	EXPLANATION
1	Interest Income	Details of all the different **Interest Incomes** earned by the business
2	Interest Expense	Details of all the different **Interest Expenses** accrued by the business
3	Fixed/Tangible Assets	Details of all the **Fixed/Tangible Assets** of the business
4	Inventories	Details of the balance of **Inventories** (Trading Stock Account balance and the Consumable Store on Hand Account balance)
5	Trade & Other Receivables	Details of all the **amounts owed** to the business
6	Cash and Cash Equivalents	Details of all the **Cash** and **Cash Equivalents** available

For a Sole Trader

7	Owner's Equity	Details of all the **Owner's Equity** of a Sole Trader
8	Trade and Other Payables	Details of all the **amounts owed** by the business

For a Partnership ⑪

7a	Capital	Details of **Capital** contributed by the Partners of a Partnership
8a	Current Accounts	Details of the **Current Accounts** of a Partnership
9	Trade and Other Payables	Details of all the **amounts owed** by the business

For a Company ⑫

7b	Share Capital	Details of the **Shares** of a Company
8b	Retained Income	Details of the **Retained Income** of a Company
9	Trade and Other Payables	Details of all the **amounts owed** by the business

EXAMPLE OF NOTES TO THE INCOME STATEMENT AND BALANCE SHEET STATEMENT

RAINBOW PAINTING SUPPLIES
Notes to the Financial Statements on 31 December 2016

1. INTEREST INCOME

On Fixed Deposit/Investments The total Interest earned on Fixed Deposit and Investments during the Accounting Period	50 000
On Savings Account The total Interest earned on the Savings Account during the Accounting Period	8 000
On Current Bank Account The total Interest earned on the Current Bank Account during the Accounting Period	2 000
On Overdue Debtors The total Interest earned from amounts owed from Debtors during the Accounting Period	10 000
	70 000

2. INTEREST EXPENSE

On Loan from BNS Bank The total Interest accrued from Loans from the bank during the Accounting Period	100 000
Interest on Overdraft The total Interest accrued from an overdraft bank balance during the Accounting Period	5 000
Interest on Creditors The total Interest accrued from amounts owed to Creditors during the Accounting Period	15 000
	120 000

3. FIXED/TANGIBLE ASSETS

See pg 166 to learn more about Fixed/Tangible Assets.

	LAND AND BUILDINGS	VEHICLES	EQUIPMENT	TOTAL
Cost Original Cost Price of the Asset **when purchased**	600 000	1 200 000	800 000	2 600 000
Accumulated Depreciation Total Depreciation of the Assets owned at the **beginning** of the Accounting Period	–	(700 000)	(600 000)	(1 300 000)
Carrying value at beginning of year Cost – Accumulated Depreciation	600 000	500 000	200 000	1 300 000
Movements				
Additions Cost Price of Assets purchased **during** the Accounting Period	800 000	200 000	100 000	1 100 000
Disposals at carrying value Carrying value of Assets that were **disposed**	–	(50 000)	–	(50 000)
Depreciation Depreciation of Assets for the Accounting Period	–	(100 000)	(20 000)	(120 000)
Cost Cost Price of all the Assets owned on the **last day** of the Accounting Period Cost Price of Assets at beginning of year + Additions – Cost Price of Assets disposed	1 400 000	1 000 000	900 000	3 300 000
Accumulated Depreciation Total Depreciation of all the Assets owned on the **last day** of the Accounting Period	–	(450 000)	(620 000)	(1 070 000)
Carrying value at end of year Cost at beginning of year + Additions – Disposal at carrying value – Depreciation	1 400 000	550 000	280 000	**2 230 000**

4. INVENTORIES

Trading Stock Balance of Inventory available on the last day of the Accounting Period	18 000
Consumable stores on hand Total cost of Stationery, Packing Material and Consumables not used during the Accounting Period	2 000
	20 000

5. TRADE AND OTHER RECEIVABLES

Trade Debtors Debtors Control Account balance that shows the total **amount owed** by all Debtors	175 000
Provision for Bad Debts Total amount owed by Debtors that the business **does not expect to receive** in the next Accounting Period; the amount is deducted from Trade Debtors to determine the Net Trade Debtors	(20 000)
Net trade Debtors Trade Debtors − Provision for Bad Debts	155 000
SARS (Income Tax) ⑫ The **refund from SARS** if the business paid too much Income Tax for the Accounting Period	—
Expenses Prepaid (Receivable) Expenses that have been paid for by the business, that will only be incurred in the **next** Accounting Period	15 000
Accrued Income Income that has been earned but has **not yet been paid** by the customers	5 000
Deposit on Water and Electricity **Deposit** paid by the business for water and electricity	10 000
	185 000

6. CASH AND CASH EQUIVALENTS

Fixed Deposit (maturing within 12 months) The amount of the Fixed Deposit that will be paid back to the business **within 12 months**	85 000
Savings Account Cash balance in the **Savings Account** of the business	5 000
Bank Cash balance in the **Bank Account** of the business	20 000
Cash float Cash that the business has in the **tills** of their shops that is used to give customers change	3 000
Petty Cash Total amount of **Petty Cash** available to the business	2 000
	115 000

7. CAPITAL   Sole Trader only

Balance at the beginning of year Balance of the Capital Account at the **beginning** of the year	600 000
Additional Capital contributed Total of the Capital contributed **during** the year	100 000
Net Profit (Loss) for the year Net Profit (Loss) for the year found on the **last line** of the Income Statement	1 320 000
Balance at the beginning of the year + Additional Capital contributed + Net Profit (Loss) for the year	**2 020 000**
Drawings Total Drawings taken by the **Owner** during the year	(180 000)
Balance at the end of the year Balance of the Capital Account on the **last day** of the year	**1 840 000**

7a. CAPITAL Partnerships only ⑪

	PARTNER A	PARTNER B	TOTAL
Balance at the beginning of year Balance of the Capital Accounts at the **beginning** of the year	300 000	200 000	500 000
Additional Capital contributed Total Capital contributed **during** the year by each Partner	228 000	152 000	380 000
Balance at the beginning of the year + Additional Capital contributed	528 000	352 000	880 000
Decreasing of Capital Total Capital **withdrawn** by the Partners during the year	(120 000)	(80 000)	(200 000)
Balance at end of year Balance of the Capital Accounts on the **last day** of the year	**408 000**	**272 000**	**680 000**

8a. CURRENT ACCOUNTS Partnerships only ⑪   🛈 This is often asked in tests.

	PARTNER A	PARTNER B	TOTAL
Balance at the beginning of the year Balance of the Current Accounts at the **beginning** of the year. This row can also be found above the balance at the end of the year. **A Debit (negative) balance is shown in brackets.**	360 000	240 000	600 000
Net Profit (Loss) as per Income Statement The Net Profit (Loss) for the year, found on the **last line** of the Income Statement, is entered in the Total Column. **The Profit is shared between the Partners.**	792 000	528 000	1 320 000
Partners' Salaries Total Salary of **each Partner** for the year	480 000	360 000	840 000
Interest on Capital Total Interest on Capital earned by **each Partner** for the year	40 000	20 000	60 000
Partners' Bonuses Total Bonus of **each Partner** for the year	50 000	30 000	80 000
Primary distribution of Profit Shows the total amount earned during the year by **each Partner** **Partner's Salary + Interest on Capital + Partner's Bonus**	570 000	410 000	980 000
Final distribution of Profit Amount distributed to **each Partner** at the end of the year	222 000	118 000	340 000 1 320 000 − 980 000
Drawings for the year Total withdrawn by **each Partner** for the year	(552 000)	(368 000)	(920 000)
Undrawn Profits (Retained Income) for the year **Amount left** in the business by the Partners **Net Profit as per Income Statement − Drawings for the year**	240 000	160 000	400 000
Balance at end of year Balance of the Current Accounts at the **end** of the year **Balance at beginning + Retained Income**	600 000	400 000	**1 000 000**

7b. SHARE CAPITAL   Companies only ⑫   🅣 This is often asked in tests.

AUTHORISED SHARES	
Number of Authorised Shares: 3 000 000 Shares Total number of Authorised Shares of a Company; this is the total number of Shares that a Company **can issue**.	
ISSUED SHARES	
1 000 000 Ordinary Shares in issue at the beginning of the year, at an issue price of R3 each Total number of **issued** Shares at the **beginning** of the year and their price per Share **Number of Shares × Price per Share**	3 000 000
500 000 additional Shares issued during the Financial Year, at an issue price of R4 each Total number of **new issued** Shares **during** the year and their price per Share **Number of additional Shares × Price per Share**	2 000 000
340 000 Shares bought back during the year Total number of **Shares bought back** by the Company **during** the year and their price per Share **Number of Shares bought back × Average price per Share** (340 000 × R3,33)	(1 132 200)
1 160 000 Ordinary Shares in issue at end of year Total number of **issued** Shares at the **end** of the year **Issued Shares at beginning of year + Additional Shares Issued − Shares bought back**	3 867 800

8b. RETAINED INCOME   Companies only ⑫   🅣 This is often asked in tests.

Balance at beginning of the year **Balance** of the Retained Income Account at the **beginning** of the year	503 000
Net Profit (Loss) after Tax for the year **Net Profit (Loss) after Tax** for the year; this amount is found on the last line of the Income Statement	707 000
Repurchase of Shares (difference) **Difference** between the **price paid** to buy the Shares and the **issue price** of the Shares R4 − R3,33 = R0,67 340 000 × R0,67	(227 800)
Dividends on ordinary Shares	(500 000)
Paid Total amount of **Dividends paid** to the Shareholders during the Accounting Period	200 000
Recommended Total amount of **Dividends owed** to the Shareholders on the last day of the Accounting Period	300 000
Balance at the end of the year **Balance** of the Retained Income Account at the **end** of the year **Balance at the beginning of the year + Net Profit (Loss) after Tax − Repurchase of Shares − Dividends on Ordinary Shares**	482 200

Average price per Share = $\dfrac{3\ 000\ 000 + 2\ 000\ 000}{1\ 000\ 000 + 500\ 000}$

= $\dfrac{5\ 000\ 000}{1\ 500\ 000}$

= R3,33

9. TRADE AND OTHER PAYABLES This will be Note number 8 for a Sole Trader.

Trade Creditors Creditors Control Account balance that shows the **total amount owed** to Creditors	70 000
Accrued Expenses (Payable) Total amount of Expenses that have occurred but have **not yet been paid** by the business	20 000
Income Received In Advance (Deferred) Income that has been paid for by the customer to the business but **not yet earned** by the business	40 000
Shareholders for Dividends Amount of Dividends that have been **declared** but **not yet paid** to the Shareholders Only applicable for a Company	—
SARS (Income Tax) Amount of Income Tax that is **still owed to SARS** Only applicable for a Company	—
Creditors For Salaries Total of all the Salaries that **still need to be paid**	15 000
Unemployment Insurance Fund **Amount owed** to the Unemployment Insurance Fund (UIF)	1 000
SDL **Amount owed** to the Skills Development Levy (SDL)	500
Pension Fund **Amount owed** to the Pension Fund	1 500
Medical Aid Fund **Amount owed** to the Medical Aid Fund	2 000
	150 000

D. CASH FLOW STATEMENT

The Cash Flow Statement shows the **changes in the cash of the business**.

MAIN HEADINGS ON THE CASH FLOW STATEMENT
A Cash Flow Statement has a unique layout, which makes it easy to understand the effect that different activities have had on the amount of cash available to the business.

HEADINGS	EXPLANATIONS
Cash effects of Operating Activities	**Cash flows from Operating Activities include:** • **Inflow** of cash from **Operating Activities** • **Outflow** of cash from **Operating Activities**
Cash effects of Investing Activities	**Cash flows from Investing Activities include:** • **Outflow** of cash for **purchasing Fixed Assets** • **Inflow** of cash from **selling Fixed Assets** • **Outflow** of cash for **purchasing Financial Assets** • **Inflow** of cash from **Financial Assets**
Cash effects of Financing Activities	**Cash flows from Financing Activities include:** • **Inflow** of cash from a **Loan** • **Inflow** of cash from **issuing Shares** • **Outflow** of cash from **paying** back a **Loan** • **Outflow** of cash from **repurchasing Shares**
Net change in Cash and Cash Equivalents	Net effect on cash from the Activities (above) during the year The difference between total cash received and total cash paid
Cash and Cash Equivalents: beginning of the year	Total cash balance at the beginning of the year
Cash and Cash Equivalents: end of the year	Total cash balance at the end of the year

EXAMPLE OF A CASH FLOW STATEMENT

MNP LIMITED
Cash Flow Statement for the year ended 28 March 2018

	Note	Amount
CASH EFFECTS OF OPERATING ACTIVITIES		580 000
Cash generated (utilised) from operations Cash made from the **daily operations** of the business; see **#1** on pg 103 for details.	1	1 300 000
Interest paid Cash **paid** for **interest**		(120 000)
Dividends paid Cash **paid** for **Dividends**; see **#3** on pg 104 for details.	3	(400 000)
Income Tax paid Cash **paid** for **Tax**; see **#4** on pg 104 for details.	4	(200 000)
CASH EFFECTS OF INVESTING ACTIVITIES		(250 000)
Purchase of Fixed Assets Cash **paid** to purchase **Fixed Assets**; see **#5** on pg 104 for details.	5	(900 000)
Proceeds from disposal of Fixed Assets Cash **received** for any **Fixed Assets** that were sold		400 000
Investments matured/placed Cash **received** from any **investment payouts**		250 000
CASH EFFECTS OF FINANCING ACTIVITIES		140 000
Proceeds of Shares issued Cash **received** from the **sale** of **Shares**		2 000 000
Repurchase of Shares Cash **paid** for the **purchasing** of **Shares**		(1 360 000)
Long term Loans received Cash from **Loans received**		–
Long term Loans paid Cash **paid** on **Loans**		(500 000)
NET CHANGE IN CASH AND CASH EQUIVALENTS Change in cash **during** the Accounting Period; see **#2** on pg 104 for details. **Cash effects of Operating Activities + Cash effects of Investing Activities + Cash effects of Financing Activities**	2	470 000
CASH AND CASH EQUIVALENTS: BEGINNING OF THE YEAR Cash **balance** at the **beginning** of the year; see **#2** on pg 104 for details.	2	275 000
CASH AND CASH EQUIVALENTS: END OF THE YEAR Cash **balance** at the **end** of the year; see **#2** on pg 104 for details. **Net change in Cash and Cash Equivalents + Cash and Cash Equivalents: beginning of the year**	2	745 000

E. NOTES TO THE CASH FLOW STATEMENT

Notes to the Cash Flow Statement provide additional details about the totals shown on the Cash Flow Statement.

HEADINGS OF THE NOTES TO A CASH FLOW STATEMENT
The Notes to the Cash Flow Statement are listed in the order shown below.

NOTE	HEADING	COMMENTS
1	Reconciliation between Profit before Taxation and cash generated from Operations	Details of the cash flow from Operating Activities
2	Cash and Cash Equivalents	Details of the different forms of cash available to a business at the beginning of the year, cash changes during the year and cash balances at the end of the year
3	Dividends paid	Details of the amount of cash that was paid for Dividends during the year
4	Income Tax paid	Details of the amount of Income Tax that was paid to SARS during the year
5	Fixed Assets purchased	Details of the amount of cash that was paid for Fixed Assets during the year

MNP LIMITED
Notes to the Cash Flow Statement for the year ended 28 March 2018

	Amount
1. RECONCILIATION BETWEEN PROFIT BEFORE TAXATION AND CASH GENERATED FROM OPERATIONS	
Net Profit before Taxation Net Profit before Tax is found on the last line of the Income Statement. It is important to note that the amount **before** Tax is used.	1 010 000
Adjustments in respect of: Adjustments are made to the Net Profit before Taxation amount.	
Depreciation No cash is paid when Depreciating Assets. The amount of Depreciation is added.	250 000
Interest Expense The amount of Interest Expense paid is not part of Operating Activities. The amount of Interest Expense is added.	120 000
Operating Profit before changes in Working Capital Net Profit before Taxation + Depreciation + Interest Expense	1 380 000
Cash effects of changes in Working Capital	
Change in Inventory — Remember to include Consumable Stores on Hand. Balance of Trading Stock Account at beginning of the year – Balance of Trading Stock Account at the end of the year	(100 000)
Change in Trade and Other Receivables Balance of Trade and Other Receivables at beginning of the year – Balance of Trade and Other Receivables at the end of the year *Don't include SARS Debit balance, or Expenses paid if it is for Interest Expense.*	(50 000)
Change in Trade and Other Payables Balance of Trade and Other Payables at beginning of the year – Balance of Trade and Other Payables at the end of the year *Don't include SARS Credit balance, Shareholders for Dividends, or Expenses accrued if it is for Interest Expense.*	70 000
Cash generated from Operations TOTAL NET CASH FLOW from Operations for the year	1 300 000

2. CASH AND CASH EQUIVALENTS	Net change	Year 2	Year 1
Bank Bank balance of the business	465 000	730 000	265 000
Cash Float Amount of cash in the till of a business	5 000	10 000	5 000
Petty Cash Amount of Petty Cash of the business	0	5 000	5 000
	470 000	745 000	275 000

3. DIVIDENDS PAID	
Dividends for the year as reflected in Financial Statements Total Dividends that the Company has **declared** for the year	500 000
Balance at beginning of year Total amount of Dividends owed at the **beginning** of the year	100 000
Balance at end of year Total amount of Dividends owed at the **end** of the year	(200 000)
Amount paid Total Dividends **paid** for the year	400 000

4. INCOME TAX PAID	
Income Tax for year as reflected in Financial Statement Amount owed to SARS at the end of the previous year (this is called Income Tax and is found on the Income Statement)	303 000
Balance at beginning of year Amount owed to/by SARS at the **beginning** of the year	57 000
Balance at end of year Amount owed to/by SARS at the **end** of the year	(160 000)
Amount paid The total amount of Income Tax **paid** for the year	200 000

5. FIXED ASSETS PURCHASED	
Land and Buildings Amount of cash spent on the **purchase** of Land and Buildings during the year	600 000
Vehicles Amount of cash spent on the **purchase** of Vehicles during the year	140 000
Equipment Amount of cash spent on the **purchase** of Equipment during the year	160 000
Amount paid Land and Buildings + Vehicles + Equipment	900 000

 Remember that Credit can also be used to purchase Fixed Assets, so the Cost Price of a new Fixed Asset purchased is not always the same as the total amount of cash paid for the Fixed Asset.

This concludes the chapter on Financial Statements and Notes!

ANALYSIS AND INTERPRETATION OF FINANCIAL STATEMENTS
SUMMARY OF CONTENTS

1. **OVERVIEW OF THE FINANCIAL INDICATORS** 106
2. **STEPS TO ANALYSE AND INTERPRET FINANCIAL INDICATORS** 107

   A PROFITABILITY INDICATORS 107
   1. Gross Profit Margin
   2. Gross Profit on Cost of Sales 108
   3. Operating Expenses on Sales
   4. Operating Profit on Sales 109
   5. Net Profit on Sales

   B EFFICIENCY INDICATORS 110
   1. Stock Turnover Rate
   2. Stock Holding Period
   3. Average Debtors' Collection Period 111
   4. Average Creditors' Payment Period

   C LIQUIDITY INDICATORS 112
   1. Current Ratio
   2. Acid Test Ratio
   3. Net Working Capital (Net Current Assets) 113

   D MARKET VALUE INDICATORS 113
   1. Net Asset Value per Share
   2. Earnings per Share 114
   3. Dividends per Share

   E RETURN INDICATORS 115
   1. Return on Owner's Equity
   2. Return on Partners' Equity
   3. Partners' Earnings 116
   4. Return on Shareholders' Equity (ROE)
   5. Return on Capital Employed (ROCE) 117

   F SOLVENCY INDICATORS 117
   1. Solvency Ratio
   2. Net Assets (Owner's Equity) 118
   3. Debt-Equity Ratio (Risk/Gearing Ratio)
      a. Sole Trader
      b. Partnership 119
      c. Company

ANALYSIS AND INTERPRETATION OF FINANCIAL STATEMENTS

Financial Indicators are used to better understand the Financial Statements of a business.
Financial Indicators are **percentages** or **ratios** that are calculated using the amounts found on the Financial Statements of a business.

1. OVERVIEW OF THE FINANCIAL INDICATORS

It is important to look at **different** Financial Indicators when analysing Financial Statements.
The Financial Indicators are divided into **six** main **categories**.

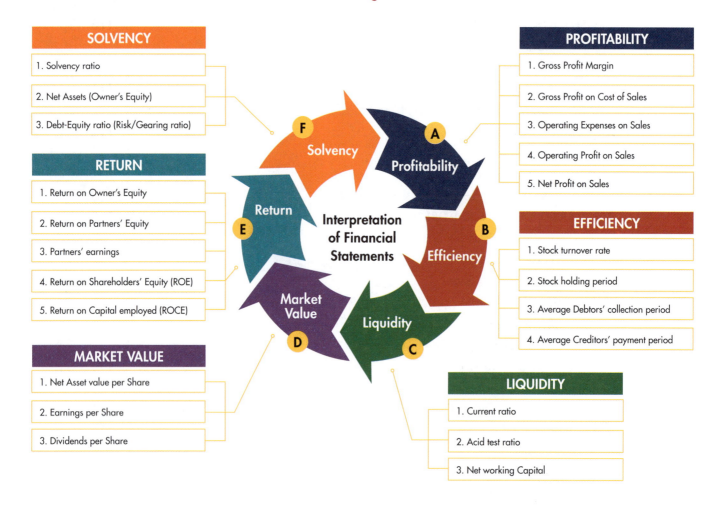

If you are asked a question about the **Liquidity** of a company in a test, you must include comments about the **Efficiency** of the company. The same is true if you are asked a question about the **Profitability** of a company – make sure you include comments about the company's **Efficiency**.

2. STEPS TO ANALYSE AND INTERPRET FINANCIAL INDICATORS

> In a test, you will be given the name of the Financial Indicator. You will be asked to calculate the Financial Indicator for the current period and previous periods and to comment on the results.

1. **Write down the formula for the Financial Indicator that needs to be determined.**
   Memorise the **formulas** on the pages that follow for each different Financial Indicator.

2. **Find the amounts on the Financial Statements and calculate the Financial Indicators.**
   Make sure that you know where to find the amounts on the Financial Statements. The answer must always be shown using the correct units. Financial Indicators are either a **percentage** or a **ratio**.

3. **Interpret the results of the Financial Indicators.**
   The following points are general guidelines to interpret a Financial Indicator in a test:
   - **Mention** what the Financial Indicator shows.
   - **Comment** on whether a higher or lower Financial Indicator is better. Look at the formula to determine which Account balances will increase or decrease the Financial Indicator.
   - **Compare** the Financial Indicator to the previous year's Financial Indicator and comment on the difference. Suggest what possible factors caused the Financial Indicator to increase or decrease. State whether it is favourable or unfavourable.
   - **Compare** the Financial Indicator to a norm – if there is one – and comment on the difference.

   The tables that follow provide more comments that can be made for each Financial Indicator.

A. PROFITABILITY INDICATORS
The Profitability of a business is also shown by Efficiency Indicators.

Profitability Indicators show how Profitable a business is and how efficiently the business operates.
The following questions can be answered using Profitability Indicators:
- How well did the business **perform**?
- How well did the business **manage** Expenses?

The amounts for the Profitability Indicators are found on the **Income Statement**.

1. GROSS PROFIT MARGIN
The Gross Profit as a percentage of Sales

FORMULA	TIPS TO INTERPRET THE FINANCIAL INDICATOR
$\dfrac{\text{Gross Profit}}{\text{Sales}} \times 100$ • **Gross Profit** = Sales − Cost of Sales When the difference between Sales and Cost of Sales (Gross Profit) increases, the percentage increases. **Remember:** **Sales** = Sales − Debtors Allowances	The Indicator shows whether or not the business has achieved its Profit Margin. A **higher percentage** is **better** because this shows that the percentage of Profit made on Inventory sold is higher (higher Profit Mark-Up). A **lower percentage** is **worse** because this shows that the percentage of Profit made on Inventory sold is lower (lower Profit Mark-Up). The following points are possible reasons for a lower percentage: • **Lower Sales Price** due to **competition** • **Higher Cost Price** due to **increased prices** from **suppliers** or **lower efficiency** • **Higher discounts allowed** to customers • **Inventory lost** or **damaged**, which increases the Cost Price **Compare** the Indicator with **previous years** and comment on the differences.

2. **GROSS PROFIT ON COST OF SALES** This provides the same information as the Percentage Gross Profit on Sales. The Gross Profit as a percentage of Cost of Sales

FORMULA	TIPS TO INTERPRET THE FINANCIAL INDICATOR
$$\frac{\text{Gross Profit}}{\text{Cost of Sales}} \times 100$$ • **Gross Profit** = Sales − Cost of Sales When the difference between Sales and Cost of Sales (Gross Profit) increases, the percentage increases. 💡	The Indicator shows whether or not the business has achieved its Profit Margin. A **higher percentage** is **better** because this shows that the percentage of Profit made on Inventory sold is higher (higher Profit Mark-Up). A **lower percentage** is **worse** because this shows that the percentage of Profit made on Inventory sold is lower (lower Profit Mark-Up). The following points are possible reasons for a lower percentage: • **Lower Sales Price** due to **competition** • **Higher Cost Price** due to **increased prices** from **suppliers** or **lower efficiency** • Higher **discounts allowed** to customers • **Inventory** is **lost** or **damaged**, which increases the Cost Price **Compare** the Indicator with **previous years** and comment on the differences.

3. **OPERATING EXPENSES ON SALES**
   The percentage of Sales that is spent on Operating Expenses

FORMULA	TIPS TO INTERPRET THE FINANCIAL INDICATOR
$$\frac{\text{Operating Expenses}}{\text{Sales}} \times 100$$ When Operating Expenses increase relative to Sales, the percentage increases. 💡	The Indicator shows what percentage of Sales has been spent on Operating Expenses. A **lower percentage** is **better**. This shows **better management** of costs (**Operating Expenses**). If the **percentage** has **increased**, the business needs to look at how to control its **Expenses** more efficiently. A business will want to **minimise** its **Operating Expenses** and **maximise** its **Sales**. Look at the **individual Expenses** that have been included in the Operating Expenses and comment on the **Expenses** that have had the greatest **effect** on the change in Operating Expenses. **Compare** the Indicator with **previous years** and comment on the differences.

4. **OPERATING PROFIT ON SALES** This is also called **EBIT** (**E**arnings **B**efore **I**nterest and **T**ax).
   The Operating Profit as a percentage of Sales

FORMULA	TIPS TO INTERPRET THE FINANCIAL INDICATOR
$\dfrac{\text{Operating Profit}}{\text{Sales}} \times 100$ • **Operating Profit** = Gross Profit − Operating Expenses − Operating Income When Operating Profit increases relative to Sales, the percentage increases. 💡	The Indicator shows how effectively a business has controlled its Operating Expenses. A **higher percentage** is **better** because this shows **better operating efficiency** (costs better managed). Compare the **Operating Profit** on **Sales** with the **Gross Profit** on **Sales**. If the Percentage Gross Profit on Sales is a lot higher, then it shows that the Operating Expenses are not well controlled. **Compare** the Indicator with **previous years** and comment on the differences.

5. **NET PROFIT ON SALES**
   The Net Profit as a percentage of Sales
   This is nearly the same as Operating Profit on Sales. The only difference is that it includes Interest Income and Interest Expenses.

FORMULA	TIPS TO INTERPRET THE FINANCIAL INDICATOR
$\dfrac{\text{Net Profit}}{\text{Sales}} \times 100$ • **Net Profit** = Total Income − Total Expenses When Net Profit increases relative to Sales, the percentage increases. 💡	The Indicator shows how effectively a business has controlled its Expenses. A **higher percentage** is **better** because this shows that a higher percentage of Sales is Profit. A business will **aim** to **increase** its **Net Profit** by as much as possible each year. **Compare** the Indicator with **Operating Profit on Sales** to determine the effects that Interest Income and Interest Expenses have. **Compare** the Indicator with **previous years** and comment on the differences.

B. EFFICIENCY INDICATORS

These Indicators also show the Profitability and Liquidity of a business.

Efficiency Indicators show how well a business is managing its Working Capital.
The following questions can be answered using Efficiency Indicators:
- Is the business **managing** its **Inventory** well?
- Is the business **managing** the **payments to Creditors** and **payments from Debtors** well?

The amounts for the Efficiency Indicators are found on the **Income Statement** and the **Balance Sheet Statement**.
Working Capital refers to the Current Assets and Current Liabilities of a business.

1. STOCK TURNOVER RATE
The Cost of Sales divided by the average Trading Stock.

FORMULA	TIPS TO INTERPRET THE FINANCIAL INDICATOR
$$\frac{\text{Cost of Sales}}{\text{Average Stock}}$$ • **Average Stock** = (Opening Trading Stock balance + Closing Trading Stock balance) ÷ 2 If no opening Trading Stock is provided then use the balance of Trading Stock on the Balance Sheet and do not divide by 2. **When Cost of Sales increases relative to average Stock, the ratio increases.**	The Indicator shows the number of times per year that the business has to replace all of its available Inventory (Trading Stock). The **higher** the **ratio** the **better.** This **shows** that **Inventory** has been **sold** more **regularly.** For businesses such as **supermarkets** and **bakeries** that sell **perishable** Inventory such as milk, you can **expect** a **high Stock turnover ratio.** For businesses such as **expensive car retailers,** you can expect a **low Stock turnover** ratio because Inventory is not sold as regularly. **Compare** the Indicator with **previous years** and comment on the differences.

2. STOCK HOLDING PERIOD
The average Trading Stock divided by Cost of Sales, multiplied by 365 days

FORMULA	TIPS TO INTERPRET THE FINANCIAL INDICATOR
$$\frac{\text{Average Stock}}{\text{Cost of Sales}} \times 365$$ • **Average Stock** = (Opening Trading Stock balance + Closing Trading Stock balance) ÷ 2 If no opening Trading Stock balance is provided, use the balance of Trading Stock on the Balance Sheet and do not divide by 2. **When average Stock increases relative to Cost of Sales, the number of days increases.**	The Indicator shows the average time period that the business keeps its Inventory for, before selling it. The **lower** the **number** the **better.** This shows that the business takes less time to **sell** its **Inventory**. This is an advantage because holding Inventory often comes with many Expenses; e.g. renting of storage, insurance. For businesses such as **supermarkets** and **bakeries** that sell **perishable** Inventory such as milk, you can **expect** a **low Stock holding period.** For businesses such as **car retailers** that sell **expensive Inventory**, you can expect a **high Stock turnover** ratio because Inventory is not sold as regularly. **Compare** the Indicator with **previous years** and comment on the differences.

3. AVERAGE DEBTORS' COLLECTION PERIOD
The average Debtors Control Balance divided by the Credit Sales, multiplied by 365 days

FORMULA	TIPS TO INTERPRET THE FINANCIAL INDICATOR
$\dfrac{\text{Average Debtors}}{\text{Credit Sales}} \times 365$ • **Average Debtors** = (Opening trade Debtors + Closing trade Debtors) ÷ 2 If no opening Debtors Control balance is provided, use the balance of Debtors Control on the Balance Sheet and do not divide by 2. • **Credit Sales** = Total Sales − Cash Sales When Average Debtors increases relative to Credit Sales, the number of days increases.	The Indicator shows the average number of days that it takes a Debtor to pay their Account. The **lower** the **number** of days the **better.** This shows that Debtors are paying back their Accounts quicker. The **norm** is **30** to **60** days. A business will aim to receive cash from Debtors between 30 and 60 days. **Compare** the Indicator with **previous years** and comment on the differences.

4. AVERAGE CREDITORS' PAYMENT PERIOD
The average Creditors Control Balance divided by the Purchases on credit, multiplied by 365 days

FORMULA	TIPS TO INTERPRET THE FINANCIAL INDICATOR
$\dfrac{\text{Average Creditors}}{\text{Credit Purchases}} \times 365$ • **Average Creditors** = (Opening trade Creditors balance + Closing trade Creditors balance) ÷ 2 If no opening Creditors Control balance is provided, use the balance of Creditors Control on the Balance Sheet and do not divide by 2. • **Credit Purchases** = Total Purchases − Cash Purchases When the value of Average Creditors increases relative to Credit Purchases, the number of days increases.	The Indicator shows the average number of days that it takes the business to pay its Creditors. In general, the **higher** the number of days the **better**. This shows that the business takes longer to pay back their Accounts which will make the business more liquid. However, the business must make use of discounts if this will decrease the amount of cash the business needs to pay. Suppliers often offer discounts to encourage businesses to pay the outstanding amounts as soon as possible. The **norm** is **30** to **60** days. A business will aim to pay their Creditors between 30 and 60 days. **Compare** the Indicator with **previous years** and comment on the differences.

C. LIQUIDITY INDICATORS

The Liquidity of a business is also shown by Efficiency Indicators.

Liquidity Indicators show whether a business is able to pay back its short term Debts and how well the Current Assets and Current Liabilities are being managed.

The following questions can be answered using Liquidity Indicators:
- Is the business able to **pay back** its short term Debts?
- Is the business **managing** its Current Assets and Current Liabilities well?

The amounts for the Liquidity Indicators are found on the **Balance Sheet Statement**.

1. CURRENT RATIO
The ratio between Current Assets and Current Liabilities

FORMULA	TIPS TO INTERPRET THE FINANCIAL INDICATOR
Current Assets : Current Liabilities - **Current Assets** = Inventory + Trade and other receivables + Cash and cash equivalents - **Current Liabilities** = Trade and other payables + Bank overdraft **Divide both sides by the number on the right hand side (Current Liabilities) to find the ratio.**	The Indicator shows whether or not the business can pay its short-term Debts. **Short-term Debt is usually money owed to Creditors.** The Norm is **2:1**. A business will aim to have close to this ratio. - A **higher ratio** (e.g. 3:1) could mean that the business has invested **too much** in **Trading Stock**. Remember that there is a cost to holding too much Stock. - A **lower ratio** (e.g. 1:1) could mean that the business will **struggle** to **pay** its short-term **Debts.** **Compare** the Indicator with **previous years** and comment on the differences.

2. ACID TEST RATIO
The ratio between Current Assets minus Inventory, and Current Liabilities

The Acid Test Ratio and Current Ratio are similar. The only difference is that Inventory is subtracted from Current Assets when calculating the Acid Test Ratio.

FORMULA	TIPS TO INTERPRET THE FINANCIAL INDICATOR
Current Assets – Inventory : Current Liabilities or **Cash and cash equivalents + Trade and other receivables : Current Liabilities** - **Current Assets** = Inventory + Trade and other receivables + Cash and cash equivalents - **Current Liabilities** = Trade and other payables + Bank overdraft **If the left hand side is greater than the right side then the difference is a positive value.**	The Indicator shows whether or not the business can pay its short-term Debts. The **Norm** is **1:1**. A business will aim to have close to this ratio. - A **higher ratio** shows that the business is **more liquid**. - A **lower ratio** could mean that the business will **struggle** to **pay** short-term **Debts**. **Compare** the Indicator with **previous years** and comment on the differences. This ratio removes Inventory as it is the least liquid Asset.

3. NET WORKING CAPITAL (NET CURRENT ASSETS)
The difference between Current Assets and Current Liabilities

FORMULA	TIPS TO INTERPRET THE FINANCIAL INDICATOR
Current Assets – Current Liabilities • **Current Assets** = Inventory + Trade and other receivables + Cash and cash equivalents • **Current Liabilities** = Trade and other payables + Bank overdraft If the left hand side is greater than the right side then the difference is a positive value.	The Indicator shows whether or not the business has sufficient Current Assets to pay its Current Liabilities. The **higher** the **positive difference**, the **more liquid** the business is. The difference should be positive. **Compare** the Indicator with **previous years** and comment on the differences.

D. MARKET VALUE INDICATORS

The Market Value Indicators are important Indicators for a Company.
The following questions can be answered using Market Value Indicators:
- Is the **Share price** overvalued or undervalued?
- What are the **Earnings** and **Dividends** per Share?

The amounts for the Market Value Indicators are found on the **Balance Sheet Statement**.

1. NET ASSET VALUE PER SHARE
The Shareholders' Equity divided by the number of Shares issued, multiplied by 100 (to convert the value from Rands to Cents)

FORMULA	TIPS TO INTERPRET THE FINANCIAL INDICATOR
$\dfrac{\text{Shareholders' Equity}}{\text{No. of Shares issued}} \times 100$ • **Shareholders' Equity** = Ordinary Share Capital + Retained Income When Shareholders' Equity increases relative to the number of Shares issued, the value increases.	The Indicator shows the value of each Share according to the books of the business. This is not the Market Value (price listed on the Stock Exchange), as that includes speculation. The **higher** the amount the **better**. This shows that each Share is worth more. The amount should be **compared** with the **Market Value** of the Share: • If the amount is **higher** than the Market Value, then the Market Value is **undervalued**. • If the amount is **lower** than the Market Value, then the Market Value is **overvalued**. **Compare** the Indicator with **previous years** and comment on the differences.

2. **EARNINGS PER SHARE**
   The Net Profit after Tax divided by the number of issued Shares, multiplied by 100 (to convert the value from Rands to Cents)

FORMULA	TIPS TO INTERPRET THE FINANCIAL INDICATOR
$\dfrac{\text{Net Profit after Tax}}{\text{No. of Shares issued}} \times 100$ When Net Profit after Tax increases relative to the number of Shares issued, the value increases.	The Indicator shows how much Net Profit each Share has earned after Tax. The **higher** the amount the **better**. This shows that the Net Profit earned for each Share is higher. **Compare** this with the **Dividends Per Share** – if the Dividends are low compared with the Earnings, then the Company has a large amount of Retained Income. **This usually indicates that the Company wants to keep cash for new projects.** **Compare** the Indicator with **previous years** and comment on the differences.

3. **DIVIDENDS PER SHARE**
   Total Dividends divided by the number of issued Shares, multiplied by 100 (to convert the value from Rands to Cents)

FORMULA	TIPS TO INTERPRET THE FINANCIAL INDICATOR
$\dfrac{\text{Dividends paid and declared}}{\text{No. of Shares issued}} \times 100$ When Dividends paid and declared increases relative to the number of Shares issued, the value of the Dividends per Share increases.	The Indicator shows the amount of Dividends per Share that the Shareholders have received. **Shareholders want high Dividends**. However, a business might want to keep cash to expand and grow. **Compare** with the **Earnings per Share** – if the Dividends are low compared with the Earnings, then the Company has a large amount of Retained Income. **This usually indicates that the Company wants to keep cash for new projects.** **Compare** the Indicator with **previous years** and comment on the differences.

E. RETURN INDICATORS

Return Indicators show what **return** the Owners are earning on their investments.
The following question can be answered using Return Indicators:
- Is the business a **good investment** for the Owners?

The amounts for the Return Indicators are found on the **Balance Sheet Statement** and the **Income Statement**.
A different formula is used to determine the Return Indicators for each form of ownership.

1. RETURN ON OWNER'S EQUITY — This is used for a Sole Trader.
The Net Profit as a percentage of the average Owner's Equity

FORMULA	TIPS TO INTERPRET THE FINANCIAL INDICATOR
$$\frac{\text{Net Profit}}{\text{Average Owner's Equity}} \times 100$$ • **Average Owner's Equity** = (Opening balance of Capital Account + Closing balance of Capital Account) ÷ 2 When Net Profit increases relative to average Owner's Equity, the percentage increases.	The Indicator shows the return the Owners have made on their investment in the business. The **higher** the **percentage** the **better**. This shows that the Owners have received a high return on their investment. **Compare** the Indicator with the **return** on **other investments** (e.g. **Fixed Deposit**) and comment on whether an investment in the business is good or not. **Compare** the Indicator with **previous years** and comment on the differences.

2. RETURN ON PARTNERS' EQUITY — This is used for a Partnership.
The Net Profit as a percentage of the Partners' average Owners' Equity

FORMULA	TIPS TO INTERPRET THE FINANCIAL INDICATOR
$$\frac{\text{Net Profit}}{\text{Partners' Average Owners' Equity}} \times 100$$ Use all the Partners' Accounts • **Partners' Average Equity** = (Opening balance of Capital Accounts + Closing balance of Capital Accounts + Opening balance of Current Accounts + Closing balance on Current Account) ÷ 2 When Net Profit increases relative to Partners' average Owners' Equity, the percentage increases.	The Indicator shows the return the Partners have made on their investment in the business. The **higher** the **percentage** the **better**, because this shows that the Partners have received a high return on their investment. **Compare** the Indicator with the **return** on **other investments** (e.g. **Fixed Deposit**) and comment on whether an investment in the business is good or not. **Compare** the Indicator with **previous years** and comment on the differences.

3. PARTNERS' EARNINGS This is only used for a Partnership.
A Partner's total Earnings as a percentage of the Partner's average Owner's Equity

FORMULA	TIPS TO INTERPRET THE FINANCIAL INDICATOR
$$\frac{\text{Total Earnings by Partner}}{\text{Partner's Average Owner's Equity}} \times 100$$ **Use only the specific Partner's Accounts** • **Total Earnings by Partner** = Salary + Interest on Capital + Remaining Profit • **Partner's Average Owner's Equity** = (Partner's Capital Account opening balance + Partner's Capital Account closing balance + Partner's Current Account opening balance + Partner's Current Account closing balance) ÷ 2 When the Total Earnings by a Partner increases relative to the Partner's average Owner's Equity, the percentage increases.	The Indicator shows the return the Partner has made on their investment in the business. Notice that this Indicator is calculated for a specific Partner. The **higher** the **percentage** the **better**, because this shows that the Partner has received a high return on their investment. **Compare** the Indicator with the **return** of **other investments** (e.g. **Fixed Deposits**) and comment on whether an investment in the business is good or not. 🅣 These will usually be provided in a test. **Compare** the Indicator with **previous years** and comment on the differences.

4. RETURN ON SHAREHOLDERS' EQUITY (ROE) This is used for a Company.
The Net Profit as a percentage of the average Shareholders' Equity

FORMULA	TIPS TO INTERPRET THE FINANCIAL INDICATOR
$$\frac{\text{Net Profit after Tax}}{\text{Average Shareholders' Equity}} \times 100$$ • **Shareholders' Equity** = Ordinary Share Capital + Retained Income When Net Profit increases relative to average Shareholders' Equity, the percentage increases.	The Indicator shows the return the Shareholders have made on their investment in the Company. The **higher** the percentage the **better.** This shows that the Shareholders have received a high return on their investment. **Compare** the Indicator with the **return** on **other investments** (e.g. **Fixed Deposits**) and comment on whether an investment in the business is good or not. 🅣 These will usually be provided in a test. **Compare** the Indicator with **previous years** and comment on the differences.

5. RETURN ON CAPITAL EMPLOYED (ROCE) ⑫
The Net Profit plus Interest Expense, as a percentage of average Capital Employed

FORMULA	TIPS TO INTERPRET THE FINANCIAL INDICATOR
$\dfrac{\text{Net Profit before Tax + Interest Expense}}{\text{Average Capital Employed}} \times 100$ • **Capital Employed** = Non-Current Liabilities + Shareholders' Equity (Shareholders' Equity = Ordinary Share Capital + Retained Income) When the sum of Net Profit and Interest Expense increases relative to average Capital, the percentage increases. 💡	The Indicator shows the return on all the Capital that has been invested in the Company. **Compare** the Indicator to the **Interest rate** on the **Loan**: • If ROCE > Interest rate on Loan, then it is favourable to borrow. This is called **positive gearing**. • If ROCE < Interest rate, it is unfavourable to borrow. This is called **negative gearing**. **Compare** the Indicator with **previous years** and comment on the differences.

F. SOLVENCY INDICATORS

Solvency Indicators show whether or not a business is expected to survive in the long term (whether the business is solvent or not).
The following questions can be answered by using Solvency Indicators:
- Is the business able to **pay back** its long-term Debt?
- **How** is the business being **financed** – with Equity or Debt?

The amounts for Solvency Indicators are found on the **Balance Sheet Statement**.

1. SOLVENCY RATIO
The ratio between Total Assets and Total Liabilities

FORMULA	TIPS TO INTERPRET THE FINANCIAL INDICATOR
Total Assets : Total Liabilities • **Total Assets** = Fixed Assets + Current Assets • **Total Liabilities** = Non-Current Liabilities + Current Liabilities Divide both sides by the number on the right hand side (Total Liabilities) to find the ratio. 💡	The Indicator shows whether or not the business is able to pay all the amounts it owes. • The **Norm** is **2:1**. A business will aim to have approximately twice as many Assets as Liabilities. The ratio needs to be **at least 1:1** for the business to be **solvent**. **Compare** the Indicator with **previous years** and comment on the differences.

2. NET ASSETS (OWNER'S EQUITY)
The difference between Total Assets and Total Liabilities
The Net Assets Indicator shows the same information as the Solvency Indicator. The only difference is that the Solvency Indicator is expressed as a ratio and the Net Assets Indicator is expressed in Rands.

FORMULA	TIPS TO INTERPRET THE FINANCIAL INDICATOR
Total Assets – Total Liabilities • **Total Assets** = Fixed Assets + Current Assets • **Total Liabilities** = Non-Current Liabilities + Current Liabilities When Total Assets are more than Total Liabilities, the value will be positive.	**The Indicator shows whether or not the business is able to pay all the amounts that it owes.** The difference needs to be 0 or positive for the business to be **solvent**. **Compare** the Indicator with **previous years** and comment on the differences.

3. DEBT-EQUITY RATIO (RISK/GEARING RATIO)
The ratio between Long-Term Liabilities and Owner's Equity
The Accounts used to calculate Owner's Equity are **different for each form of Ownership**.

a. Sole Trader

FORMULA	TIPS TO INTERPRET THE FINANCIAL INDICATOR
Long-Term Liabilities : Owner's Equity • Long-Term Liabilities are also called Non-Current Liabilities • **Long-Term Liabilities** = Debt (long-term) • **Owner's Equity** = Capital Account balance Divide both sides by the number on the right hand side (Owner's Equity) to find the ratio.	**The Indicator shows to what degree the Sole Trader is dependent on Debt or Equity to finance the business.** The **lower** the ratio, the **better** the **chance** the business has of **receiving** a **Loan**. This is because there is a better chance that the business will have enough money to pay back the Loan. The **higher** the ratio, the **more dependent** a Sole Trader is on **debt** to finance the business. The **norm** is **between 0,5 : 1** and **1 : 1**. **Compare** the Indicator with **previous years** and comment on the differences.

b. Partnership ⑪

FORMULA	TIPS TO INTERPRET THE FINANCIAL INDICATOR
Long-Term Liabilities : Owners' Equity • Long-Term Liabilities are also called Non-Current Liabilities • **Long-Term Liabilities** = Debt (long-term) • **Owners' Equity** = Capital Accounts balances + Current Accounts balances Divide both sides by the number on the right hand side (Owners' Equity) to find the ratio.	**The Indicator shows to what degree the Partnership is dependent on Debt or Equity to finance the business.** The **lower** the ratio, the **better** the **chance** the business has of **receiving** a **Loan**. This is because there is a better chance that the business will have enough money to pay back the Loan. The **higher** the ratio, the **more dependent** a Partnership is on **Debt** to finance the business. The **norm** is **between 0,5 : 1** and **1 : 1**. **Compare** the Indicator with **previous years** and comment on the differences.

c. Company   The Owners' Equity of a Company is called Shareholders' Equity. ⑫

FORMULA	TIPS TO INTERPRET THE FINANCIAL INDICATOR
Long-Term Liabilities : Shareholders' Equity • Long-Term Liabilities are also called Non-Current Liabilities • **Debt (long-term)** = Non-Current Liabilities • **Shareholders' Equity** = Ordinary Share Capital Account balance + Retained Income Account balance Divide both sides by the number on the right hand side (Shareholders' Equity) to find the ratio.	**The Indicator shows to what degree the Company is dependent on Debt or Equity to finance the business.** The **lower** the ratio, the **better** the **chance** the business has of **receiving** a **Loan**. This is because there is a better chance that the business will have enough money to pay back the Loan. The **higher** the ratio, the **more dependent** a Company is on **Debt** to finance the business. This is high risk because the Company may not be able to pay back its Debt. The **norm** is **between 0,5 : 1** and **1 : 1**. **Compare** the Indicator to **previous years** and comment on the differences.

T Practise past papers to familiarise yourself with calculations and commenting.

YEAR-END PROCEDURES
SUMMARY OF CONTENTS

A ADJUSTMENTS 122

    1. Correction of mistakes

    2. Update the balances of Accounts (Adjusting Entries) 123

        a. Depreciation

        b. Trading Stock Deficit/Surplus 124

        c. Provision for Bad Debts 125

            i. Bad Debts to write off

            ii. Bad Debts Recovered

            iii. Provision for Bad Debts Adjustment

        d. Accrued Income 126

        e. Accrued Expenses 127

        f. Income received in advance

        g. Prepaid Expenses 128

        h. Consumable Stores on hand

B FINAL ACCOUNTS 129

Steps to prepare the Final Accounts

Details of the steps to prepare the Final Accounts of a Sole Trader 130

    1. Debtors Allowances Account ⟶ Sales Account

    2. Sales Account, Cost of Sales Account ⟶ Trading Account

    3. Trading Account (Gross Profit), All Income Accounts, All Expense Accounts

       ⟶ Profit and Loss Account 131

    4. Profit and Loss Account (Net Profit), Drawings Account ⟶ Capital Account

C REVERSALS 132

YEAR-END PROCEDURES 🔟

A bookkeeper completes a number of tasks at the end of the Accounting Period.
The tasks that are completed are known as **Year-End Procedures**.
Year-End Procedures are completed at the end of the Accounting Period to:
- ensure that all the **information** has been recorded and is **accurate**
- prepare Final Accounts to **summarise** the business's **Profitability** for the Accounting Period and **Financial Position** at the end of the Accounting Period
- **reverse** specific entries to **prepare** the **books** for the **start** of the **new Accounting Period**.

In this chapter, the focus is on the different **Adjustments** recorded (Step 7), **Final Accounts** prepared (Step 9) and **Reversals** recorded (Step 13) at the end of the Accounting Period.

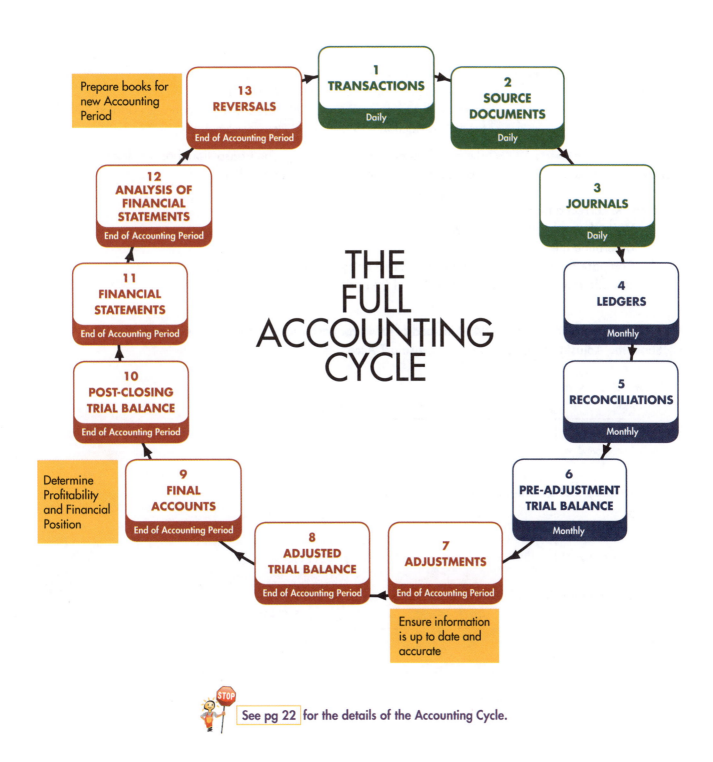

A. ADJUSTMENTS

Adjustments are made to correct mistakes and to update Account balances (Adjusting Entries) at the end of the Accounting Period.

1. CORRECTION OF MISTAKES

Any mistakes found are corrected in the General Journal.

MISTAKE	EXPLANATION	CORRECTION IN GENERAL JOURNAL
Incorrect Account has been used	The bookkeeper used the wrong Account to record the transaction.	• The incorrect Account that was used is adjusted to cancel out the incorrect transaction. • The correct Account is updated.
Incorrect amount has been recorded	The bookkeeper recorded the wrong amount for the transaction.	• The Accounts are updated to show the correct amounts.
Incorrect Account has been used and incorrect amount has been recorded	The bookkeeper used the wrong Account to record the transaction and also recorded the wrong amount for the transaction.	• The Account that was used incorrectly is adjusted to cancel out the incorrect transaction. • The correct Account is updated with the correct amount.
An entry has not been recorded (omission)	The bookkeeper did not record the transaction.	• The transaction that was left out is now recorded.

Steps to correct a mistake
1. Write down the incorrect entry.
2. Determine the correct entry.
3. Compare the incorrect entry with the correct entry to find the difference.
   The difference is corrected in the General Journal.

AMISHA incorrectly recorded R490 instead of R940 for cash received for Current Income.
Show the Adjustment to correct the error using T Accounts.

Incorrect entry recorded

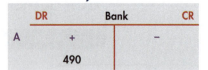

Correct entry that should have been recorded

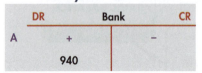

Adjustment in the General Journal to correct the error

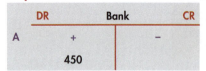

In the General Journal, the Bank Account should be debited by R450 and the Current Income Account should be credited by R450 to correct the mistake.

2. UPDATE THE BALANCES OF ACCOUNTS (ADJUSTING ENTRIES)

The balances of certain Accounts need to be updated before the end of the Accounting Period.

The Accounts are updated to **comply** with the **Matching Principle** or to record any **outstanding transactions**.
See pg 153 to find out more about the Matching Principle.

	NAME	DETAILS
a	Depreciation	The **loss** in the **value** of **Assets** for the Accounting Period
b	Trading stock deficit/ surplus	The **Trading Stock Account** is updated to record the actual amount of Stock available according to a stocktake
c	Provision for bad debts	The amount that the business **cannot expect** to **receive** from outstanding **Debtors**
d	Accrued income	The **Income** that has been **earned** by the business but that has **not** yet been **paid** by the customer
e	Accrued expenses	The **Expenses** that have **occurred** but that have **not** yet been **paid** by the business
f	Income received in advance	The amount of **cash** that has been **received** by the business for **Income** that has **not** yet been **earned**
g	Prepaid expenses	**Expenses** that have **not occurred** during the Accounting Period but that have **already been paid** by the business
h	Consumable stores on hand	The cost of **Stationery**, **Packing Material** and **Consumable Stores** purchased that have not yet been used

a. DEPRECIATION   See pg 168 to learn more about Depreciation methods and calculations.

Depreciation is the loss in the value of an Asset.

Depreciation is recorded for **equipment** and **vehicles** at the end of each Accounting Period.

The **Depreciation Account** is an **Expense Account** that is used to record the amount of Depreciation for the Accounting Period.

The **Accumulated Depreciation Account** is known as a **Negative Asset Account** because it decreases the value of an Asset (vehicles or equipment). The balance of the Accumulated Depreciation Account shows the total Depreciation recorded for the Asset by the business.

Land and buildings are the only Long-Term Assets that do not depreciate, since these do not lose value over time.

JOHN recorded R20 000 Depreciation for vehicles.

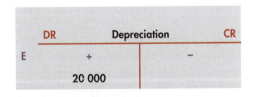

b. **TRADING STOCK DEFICIT/SURPLUS**   See pg 154 to learn more about Trading Stock (Inventory).

The amount of Trading Stock left over is physically counted at the end of each Accounting Period.
The amount of Trading Stock counted is compared with the Trading Stock Account balance in the General Ledger.
- If **Trading Stock Counted** is **more** than the **Trading Stock Account balance** then the difference is recorded as an **Income**. This can occur if there is more Inventory than the books of the business shows.
  The Trading Stock Surplus Account is an **Income Account** that is used to record the difference.
- If the **Trading Stock Account balance** is **less** than the **Trading Stock counted** then the difference is recorded as an **Expense**. This can occur if Inventory is taken/stolen and not recorded by the bookkeeper.
  The Trading Stock Deficit Account is an **Expense Account** that is used to record the difference.

NADIA counted that there was R5 000 more Trading Stock than the Trading Stock balance showed. She recorded an adjustment using T Accounts to correct the difference.

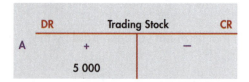 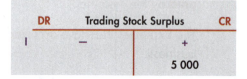

ANELE counted that there was R2 000 less Trading Stock than the Trading Stock balance showed. She recorded an adjustment using T Accounts to correct the difference.

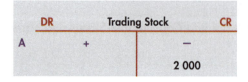 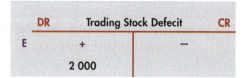

The process of counting Trading Stock is referred to as 'Stock Taking'.

c. **PROVISION FOR BAD DEBTS**
Bad Debts refers to the amount of cash owed to the business by Debtors, which the business does not expect to receive.

There are three different transactions that can be recorded for Bad Debts.

i. **Bad Debts to write off**
During the Accounting Period, the business writes off Bad Debts if cash has not been received from a Debtor for a certain period of time.
This happens when the Debtor is **insolvent** and his or her debt is **irrecoverable**. The Bad Debts Account is an **Expense Account** that shows the amount of Bad Debts written off during the Accounting Period.

> **JEFF** writes off Bad Debts to the value of R5 000 for all Debtors who have not paid after three months.
>
> | | DR | Bad Debts | CR | | DR | Debtors Control | CR |
> |---|---|---|---|---|---|---|---|
> | E | + | | − | A | + | | − |
> | | 5 000 | | | | | | 5 000 |

ii. **Bad Debts Recovered**
Bad Debts Recovered refers to the amount of cash received from Debtors who had previously been written off as Bad Debts. In some cases, Debtors will pay the business after they have been written off. The Bad Debts Recovered Account is an Income Account that shows any payments received from Debtors who had previously been written off as Bad Debts.

> **MAC TRADERS** wrote off R2 000 for L. Phillips after she had not paid for three months.
> L. Phillips then paid MAC Traders the outstanding amount a year later. The amount received is recorded as Bad Debts Recovered.
>
> | | DR | Bank | CR | | DR | Bad Debts Recovered | CR |
> |---|---|---|---|---|---|---|---|
> | A | + | | − | I | − | | + |
> | | 2 000 | | | | | | 2 000 |

iii. **Provision for Bad Debts Adjustment**
At the end of the Accounting Period, the business adjusts the balance of the Provision for Bad Debts Account, to show the amount of Bad Debts that the business expects it will not receive.
The Provision for Bad Debts Account is a negative Asset because it decreases the balance of the Debtors Control Account (Asset). **The Account shows the amount that the business does not expect to receive from Debtors.**
At the end of the Accounting Period, the business uses the balance of the Debtors Control Account and a percentage to calculate the amount it expects not to receive. An adjustment is made to either increase or decrease the balance of the Provision for Bad Debts Adjustment Account.
The **Provision for Bad Debts Adjustment** Account is used to record the difference.
- If the balance of the Provision for Bad Debts Account is **more** than the amount that the business calculates, then the difference is recorded as an **Income**.
- If the balance of the Provision for Bad Debts Account is **less** than the amount that the business calculates, then the difference is recorded as an **Expense**.

Notice that the Provision for Bad Debts Adjustment Account can be either an Income or an Expense Account.

Show the entries to adjust the Provision for Bad Debts Account for **COOL RUNNINGS LTD.** at the end of the Accounting Period.

Extract from the Trial Balance of Cool Runnings CC at the end of the Accounting Period:

Balance Sheet Accounts	Debit	Credit
Debtors Control	20 000	
Provision for Bad Debts		900

Provision for Bad Debts must be adjusted to 6% of outstanding Debtors.

Solution
1. The balance of the Provision for Bad Debts Account should be: 20 000 x 6% = R1 200
2. Provision for Bad Debts calculated > Current Provision for Bad Debts Account
3. The Provision for Bad Debts Account needs to increase by R300 (1 200 – 900)
   - Debit: Provision for Bad Debts Adjustment Account R300
   - Credit: Provision for Bad Debts Account R300

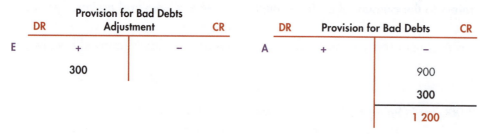

The balance of the Provision for Bad Debts Account is R1 200 after the adjustment.

d. ACCRUED INCOME
Accrued Income is Income that has been earned by the business but that has not yet been paid by the customer. According to the **Matching Principle**, all Income earned during the Accounting Period must be recorded.

The Accrued Income Account is an **Asset Account** that is used to record the amount that is **owed to the business** for **Income** that has been **earned** but that has not yet been paid.

 The Accrued Income Account is similar to the Debtors Control Account because they are both Asset Accounts that show how much is owed to the business.

THATO rents out an office for R4 000 per month. On the last day of the Accounting Period he calculates that he has received R44 000 (11 months) for rent. Make the necessary Adjustment at the end of the year.

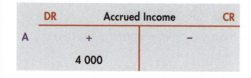

The 44 000 shows the amount of Rent Income already recorded by the bookkeeper.
The Rent Income Account increases by R4 000 to report the total (R48 000) Rent Income earned during the Accounting Period.

e. **ACCRUED EXPENSES**   Accrued Expenses are also called **Expenses Payable**.
Accrued Expenses are Expenses that have occurred but that have not yet been paid for by the business. According to the **Matching Principle**, all Expenses that occur during the Accounting Period must be reported. The Accrued Expenses Account is a **Liability Account** that is used to record how much the **business owes** for the **Expenses** that have **occurred** but that have not yet been paid for.
The Accrued Expense Account is similar to the Creditors Control Account, because they are both Liability Accounts that show how much the business owes.

On the last day of the Accounting Period, THANDI received a Telephone Account for R400. She decides only to pay the Account in two weeks' time. Make the necessary adjustment.

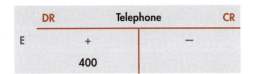

The Telephone Account increases by R400 to record the total telephone Expenses for the Accounting Period.
The Accrued Expense Account increases by R400 to show how much the business owes for the Telephone Account.

f. **INCOME RECEIVED IN ADVANCE**   Income Received in Advance is also called **Deferred Income**.
Income Received in Advance is cash that has been received by the business for Income that has not yet been earned. According to the **Matching Principle**, Income must only be recorded once it has been earned.
The Income Received in Advance Account is a **Liability Account** that is used to record how much a **business owes** a customer for **Inventory** or a **service** that has already been paid for.

THOMSON LAWYERS received R2 000 for services that they will provide in the first month of the following year. Make the necessary end-of-year adjustment.
The amount that is not in bold is the previous balance of the Account.

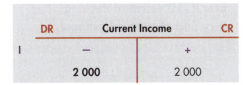

- The Current Income Account decreases by R2 000 to show that the Income was not earned during the Accounting Period.
- The Income Received in Advance Account increases by R2 000 to show that the business owes R2 000 worth of services.

g. **PREPAID EXPENSES**

Prepaid Expenses are Expenses that have not occurred during the Accounting Period but that have already been paid by the business. According to the Matching Principle, Expenses must only be recorded once they have occurred.

The Prepaid Expenses Account is an **Asset Account** that is used to record how much the business has **paid** for **Expenses** that have **not yet occurred**.

BHAVNA AND JONES CC decided to pay their rent of R8 000 in advance on the last day of the current Accounting Period. Make the necessary end-of-year adjustment.

The amount that is not in bold is the previous balance of the Account.

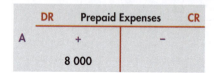
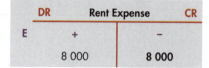

- The Prepaid Expenses Account increases by R8 000 to show that the business has paid R8 000 rent in advance.
- The Rent Expense Account decreases by R8 000 to show that the Expense did not occur during the Accounting Period.

---

h. **CONSUMABLE STORES ON HAND**

Consumable Stores on Hand is the amount of Stationery, Packing Material and Consumable Stores that is left over at the end of the Accounting Period.

According to the Matching Principle, the Expenses must only be recorded in the Accounting Period in which they are used.

The Consumable Stores on Hand Account is an **Asset Account** that is used to record the **costs** of all **Stationery, Packing Material** and **Consumable Stores available** at the end of the Accounting Period.

GATSBY TRADERS calculated that there was R400 worth of Stationery and R250 worth of Packing Material left over at the end of the Accounting Period. Make the necessary end-of-year adjustment.

The amounts that are not in bold are the previous balances of the Accounts.

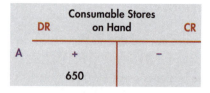
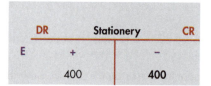

	Consumable Stores on Hand			Stationery			Packing Material	
A	+	–	E	+	–	E	+	–
	650			400	**400**		250	**250**

The Stationery and Packing Material Accounts are decreased to report that the Expenses did not occur during the current Accounting Period.

 Adjustments are often asked in tests in Grades 10–12. Make sure you revise this section and practise as many examples as possible.

B. FINAL ACCOUNTS

Closing transfers are recorded in the General Journal to prepare the Final Accounts at the end of the Accounting Period.
- The balances of Sales and Cost of Sales are closed off to the Trading Account.
- The balances of the **Income** and **Expense** Accounts are **closed off** to the **Profit and Loss Account** to determine the business's **Profitability** for the Accounting Period.
- The **Profit and Loss Account** is then closed off to the **Owner's Equity Accounts** to determine the **Financial Position** of the business on the last day of the Accounting Period.

STEPS TO PREPARE THE FINAL ACCOUNTS   See pg 130 for more detailed explanations.

1. Debtors Allowances Account ⟶ Sales Account

2. Sales Account
   Cost of Sales Account ⟶ Trading Account (Gross Profit)

3. Trading Account (Gross Profit)
   All Income Accounts
   All Expense Accounts ⟶ Profit and Loss Account

4. This is the final step to determine what belongs to the Owners. It is different for each form of ownership.

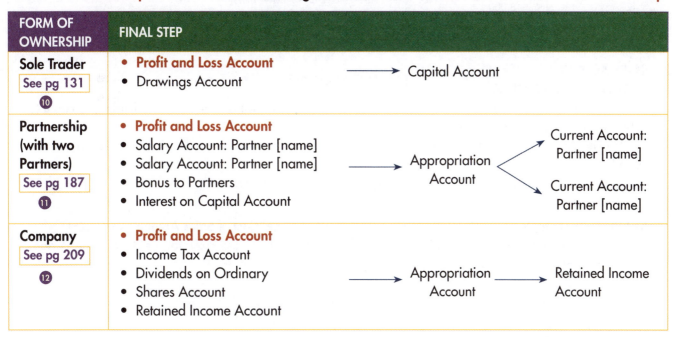

FORM OF OWNERSHIP	FINAL STEP		
Sole Trader See pg 131 ⑩	• Profit and Loss Account • Drawings Account	⟶ Capital Account	
Partnership (with two Partners) See pg 187 ⑪	• Profit and Loss Account • Salary Account: Partner [name] • Salary Account: Partner [name] • Bonus to Partners • Interest on Capital Account	⟶ Appropriation Account	⟶ Current Account: Partner [name] ⟶ Current Account: Partner [name]
Company See pg 209 ⑫	• Profit and Loss Account • Income Tax Account • Dividends on Ordinary Shares Account • Retained Income Account	⟶ Appropriation Account	⟶ Retained Income Account

DETAILS OF THE STEPS TO PREPARE THE FINAL ACCOUNTS OF A SOLE TRADER

1. **DEBTORS ALLOWANCES ACCOUNT ⟶ SALES ACCOUNT**

   Debtors Allowances is an Expense to the business. It shows the total **sales returns** from the customers. The **balance** of the Debtors Allowances Account is **transferred** to the Sales Account to show the Net Sales for the Accounting Period.

   > It is important for a business to know what the Net Sales are for the Accounting Period, to see how much was made from the sale of Inventory minus any returns and discounts allowed (Debtors Allowances).

   The following example uses T Accounts to show how the Debtors Allowances Account (with a balance of R2 000) in the books of TEBS CAKES is closed off to the Sales Account (with a balance of R20 000).

   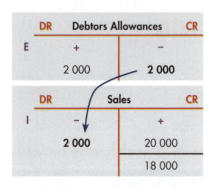

   The amounts that are not in bold are the previous balances of the Accounts.

   An Account has a balance of zero after it has been closed off.

   The new balance of R18 000 shows the Net Sales (Sales – Debtors Allowances) for the Accounting Period.

2. **SALES ACCOUNT**
   COST OF SALES ACCOUNT ⟶ TRADING ACCOUNT

   The balances of the Sales Account and the Cost of Sales Account are transferred to the Trading Account to determine the Gross Profit for the year.

   The Trading Account is a **Temporary Account** that is used to **calculate** the **Gross Profit** for the Accounting Period.

   Temporary Accounts are only used to determine differences between Accounts.

   The following example uses T Accounts to show how the Sales and Cost of Sales Accounts of NIRESH ARCHITECTS are closed off to the Trading Account, to determine the Gross Profit for the Accounting Period. The amounts that are not in bold are the previous balances of the Accounts.

   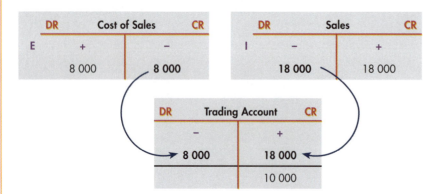

   The difference of R10 000 between Sales and Cost of Sales is the Gross Profit for the year.

3. **TRADING ACCOUNT (GROSS PROFIT)**
   ALL INCOME ACCOUNTS → **PROFIT AND LOSS ACCOUNT**
   ALL EXPENSE ACCOUNTS

   The Trading Account (Gross Profit), all the other Income Accounts and all the other Expense Accounts are closed off to the Profit and Loss Account to determine whether the business made a Profit or a Loss.
   The Profit and Loss Account is a **Temporary Account** that is used to determine the Net Profit and Loss for the Accounting Period. The balances of all the Expense Accounts are recorded on the Debit side and the balances of all the Income Accounts are recorded on the Credit side.

   The following example uses T Accounts to show how the balances of the Trading Account (R600 000), Income Accounts (R400 000) and Expense Accounts (R300 000) of THAPELO TRADERS are closed off to the Profit and Loss Account at the end of the Accounting Period.
   The amounts that are not in bold are the previous balances of the Accounts.

DR	Trading Account	CR
–		+
600 000		600 000

DR	Income	CR
I	–	+
	400 000	400 000

DR	Expense	CR
E	+	–
	300 000	300 000

DR	Profit and Loss	CR
–		+
300 000		600 000
700 000		400 000
1 000 000		1 000 000

   The difference of R700 000 is the Net Profit for the year. If the business makes a Loss, the difference will be on the Credit side of the Profit and Loss Account. The difference is transferred to an Owner's Equity Account.

4. **PROFIT AND LOSS ACCOUNT (NET PROFIT)** → **CAPITAL ACCOUNT**
   DRAWINGS ACCOUNT

   There is only one Owner in a Sole Trader Business.
   The balances of the **Profit and Loss Account** and **Drawings Account** are **transferred** to the **Capital Account** of the Owner.

   The following example uses T Accounts to show how the balances of the Profit and Loss Account (R700 000) and the Drawings Account (R200 000) are closed off to the Capital Account (with a balance of R300 000) in the books of BONGI'S BALLOONS at the end of the Accounting Period.
   The amounts that are not in bold are the previous balances of the Accounts.

DR	Profit and Loss	CR
–		+
700 000		700 000

DR	Drawings	CR
O	–	+
	200 000	200 000

DR	Capital	CR
O	–	+
	200 000	300 000
		700 000
		800 000

   R300 000 belongs to the Owner at the beginning of the Accounting Period.
   R800 000 belongs to the Owner at the end of the Accounting Period.

> Make sure that you know how to do closing entries in the General Journal and how to prepare the Trading Account and Profit and Loss Account.

C. REVERSALS

Reversals are recorded in the General Journal before the start of the new Accounting Period.
Reversals are made **before** a new Accounting Period in order to **cancel out adjusting entries** that were made.
To cancel out an adjusting entry, reverse the entry that was recorded.
Reversals make it easier to record transactions during the new Accounting Period.
Reversals allow the bookkeeper to record all transactions that occur during the new Accounting Period, without having to worry that something was also recorded in the previous Accounting Period.

Pierre: Hey, Kate. I don't know what to do. A client paid us today for services we offered in the last Accounting Period. If I record the transaction now it will show that the Income Account increased for this Accounting Period. This is wrong because the Income was earned in the last Accounting Period.

Kate: Don't worry, Pierre! I reversed the entry by decreasing the Income Account before the start of this Accounting Period. Enter the transaction like you normally do. It will cancel out my reversing entry, so it will not show that Income increased for this transaction during the current Accounting Period.

EXAMPLES OF ADJUSTMENTS AND REVERSALS RECORDED BY THE BOOKKEEPER OF N&P PARTNERS
The amounts that are not in bold are the previous balances of the Accounts.

1. **ACCRUED INCOME**
   b. Adjustment

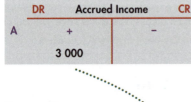
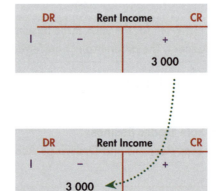

   b. Reversal

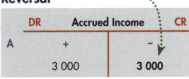

2. **ACCRUED EXPENSES**
   c. Adjustment

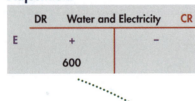
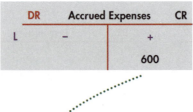

   b. Reversal

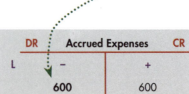

Notice that to do a reversal, you simply record the amounts on the opposite side.

3. **INCOME RECEIVED IN ADVANCE**
   d. Adjustment

   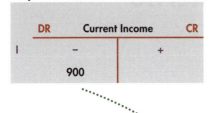 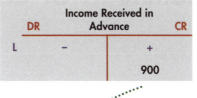

   b. Reversal

   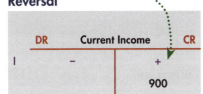 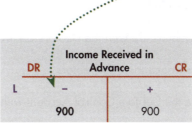

4. **PREPAID EXPENSES**
   e. Adjustment

   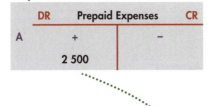 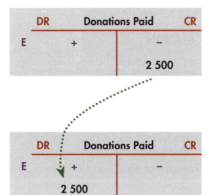

   b. Reversal

   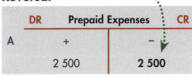

5. **CONSUMABLE STORES ON HAND**
   f. Adjustment recorded at the end of the Accounting Period

   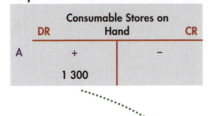 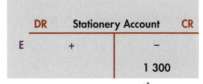

   b. Reversal

   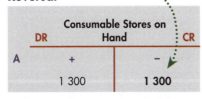 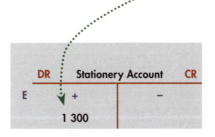

 Watch out for reversals that have not yet been done on a Pre-Adjustment Trial Balance.

RECONCILIATIONS
SUMMARY OF CONTENTS

A DEBTORS RECONCILIATION 135

    1. Reconciling the Debtors List with the Debtors Control Account

       Steps to record transactions with Debtors

       Steps to reconcile the Debtors Control Account with the Debtors List 136

    2. Debtors Age Analysis 138

       Credit Policy

       Format of the Debtors Age Analysis

B CREDITORS RECONCILIATION 139

    1. Reconciling the Creditors List with the Creditors Control Account

       Overview of how to record transactions with Creditors

       Steps to reconcile the Creditors Control Account with the Creditors List 140

    2. Reconciling the Account of the Creditor in the Creditors Ledger with the Creditor's Statement 142

       Steps to reconcile the Account of the Creditor with the Creditor's Statement 143

C BANK RECONCILIATION 146

   Steps to complete the Bank Reconciliation Statement 147

RECONCILIATIONS

Reconciliation is the process of finding the differences between two financial Accounts and correcting these so that the Accounts agree with each other. Reconciliation is an important part of the **Internal Control** process.
A business prepares three different Reconciliations at the end of each month.
A. Debtors Reconciliation
B. Creditors Reconciliation
C. Bank Reconciliation

To reconcile means to correct. Records are compared and corrected so that they agree with each other.

A. DEBTORS RECONCILIATION

The **Debtors List** is reconciled with the **Debtors Control Account** in the General Ledger at the end of each month to complete the **Debtors Reconciliation**. The Debtors List is taken from the Debtors Ledger.
The **Debtors Age Analysis** is also prepared, to show a summary of the Debtors. See pg 138

1. RECONCILING THE DEBTORS LIST WITH THE DEBTORS CONTROL ACCOUNT
The bookkeeper finds and corrects mistakes to ensure that the transactions with Debtors have been recorded correctly.
A mistake has been made if the balances of the Debtors List and the Debtors Control Account are different.

Debtors List  **Debtors Control Account**

The Debtors List shows the individual balances owed by each Debtor.
These balances are taken from the Debtors Ledger. The **total outstanding balance** is calculated at the end of the month by adding up the list of all the Debtors' balances.
It is important to remember that the Debtors List is taken from the Debtors Ledger.

The Debtors Control Account shows a summary of all transactions that affect the Debtors.
The **total outstanding balance** is calculated at the end of each month.

STEPS TO RECORD TRANSACTIONS WITH DEBTORS

 Understanding the steps that are followed to record transactions with Debtors will help you to learn how to reconcile the Debtors List and the Debtors Control Account.

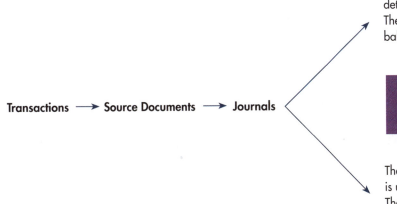

The **Debtors Ledger** is updated **daily** to show the details of the individual Accounts of each Debtor.
The **Debtors List** is updated **monthly** to show the balance of each Debtor in the Debtors Ledger.

The Debtors List is compared with the Debtors Control Account to find and correct any mistakes

The **Debtors Control Account** in the **General Ledger** is updated at **the end of every month**.
The balance of the Debtors Control Account shows the total owed by all the Debtors.

All transactions are recorded on Source Documents and then recorded in the Journals.
- The individual **transactions** in the **Journals** are used to **prepare** the **Debtors Ledger** (which is used to prepare the **Debtors List**).
- The **totals** of the **Journals** are used to **prepare** the **Debtors Control Account** in the **General Ledger**.

STEPS TO RECONCILE THE DEBTORS CONTROL ACCOUNT WITH THE DEBTORS LIST

a. **Determine whether each mistake is in the Debtors Control Account or in the Debtors List, or in both.**

b. **Correct the mistakes.** Look at the next page for examples of mistakes and how to correct them.
   i. Determine what the **correct entry** should be.
   ii. Compare the **mistake** with the **correct entry** and **reconcile** the difference.
      - To correct a mistake in the **Debtors list**, add or subtract the difference from the amount owed by the Debtor.
      - To correct a mistake in the **Debtors Control Account**, increase (Debit) or decrease (Credit) the difference in the Debtors Control Account.

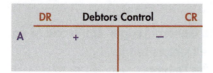

c. **After the mistakes have been corrected, confirm that the new balances of the Debtors Control Account and Debtors List are the same.**
   i. Determine the **new balances** of the **Debtors Control Account** and the **Debtors List**.
   ii. **Compare** the balances to check that they have been reconciled correctly.

> In a test you will be provided with the Debtors Control Account, Debtors List and a list of the mistakes made by the business. You will need to reconcile the mistakes so that the balances of the Debtors Control Account and Debtors List are equal after corrections have been made.

 In a business, it is a good idea to have two separate clerks working on Debtors. One clerk will post to the General Ledger and the other will post to the Debtors Ledger. This is a very good means of Internal Control, which is called '**division of duties**'.

EXAMPLES OF MISTAKES THAT CAN BE MADE AND HOW TO CORRECT THEM

1. **N. DUBE** paid R850 to settle his Account. The amount recorded on the Receipt is R580.
   The Source Document is incorrect, so it affects **both** the General Ledger and Debtors List.

General Ledger	Debtors List
Decrease the Debtors Control Account (Credit) and increase the Bank Account (Debit) by R270 (850 – 580) to correct the mistake.	**Decrease** N. Dube's Account balance in the Debtors List by R270 (850 – 580).

DR	Debtors Control	CR		DR	Bank	CR
A	+	–		A	+	–
		580			580	
		270			270	
		850			850	

2. An Invoice issued to **G. RYK** was undercast by R150. *If an amount is undercast, it is lower than it should be.*

General Ledger	Debtors List
Increase the Debtors Control Account (Debit) and increase the Sales Account (Credit) by R150 to correct the mistake.	**Increase** G. Ryk's Account balance in the Debtors List by R150.

DR	Debtors Control	CR		DR	Sales	CR
A	+	–		I	–	+
	150					150

3. The Sales Column in the Debtors Journal of **PNG LIMITED** was undercast by R900.

General Ledger	Debtors List
Increase the Debtors Control Account (Debit) and increase the Sales Account (Credit) by R900 to correct the mistake.	**No Adjustment** required. **Mistakes of totals in the Journals do not affect the Debtors List. Only individual transactions affect the Debtors List.**

DR	Debtors Control	CR		DR	Sales	CR
A	+	–		I	–	+
	900					900

4. The Debtors Allowances Column in the Debtors Allowances Journal of **TIM'S TYRES** was overcast by R400. *If an amount is overcast, it is higher than it should be.*

General Ledger	Debtors List
Increase the Debtors Control Account (Debit) and decrease the Debtors Allowances Account (Credit) by R400 to correct the mistake.	**No Adjustment** required. **Mistakes of totals in the Journals do not affect the Debtors List. Only individual transactions affect the Debtors List.**

DR	Debtors Control	CR		DR	Debtors Allowances	CR
A	+	–		E	+	–
	400					400

Remember that the Debtors Allowances Journal shows returns by Debtors and discounts/allowances given. If the total was too high, then the Debtors Control Account will have been decreased by too much.

5. An Invoice issued to P. Pillay for R300 was correctly recorded in the Debtors Journal of **VV PARTNERS**. The transaction was then incorrectly posted to the Account of P. Phillips.

General Ledger	Debtors List
No Adjustment required.	**Increase** the Account of P. Pillay in the Debtors List by R300. **Decrease** the Account of P. Phillips in the Debtors List by R300.

2. DEBTORS AGE ANALYSIS

A **Debtors Age Analysis is an overview of how much the Debtors owe and for how long the amounts have been outstanding.** It is an important part of the business's **Internal Control** of Debtors.

An amount that is outstanding is an amount that is still owed.

CREDIT POLICY

Each business will have a Credit Policy that explains to customers what the conditions are when they buy on credit.

A customer will be required to sign a form to show that he or she has read and understood this Credit Policy.

- Debtors are expected to **pay** their outstanding amounts **within a certain number of days**.
  Businesses generally give Debtors 30, 60 or 90 days to pay their outstanding amounts.
- A business will **give discounts** to Debtors who **pay within this time period**, to encourage Debtors to pay as soon as possible.
- A business may **charge interest** on amounts that are **not paid within the time period**. The interest charged discourages Debtors to make late payments.

FORMAT OF THE DEBTORS AGE ANALYSIS

DEBTORS AGE ANALYSIS					
Debtors	Total Owed	Current	30 days	60 days	90 days
L. Simmons	R4 000	R3 000	R1 000		
M. Mthombeni	R12 000	R4 000	R3 000	R2 000	R3 000
C. Pienaar	R6 000		R1 000	R5 000	
T. Tickly	R2 000	R1 000	R500	R500	
	R24 000	**R8 000**	**R5 500**	**R7 500**	**R3 000**

Total Owed:
R24 000

- Current — R8 000 (owed from current month)
- 30 Days — R5 500 (owed from previous month)
- 60 Days — R7 500 (owed from 2 months ago)
- 90 Days — R3 000 (owed from 3 months ago)

In a test, you will be given a Debtors Age Analysis and you will be asked to interpret it. Make sure you understand what each column is for.
You will also need to know how to prepare a Debtors Age Analysis for a particular Debtor.

B. CREDITORS RECONCILIATION

There are two Creditors Reconciliations done by a business at the end of each month.

The **Creditors List** is reconciled with the **Creditors Control Account**. See below
A reconciliation is done to check that the transactions have been recorded correctly in the Creditors Control Account and the Creditors Ledger. The Creditors List is taken from the Creditors Ledger.
The same process is followed as with the Debtors Reconciliation.

The **Account of the Creditor** is reconciled with the **Creditor's Statement**. See pg 142
A reconciliation is done to check that the transactions that have been recorded by the business agree with the transactions that have been recorded by each Creditor.

1. RECONCILING THE CREDITORS LIST WITH THE CREDITORS CONTROL ACCOUNT
The Creditors List is reconciled with the Creditors Control Account in the General Ledger at the end of each month. The bookkeeper checks that all transactions with Creditors have been recorded correctly.

The **Creditors List** shows the individual balances owed to each Creditor.
These balances are taken from the Creditors Ledger. The **total outstanding balance** is calculated at the end of the month by adding up the list of all the Creditors' balances.

The **Creditors Control Account** shows a summary of all transactions that affect the Creditors.
The **total outstanding balance** is calculated at the end of each month.

OVERVIEW OF HOW TO RECORD TRANSACTIONS WITH CREDITORS

 Understanding the steps that are followed to record transactions with Creditors will help you to learn how to reconcile the Creditors List and the Creditors Control Account.

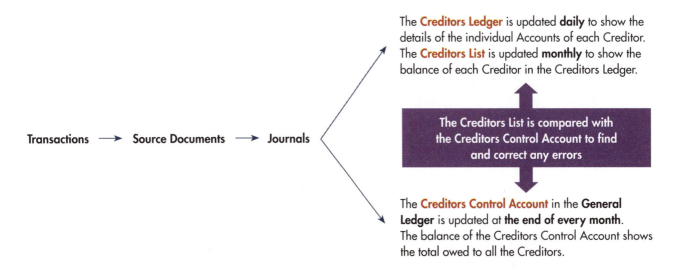

All transactions are recorded on Source Documents and then recorded in the Journals.
- The **transactions** in the **Journals** are used to prepare the Creditors Ledger (which is used to prepare the **Creditors List**).
- The **totals** in the **Journals** are used to prepare the **Creditors Control Account** in the General Ledger.

STEPS TO RECONCILE THE CREDITORS CONTROL ACCOUNT WITH THE CREDITORS LIST

A mistake has been made if the balance of the Creditors Control Account is not the same as the balance of the Creditors List. The mistakes are found and corrected during the Reconciliation.

a. **Determine whether each mistake is in the Creditors Control Account or in the Creditors List, or in both.**

b. **Correct the mistakes. Look at the next page for examples of mistakes and how to correct them.**
   i. Determine what the **correct entry** should be.
   ii. Compare the **mistake** with the **correct entry** and **reconcile** the difference.
      - To correct a mistake in the Creditors List, add or subtract the difference from the amount owed to the Creditor.
      - To correct a mistake in the Creditors Control Account, increase (Credit) or decrease (Debit) the difference in the Account.

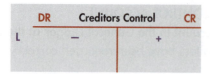

c. **After the Creditors Control Account and Creditors List have been reconciled, confirm that their balances are the same.**
   i. Determine the **new balance** of the **Creditors Control Account** and the **Creditors List**.
   ii. **Compare** the balances to check that they have been reconciled correctly.

 In a test you will be provided with the Creditors Control Account and the Creditors List. A list of the mistakes made by the business will also be provided. You will need to reconcile the mistakes so that the balances of the Creditors Control Account and Creditors List are equal after the corrections have been made.

 In a business, it is a good idea to have two separate clerks working on Creditors. One clerk will post to the General Ledger and the other will post to the Creditors Ledger. This is a very good means of Internal Control, which is called '**division of duties**'.

EXAMPLES OF THE POSSIBLE DIFFERENCES AND HOW TO MAKE THE NECESSARY CORRECTIONS FOR EACH SITUATION.

1. The Creditor, R. Myles, was paid R650 to settle an outstanding balance. The amount was incorrectly recorded as R950 on the Cheque Counterfoil by the bookkeeper of **TX TRADERS**.

   General Ledger
   Increase the Creditors Control Account (Credit) and increase the Bank Account (Debit) to correct the mistake.

DR	Creditors Control	CR
L	−	+
	950	
		300
	650	

DR	Bank	CR
A	+	−
		950
	300	
		650

   Creditors List
   Increase R. Myles' Account balance in the Creditors List by R300.

   The unbolded amounts show the balances of the Accounts from previous transactions.

2. An Invoice received from a Creditor, N. Smith, for stationery purchased was undercast by R250 in the books of **PULE BIKES**.

   General Ledger
   Increase the Creditors Control Account (Credit) and increase the Stationery Account (Debit) to correct the mistake.

DR	Creditors Control	CR
L	−	+
		250

DR	Stationery	CR
E	+	−
	250	

   Creditors List
   Increase N. Smith's Account balance in the Creditors List by R250.

3. The Creditors Control Column in the Creditors Journal of **SANTIX** was overcast by R550.

   General Ledger
   Decrease the Creditors Control Account (Debit).

DR	Creditors Control	CR
L	−	+
	550	

   Creditors List
   Mistakes of totals in the Journals do not affect the Creditors List. Only Individual transactions affect the Creditors List.

4. The Creditors Allowances Column in the Creditors Allowances Journal of **BT PAINTS** was undercast by R120.

   General Ledger
   Decrease the Creditors Control Account (Debit) and increase the Creditors Allowances (Credit) to correct the mistake.

DR	Creditors Control	CR
L	−	+
	120	

   Creditors List
   Mistakes of totals in the Journals do not affect the Creditors List. Only Individual transactions affect the Creditors List.
   Creditors Allowances is for discounts received or items returned to the Creditors.

If an amount is undercast, it is lower than it should be. If an amount is overcast, it is higher than it should be.

5. An Invoice received from L. Jacobs for R950 was correctly recorded in the Creditors Journal of **TUTORS24**. The entry was then incorrectly posted to the Account of L. Jenks.

   General Ledger
   The Accounts in the General Ledger are **not** affected.

   Creditors List
   Increase the Account of L. Jacobs in the Creditors List by R950.
   Decrease the Account of L. Jenks in the Creditors List by R950.

6. An amount of R810 in the Creditors Journal of **BV MEDIA** was incorrectly posted as R910 to the Account of S. Rhadebe.

   General Ledger
   The Accounts in the General Ledger are **not** affected.

   Creditors List
   Decrease the Account of S. Rhadebe in the Creditors List by R100 (910 − 810).

2. RECONCILING THE ACCOUNT OF THE CREDITOR IN THE CREDITORS LEDGER WITH THE CREDITOR'S STATEMENT

The Creditor's Account is reconciled with the Creditor's Statement. The bookkeeper finds and corrects mistakes so that the records of the business agree with the records of the Creditors.

a. Creditor's Account

 reconcile

c. Creditor's Statement

b. Creditor's Reconciliation

a. **The Creditor's Account shows the details of the transactions with the Creditor recorded in the Creditors Ledger.**
All the transactions between the business and the Creditor are recorded under the relevant Creditor's Account. The Creditor's Account is a **Liability** Account.
- The Account **decreases** on the **Debit** side in the General Ledger.
- The Account **increases** on the **Credit** side in the General Ledger.

b. **The Creditors Reconciliation Statement is prepared at the end of each month.** See pg 145 for an example.
The business cannot make any corrections on the Creditor's Statement. This must be done **by the Creditor**. The Creditors Reconciliation Statement shows any necessary **corrections** that need to be made to the Creditor's Statement. It is also used to **check** if the Creditor's Account and Creditor's Statement agree after corrections have been made.
The following details are included on the Creditors Reconciliation Statement:
- The Creditor's Statement balance
- A list of the corrections the Creditor needs to make
- The Creditor's Account balance in the Creditors Ledger after corrections.

c. **The Creditor's Statement is prepared by the Creditor and sent to the business at the end of each month.**
It reflects all the transactions between the Creditor and the business, as recorded by the Creditor. The Creditor's Statement is sometimes also called the **Statement of Account**.
The Creditor sees the business as a Debtor, because the Creditor is owed cash by the business.
If both the business and the Creditor have recorded the transactions correctly, then the transactions in the Creditor's Account in the books of the business will mirror the transactions on the Creditor's Statement.
- Each **Debit** amount in the **Creditors Ledger** should have a **Credit** amount on the **Creditor's Statement**.
- Each **Credit** amount in the **Creditors Ledger** should have a **Debit** amount on the **Creditor's Statement**.

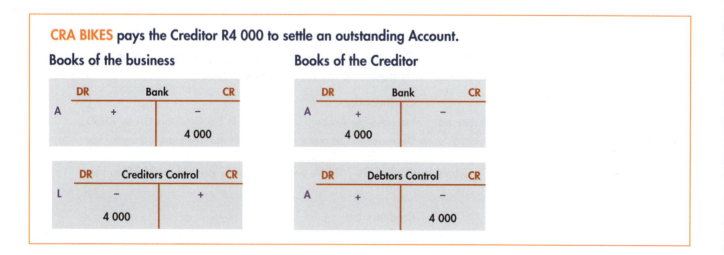

STEPS TO RECONCILE THE ACCOUNT OF THE CREDITOR WITH THE CREDITOR'S STATEMENT

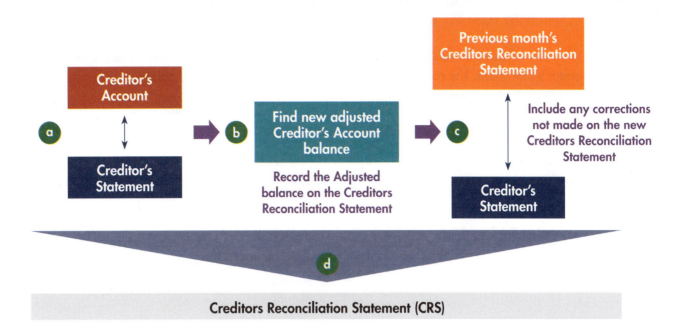

Creditors Reconciliation Statement (CRS)

a. **Compare the entries in the Creditor's Account in the Creditors Ledger with the entries on the Creditor's Statement and correct the differences.**

   i. **Circle** any **amounts** that are **different**, or any amounts that have only been shown in **one** of **either** the **Creditors Ledger** or the **Creditor's Statement**. Tick all the amounts that are the same, so that you know that you have checked them. ✓
   ii. Make adjustments to **correct** any **differences** that are circled.
   - All the **mistakes** made by the **Creditor** on the **Creditor's Statement** sent to the business are **corrected** on the **Creditors Reconciliation Statement**.
   - All the **mistakes** made in the **Creditor's Account** are **corrected** by the business in the **Creditors Ledger** using General Journal entries.

b. **Calculate the balance of the Creditor's Account after corrections.**
   The **new balance** of the Creditor's Account is determined by the business after making the corrections.

c. **Compare the previous month's Creditors Reconciliation Statement with the Creditor's Statement.**
   The **previous month's Creditors Reconciliation Statement** is compared with the Creditor's Statement. The previous month's Creditors Reconciliation Statement shows all the amounts that the Creditor needed to correct in their books. Any **corrections** that have **not** been made are **circled** and **included** in the **Creditors Reconciliation Statement** for the current month.

d. **Complete the Creditors Reconciliation Statement.**
   The **totals** on the Creditors Reconciliation Statement are **added** up to **check** that the **balances agree after** the **corrections** have been made.

EXAMPLES OF POSSIBLE DIFFERENCES WHEN COMPARING THE CREDITOR'S ACCOUNT AND CREDITOR'S STATEMENT AND HOW TO MAKE THE NECESSARY ADJUSTMENTS FOR EACH SITUATION

1. **RACHEL** circles amounts in the Debit Column of the Creditors Ledger because they are not shown on the Creditor's Statement. The reasons for the circled amounts are provided below.
   Notice that the business has recorded the transaction but the Creditor has not.

   a. Discount received from Creditor not shown on the Creditor's Statement

Books of the Business	Creditors Reconciliation Statement
No adjustment required.	Record as **outstanding discount** (amount in the Credit Column).

   b. Payment to the Creditor not shown on the Creditor's Statement

Books of the Business	Creditors Reconciliation Statement
No adjustment required.	Record as **outstanding Cheque** (amount in the Credit Column).

   c. Inventory returned by the business not shown on the Creditor's Statement

Books of the Business	Creditors Reconciliation Statement
No adjustment required.	Record as **outstanding Debit Note** (amount in the Credit Column).

2. **TOD** circles different amounts in the Creditors Ledger and in the Creditor's Statement because they are not the same. The reasons for the circled amounts are provided below.
   Notice that the business and Creditor have recorded the amounts for the transaction differently.

   a. The business has recorded an incorrect amount

Books of the Business	Creditors Reconciliation Statement
The **correction** should be made to the Creditor's Account in the **General Ledger** and the Creditor's Account in the **Creditors Ledger**. This is made in the **General Journal**.	**No adjustment** required.

   b. The Creditor has recorded an incorrect amount

Books of the Business	Creditors Reconciliation Statement
No adjustment required.	**Record** an entry on the Creditors Reconciliation Statement to **correct** the difference.

3. **PULE** circles an amount for an Invoice received from a Creditor that is not shown on the Creditor's Statement

Books of the Business	Creditors Reconciliation Statement
No adjustment required.	Record as **outstanding Invoice** (amount in the Debit Column).

4. **PICZ ARTS** receives an Invoice for an Asset purchased from a Creditor. The transaction was not recorded by the business

Books of the Business	Creditors Reconciliation Statement
The **correction** should be made to the Creditor's Account in the **General Ledger** and the Creditor's Account in the **Creditors Ledger**. This is made in the **General Journal**.	**No adjustment** required.

EXAMPLE OF A CREDITORS RECONCILIATION STATEMENT

This is often asked in tests.

M&C BRICKS CC
Creditors Reconciliation Statement on 31 December 2016

	Debit		Credit	
Debit balance on Creditor's Statement Balance on the Creditor's Statement according to the Creditor	120 000	00		
Discount received not on Creditor's Statement			4 000	00
Cheque issued not on Creditor's Statement			5 000	00
Invoice received not on Creditor's Statement	7 000	00		
Correction of error on Creditor's Statement			3 000	00
Credit balance on Creditors Ledger Account Creditor's Account balance in the Creditors Ledger after corrections have been made			115 000	00
	127 000	00	127 000	00

The Debit side must equal the Credit side.

1. All the Debit amounts are recorded under the **Debit** Column.

2. All the Credit amounts are recorded under the **Credit** Column.

3. The **Debit balance on the Creditor's Statement** is recorded. A Debit balance on the Creditor's Statement shows the amount that the business owes the Creditor, according to the Creditor.

4. **Any amounts that are not on the Creditor's Statement are recorded in the Creditors Reconciliation Statement.**
   - **Discount received not on Creditor's Statement:** If the Creditor has not recorded the discount received by the business, then the balance owed to the Creditor on the Creditor's Statement will be too high. Enter the discount on the Credit side to correct the error.
   - **Cheque issued not on Creditor's Statement:** If the Creditor has not recorded the Cheque, then the balance owed to the Creditor on the Creditor's Statement will be too high. Enter the Cheque amount on the Credit side to correct the error.
   - **Invoice received not on Creditor's Statement:** If the Creditor has not recorded the Invoice, then the balance owed to the Creditor on the Creditor's Statement will be too low. Enter the Invoice amount on the Debit side to correct the error.
   - **Correction of error on Creditor's Statement:**
     Enter the correction amount on the Debit side to increase the balance on the Creditor's Statement.
     Enter the correction amount on the Credit side to decrease the balance on the Creditor's Statement.

5. **Credit the balance of the Creditors Account in the Creditors Ledger:** The balance of the Creditors Account in the Creditors Ledger (after any corrections have been made) is recorded on the Credit side.

 Check that the total of the Debit side is equal to the total of the Credit side. If the sides are equal, the reconciliation has been done correctly.

C. BANK RECONCILIATION

The Cash Receipts Journal (CRJ), Cash Payments Journal (CPJ) and the previous month's Bank Reconciliation Statement (BRS) are reconciled with the Bank Statement.
The bookkeeper finds and corrects mistakes so that the records of the business agree with the records of the bank.

a. Cash Receipts Journal

b. Cash Payments Journal   reconcile   d. Bank Statement

c. Bank Reconciliation Statement

a. The **Cash Receipts Journal (CRJ)** shows all transactions that increase the Bank Account of the business.

b. The **Cash Payments Journal (CPJ)** shows all transactions that decrease the Bank Account of the business.

c. The **Bank Reconciliation Statement** is prepared at the end of each month. See pg 151 for an example.
   The business cannot make any corrections on the Bank Statement. This must be done **by the bank**. The Bank Reconciliation Statement shows any necessary **corrections** that need to be made to the Bank Statement.
   It is also used to **check** if the business's records and Bank Statement agree after corrections have been made.
   The following details are included on the Bank Reconciliation Statement:
   - The balance on the Bank Statement
   - A list of the corrections the bank needs to make
   - A list of outstanding Cheques
   - A list of outstanding deposits
   - The Bank Account balance in the General Ledger after corrections

d. The **Bank Statement** shows all the transactions that have affected the Bank Account of the business, as **recorded by the bank.** The bank sends the business a Bank Statement at the end of each month.
   The bank owes the business the cash that it has in the bank, so it is recorded as a Liability.
   - The **Bank Statement** shows all the **transactions** that **decrease** the **Bank Account** of the business on the **Debit** (left) side of the Bank Statement.
   - The **Bank Statement** shows all the **transactions** that **increase** the **Bank Account** of the business on the **Credit** (right) side of the Bank Statement.

The business, **MNT TRADERS**, pays out R2 000.

Books of MNT TRADERS
The transaction is recorded in the CPJ.   **Bank Statement** sent to MNT TRADERS

DR	Bank	CR		DR	Bank Statement	CR
A	+	−		L	−	+
		2 000			2 000	

The business, **MNT TRADERS**, receives a deposit of R3 000.

Books of MNT TRADERS
The transaction is recorded in the CRJ.   **Bank Statement** sent to MNT TRADERS

DR	Bank	CR		DR	Bank Statement	CR
A	+	−		L	−	+
	3 000					3 000

STEPS TO COMPLETE THE BANK RECONCILIATION STATEMENT

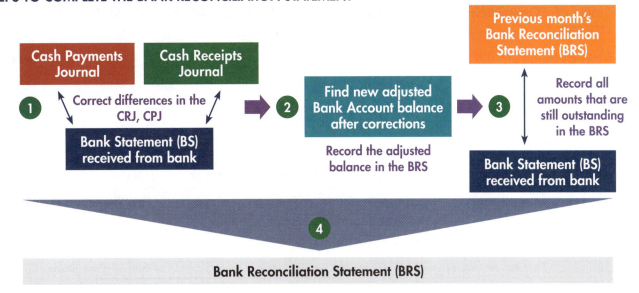

1. **Compare the Cash Receipts Journal and Cash Payments Journal with the Bank Statement.**

   a. **Compare the Cash Receipts Journal with the Credit side of the Bank Statement.**
      i. **Circle** any amounts that are **different** in the **CRJ** and the **Bank Statement.**
         Tick all the amounts that are the same, so that you know that you have checked them. ☑
      ii. Make **corrections** for the **differences** that are circled. All circled amounts require corrections.

   b. **Compare the Cash Payments Journal (CPJ) with the Debit side of the Bank Statement.**
      i. **Circle** any amounts that are **different** in the **CPJ** and the **Bank Statement.**
         Tick all the amounts that are the same, so that you know that you have checked them. ☑
      ii. Make **corrections** for the **differences** that are circled. All circled amounts require corrections.

    All amounts left out or mistakes made on the Bank Statement are recorded by the business on the Bank Reconciliation Statement.
   All amounts left out, or mistakes made by the business, are corrected by the business in the CPJ or CRJ and in the Bank Account in the General Ledger.

2. **Calculate the adjusted Bank Account balance in the General Ledger of the business.**
   The **new Bank Account balance** needs to be determined after making the corrections.
   Record the new Bank Account balance on the Bank Reconciliation Statement.

    In a test, you will be asked to do one of the following:
   - Make the corrections in the **CRJ and CPJ**: In this case the new CRJ and CPJ totals are used to find the new Bank Account balance.
   - Make the corrections to the **Bank Account** of the business in the **General Ledger**: In this case the balance of the Bank Account in the General Ledger after corrections is used to find the new Bank Account balance.

3. **Compare the previous month's Bank Reconciliation Statement with the current month's Bank Reconciliation Statement.**
   The **previous month's Bank Reconciliation Statement** is compared with the new Bank Statement, to determine if the required **corrections** from the previous month have been made by the bank. The previous month's Bank Reconciliation Statement shows all the amounts that the bank needed to correct on the Bank Statement. Any **corrections** that have **not** been made are **circled** and **included** in the **Bank Reconciliation Statement** for the current month. If these amounts have been recorded on the new Bank Statement, then they can be ticked off. ☑

    Any Cheques that are still outstanding (and are not stale/lost and needing to be cancelled) must be entered into the Bank Reconciliation Statement again.

4. **Complete the Bank Reconciliation Statement (BRS).**
   The columns on the Bank Reconciliation Statement are added up to **check** that the **balances** are the **same** after the corrections have been made and after the outstanding Cheques and deposits have been entered.

EXAMPLE OF COMPARING THE CASH RECEIPTS JOURNAL AND CASH PAYMENTS JOURNAL TO THE BANK STATEMENT.
Tick the amounts that are the same and circle the differences.

Cash Receipts Journal of MC ATTORNEYS – April 2018   CRJ 04

Doc	Day	Details	Analysis of Receipts		Bank		Current Income		Sundry Accounts		
									Amount		Details
			R	c	R	c	R	c	R	c	
BS	5	C. Pienaar	20 000	00	20 000 ✓	00	20 000	00			
Rec 35	6	Customers	45 000	00	45 000 ✓	00	45 000	00			
Rec 36	12	M. Mkize	5 000	00	(5 000)	00			5 000	00	Bad debts Recovered
Rec 37	14	K. Watson	50 000	00	50 000 ✓	00			50 000	00	Capital
CRT 90	18	T. Maseko	15 000	00	15 000 ✓	00	15 000	00			
Rec 38	30	P. van der Merwe	4 000	00	(4 000)	00			4 000	00	Rent Income
					139 000	00	80 000	00	59 000	00	

Cash Payments Journal of MC ATTORNEYS – April 2018   CPJ 04

Doc	Day	Name of payee	Bank		Equipment		Creditors Control		Sundry Accounts		
									Amount		Details
			R	c	R	c			R	c	
CC 21	2	MC Desks	8 000 ✓	00	8 000	00					
CC 22	3	L. Rhadebe	(10 000)	00					10 000	00	Drawings
CC 23	8	Turbo Tablets	12 000 ✓	00	12 000	00					
CC 24	10	Mr Stationery	300 ✓	00					300	00	Stationery
CC 25	15	AG Suppliers	(15 000)	00			15 000	00			
CC 26	25	Mozi Telekom	990 ✓	00					990	00	Telephone
			46 290	00	20 000	00	15 000	00	11 290	00	

DURBAN BANK
PO Box 2799
Bluff
Durban
4500

MC ATTORNEYS
Current Account: 1078 78787 22
25 Newlands Street
Morningside
Durban
4001

For Period: 01 April 2018 – 30 April 2018

Bank Statement						
Date	Details	Debit		Credit		Balance
01/04	Balance					35 000 00
02/04	Cheque 21	8 000	00 ✓			
05/04	Debit order: NC Insurers	(6 000)	00		✓	
06/04	Deposit			45 000	00 ✓	
06/04	Deposit		✓	20 000	00	
08/04	Cheque 23	12 000	00 ✓			
10/04	Cheque 24	300	00			
14/4	Deposit			50 000	00 ✓	
15/4	Direct deposit: M. Naude			(7 000)	00	
19/4	Deposit			15 000	00 ✓	
25/4	Cheque 26	990	00 ✓			
30/4	Bank service fees	80	00			

Notice that the CRJ is compared with the Credit side of the Bank Statement and the CPJ is compared with the Debit side of the Bank Statement.

EXAMPLES OF THE POSSIBLE DIFFERENCES WHEN COMPARING THE CRJ TO THE BANK STATEMENT AND HOW TO MAKE THE NECESSARY CORRECTIONS FOR EACH SITUATION

1. R800 was circled in the CRJ of **BENTLE CC**.

Books of the Business	Bank Reconciliation Statement
No adjustment required.	**Record** the amount as **Outstanding Deposit** in the Credit Column of the Bank Reconciliation Statement.

It often takes one to two days for a deposit made by the business to clear at the bank and to show on the Bank Statement.

2. Amounts for the following transactions were circled on the Bank Statement of **JP ELECTRONICS**:
   - R8 000 for direct deposits by customers
   - R600 for Interest on Current Account
   - R1 200 for Interest on Fixed Deposit

Books of the Business	Bank Reconciliation Statement
Record the **outstanding** transactions in the CRJ.	**No adjustment** required.

The bank immediately records amounts when it deposits money into the bank account of the business. The business will often only record these amounts after receiving the Bank Statement.

3. **BNT BAGS** received R250 from a customer. The amount was recorded correctly in the CRJ of the business, but it was recorded as R150 on the Bank Statement.

Books of the Business	Bank Reconciliation Statement
No adjustment required.	**Record** the **difference** (R100) on the Credit side.

4. **CT CAMERAS** received R650 from a customer. The amount was recorded correctly in the CRJ of the business, but it was recorded as R950 on the Bank Statement.

Books of the Business	Bank Reconciliation Statement
No adjustment required.	**Record** the **difference** (R300) on the Debit side.

5. **STEYN** received R9 000 for rent. The amount was correctly recorded on the Bank Statement, but R9 500 was recorded in the CRJ.

Books of the Business	Bank Reconciliation Statement
Record the **difference** (R500) in the CPJ to decrease the Bank Account.	**No adjustment** required.

6. **BIF CARS** received R8 000 for services. The amount was correctly recorded on the Bank Statement, but R6 000 was recorded in the CRJ.

Books of the Business	Bank Reconciliation Statement
Record the **difference** (R2 000) in the CRJ to increase the Bank Account.	**No adjustment** required.

7. The bookkeeper of **MINT DRINKS** found a stale Cheque.

Books of the Business	Bank Reconciliation Statement
Record the amount of the **Cheque** in the CRJ.	**No adjustment** required.

Stale Cheques are Cheques that are more than 6 months old. These Cheques will have been recorded in the CPJ when they were issued, so they need to be reversed in the CRJ to show that they have expired and no cash has been taken from the Bank Account of the business.

A business can also **cancel a Cheque** in the CRJ if a Cheque is lost or if the business that was being paid no longer exists.

EXAMPLES OF THE POSSIBLE DIFFERENCES YOU MAY FIND WHEN COMPARING THE CPJ TO THE BANK STATEMENT AND HOW TO MAKE THE NECESSARY CORRECTION FOR EACH SITUATION.

1. The records of **GH TRADERS** shows that there are a number of Cheques not yet presented to the bank for payment.

Books of the Business	Bank Reconciliation Statement
No adjustment required.	Record as **Outstanding Cheque** on the Debit side to decrease the Bank Account.

It takes a few days for a Cheque written by a business to clear at the bank, so the Cheque might not show on the Bank Statement before a certain time period.

2. Amounts for the following do not appear in the CPJ of **NN SPORTS**:
   - Interest on Loan
   - Interest on Overdraft
   - Bank charges
   - Debit orders
   - Stop orders
   - Dishonoured Cheques (R/D)

Books of the Business	Bank Reconciliation Statement
Record the **outstanding** transactions in the CPJ.	**No adjustment** required.

The bank deducts the amounts directly from the Bank Account of the business. The business will often only record the amounts after receiving the Bank Statement, so the CPJ of the business will need to be updated.

3. **LIZ** paid R400 for stationery. The transaction was correctly recorded in the CPJ, but an amount of R500 was recorded on the Debit side of the Bank Statement.

Books of the Business	Bank Reconciliation Statement
No adjustment required.	**Record** the **difference** (R100) on the Credit side to increase the Bank Account.

4. **DINEO** paid R8 000 for water and electricity. The transaction was correctly recorded in the CPJ, but an amount of R7 000 was recorded on the Debit side of the Bank Statement.

Books of the Business	Bank Reconciliation Statement
No adjustment required.	**Record** the **difference** (R1 000) on the Debit side to decrease the Bank Account.

5. **KHANITA** received R7 200 for rent income. The amount was correctly recorded on the Bank Statement, but R7 500 was recorded in the CRJ.

Books of the Business	Bank Reconciliation Statement
Record the **difference** (R300) in the CPJ to decrease the Bank Account.	**No adjustment** required.

6. **MOLEFE** received R12 000 for services. The amount was correctly recorded on the Bank Statement, but R11 000 was recorded in the CRJ.

Books of the Business	Bank Reconciliation Statement
Record the **difference** (R1 000) in the CRJ to increase the Bank Account.	**No adjustment** required.

7. **MIGS** issued a post-dated Cheque.

Books of the Business	Bank Reconciliation Statement
Record the amount of the Cheque in the **CPJ** to decrease the Bank Account.	**No adjustment** required.

A post-dated Cheque is a Cheque that has been written by the business with a date in the future. The bank will only reflect the amount on the Bank Statement once the Cheque has been deposited by the person who received the Cheque, on or after the due date.

EXAMPLE OF A BANK RECONCILIATION STATEMENT

STYLING SUNGLASSES LIMITED
Bank Reconciliation Statement on 31 December 2018

	Debit		Credit	
Balance on Bank Statement This is the balance at the end of the month.			200 000	00
Debit outstanding Cheques: Record all the outstanding Cheques circled in the CPJ that are not on the Bank Statement and all Cheques still outstanding from the previous month's reconciliation.				
no: 155	2 000	00		
no: 159	3 000	00		
no: 170	10 000	00		
Credit outstanding deposits Record the total of the deposits circled in the CRJ that are not on the Bank Statement.			15 000	00
Debit incorrect amount on the Bank Statement Show any corrections that the bank needs to make.	10 000	00		
Bank Account balance in the General Ledger	190 000	00		
	215 000	00	215 000	00

The Debit side must equal the Credit side.

1. All Debit amounts are recorded under the **Debit** Column.

2. All Credit amounts are entered under the **Credit** Column.

3. Record the bank balance that is found on the Bank Statement **(Balance on the Bank Statement)** on the last day of the month:
   - The balance is recorded under the Credit Column if it is positive (as shown in the example).
   - The balance is recorded under the Debit Column if it is negative.

4. All **corrections** that the bank needs to make are recorded on the Bank Reconciliation Statement.
   - **Debit outstanding Cheques:** All Cheques that do not appear on the Bank Statement are listed with their amounts in the Debit Column. A Debit amount shows that the bank needs to decrease the balance of the business on the Bank Statement.
   - **Credit outstanding deposits:** All the deposits that do not appear on the Bank Statement are listed with their amounts in the Credit Column. A **Credit** amount shows that the bank needs to **increase** the balance of the business on the Bank Statement.
   - **Debit incorrect amount on the Bank Statement:** Any errors found on the Bank Statement are corrected on the Bank Reconciliation Statement.
   Record the correction amount on the **Debit** side to show that the bank must **decrease** the **bank balance** on the Bank Statement (as shown in the example).
   (If there was an incorrect entry on the Debit side of the Bank Statement, record the correction amount on the **Credit** side to show that the bank must **increase** the **bank balance** on the Bank Statement.)

5. The new Bank Account balance (after corrections have been made) is recorded **(Bank Account balance in the General Ledger)**:
   - The balance is recorded under the Debit Column if it is positive.
   - The balance is recorded under the Credit Column if it is negative.

Notice that all the corrections that the bank needs to make are listed on the **Bank Reconciliation Statement**.

GAAP AND IFRS
SUMMARY OF CONTENTS

SIX FUNDAMENTAL CONCEPTS **153**

1. Historical Cost Concept
2. Business Entity Concept
3. Matching Concept
4. Materiality Concept
5. Going Concern Concept
6. Prudence Concept

GAAP AND IFRS

All businesses follow the same set of Accounting Standards when preparing their Financial Statements. The Accounting Standards are guidelines that help businesses to prepare the Financial Statements in a **consistent** and **reliable** manner.

IFRS (**I**nternational **F**inancial **R**eporting **S**tandards) and **GAAP** (**G**enerally **A**ccepted **A**ccounting **P**rinciples) are the most common Accounting Standards used across the world.
Both IFRS and GAAP are based on the following six fundamental concepts.

CONCEPT	EXPLANATION
HISTORICAL COST CONCEPT	The original costs (historical costs) of the Assets of a business need to be recorded. BRIXTON LTD bought a building for R450 000 ten years ago. The most recent Financial Statements of the business show the cost as R450 000 for the building, even though it is worth a lot more today.
BUSINESS ENTITY CONCEPT	The Owner and business are seen as two separate entities for Accounting purposes. The transactions of the Owner are recorded separately from the transactions of the business. MGN PARTNERS has a bank account that is used for all the transactions of the business. The Owners of MGN Partners each have their own personal bank accounts.
MATCHING CONCEPT	Income and Expenses are recorded when they take place and not when they are paid for. The bookkeeper for OP TRADERS records the Income for Inventory sold on credit on the last day of the Accounting Period, even though the cash will only be received in the next Accounting Period. Income and Expenses need to be matched. If an Expense was incurred to receive an Income, then the Expense is recorded when the Income is received. It costs OP TRADERS R600 to make their products. The products are only sold in 12 months' time. The bookkeeper only records the costs of making the products as an Expense when the products are sold.
MATERIALITY CONCEPT	All significant (material) information needs to be clearly shown in the Financial Statements of the business. The details of any items that do not have a material effect on the Financial Position of a business need not be shown. The bookkeeper of MOBILITY LTD has separate Accounts to record the costs of each Fixed Asset, but she records the costs of pens, erasers, pencils, etc. under one Stationery Account.
GOING CONCERN CONCEPT	The Accountant assumes that the business does not expect to close down in the future when preparing the Financial Statements. The Debtors Control Account shows the value of the cash that B&T PARTNERS expects to receive from Debtors. If the Accountant assumed that the business would close down soon then this value would be zero.
PRUDENCE CONCEPT	Accountants need to be conservative when recording the financial information of a business. When estimations are made: • **Income** and **Assets** should **not** be **overstated** COSTA TRADERS hopes to receive cash from a customer who is bankrupt. The business does not show the cash it expects to receive as an Asset in the Financial Statements of the business. • **Expenses** and **Liabilities** should **not** be **understated**. COSTA TRADERS expects that a customer will only pay 50% of the amount he owes the business. The business shows the 50% that it expects not to receive in the Financial Statements of the business.

INVENTORY
SUMMARY OF CONTENTS

A   **INVENTORY SYSTEMS** **155**

    1.   The Perpetual Inventory System **156**

        a.   Important Accounts used to record transactions during the Accounting Period

        b.   Adjustments at the end of the Accounting Period

    2.   The Periodic Stock System **158**

        a.   Important Accounts used to record transactions during the Accounting Period

        b.   Adjustments at the end of the Accounting Period **159**

B   **STOCK VALUATION** **164**

    1.   First In First Out Method (FIFO)

    2.   Weighted Average Cost Method (WAC)

Overview of the two different valuation methods .... **164 — 165**

INVENTORY ⑩

Inventory is the name given to the items or goods that a business sells.
Inventory is also referred to as Trading Stock, Products, Items or Goods. Inventory is sold at a **mark-up** in order to make a **Profit**.

IMPORTANT TERMS

TERM	EXPLANATION
Sales Price	The price at which an item is sold to a customer
Cost Price	The cost of an item
Gross Margin	The difference between the Sales Price and the Cost Price
Mark-up	The percentage that is added to the Cost Price to determine the Selling Price

INVENTORY SYSTEMS AND VALUATION METHODS ⑪

There are different **Inventory Systems** used to **record transactions** that involve Inventory, and there are different **Inventory Valuation Methods** used to **determine** the **cost** of Inventory sold.

A. INVENTORY SYSTEMS

An Inventory System is used to record the cost of Inventory sold and the cost of Inventory available to sell.
Remember that Cost of Sales is the term used for the cost of the Inventory sold. It is also called Cost of Goods Sold.

TWO DIFFERENT SYSTEMS USED

The **Perpetual (Continuous) Stock System** and the **Periodic Stock System** are the two different Inventory Systems used to record transactions that involve Inventory.

Overview of the two different Inventory Systems   Make sure you know the differences!
A business will decide which system to use by looking at the costs and benefits of using each system.

	PERPETUAL	PERIODIC
GENERAL	The cost of Inventory is **continuously updated** – the cost of Inventory sold and the cost of Inventory available to sell is known at all times.	The cost of Inventory is **periodically updated** – the cost of Inventory sold and the cost of Inventory available to sell is only calculated at the end of a period.
COSTS	Expensive	Not expensive
IMPLEMENT	**Difficult** to implement – requires a sophisticated computer system to be able to track all costs of Inventory as it is sold.	**Easy** to implement – no sophisticated computer system required.
STOCKTAKE	At the end of the Accounting Period, the cost of Inventory available to sell is counted to **check** that the **balance** of the **Trading Stock Account** is correct.	At the end of the Accounting Period, the cost of Inventory available is counted to **determine** how much **Inventory** was **sold**.
RECORDING TRANSACTIONS	• The **Trading Stock Account** is continuously updated. • The **Cost of Sales Account** is continuously updated to show the cost of Inventory sold.	• The **Purchases Account** is continuously updated to show the cost of Inventory purchased. • The **Trading Stock Account** is only updated at the end of the Accounting Period. • The cost of Inventory sold (**Cost of Sales**) is only determined at the end of the Accounting Period.

1. THE PERPETUAL INVENTORY SYSTEM

The **Trading Stock Account** is continuously updated to show the changes in the cost of Inventory available and the **Cost of Sales Account** is continuously updated to show the cost of Inventory sold.

Perpetual means continuous.

a. Important Accounts used to record transactions during the Accounting Period

ACCOUNT	DETAILS
Sales (I) — DR – / CR +	**The amount of Income earned from the sale of Inventory** • The Account **increases** on the **Credit** side when **Inventory** is **sold**. • The Account **balance** is **closed off** to the **Trading Account** at the end of the Accounting Period to **determine** the **Gross Profit**. **Gross Profit = Net Sales – Cost of Sales**
Debtors Allowances (E) — DR + / CR –	**The Selling Price of Inventory returned to the business** • The Account **increases** on the **Debit** side when a **Debtor returns Inventory** to the business or is **given** a **discount** by the business. • The Account **balance** is **closed off** to the **Sales** Account at the **end** of the Accounting Period to **determine Net Sales** for the Accounting Period. **Net Sales = Sales – Debtors Allowances**
Trading Stock (A) — DR + / CR –	**The cost of Inventory that is available to sell** • The Account **increases** on the **Debit** side when **Inventory** is **purchased** or Inventory sold is **returned** by a customer. • The Account **decreases** on the **Credit** side when **Inventory** is **sold** (**Cost of Sales**), or **Inventory purchased** is returned to the supplier (**Creditors Control**), or the **Owner takes Inventory** for personal use (**Drawings**), or **Inventory** is **donated** to an organisation (**Donations**).
Cost of Sales (E) — DR + / CR –	**The Cost Price of Inventory sold** • The Account **increases** on the **Debit** side to record the **Cost Price** of **Inventory sold** on credit or for cash. • The Account **decreases** on the **Credit** side when **Inventory** sold is **returned** to the business. The Account **balance** is **closed off** to the **Trading Account** at the end of the Accounting Period to **determine Gross Profit**. **Gross Profit = Net Sales – Cost of Sales**

See pg 160 for details on how different transactions are recorded using the Perpetual Stock Method.

b. Adjustments at the end of the Accounting Period See pg 122 for more details on Adjustments.

At the end of the Account Period, a business checks that the Trading Stock balance is correct and prepares the Trading Account to determine the Gross Profit (Net Sales – Cost of Sales).

iii. Physical stocktake

At the end of the Accounting Period a physical stocktake is done.

The physical stocktake is done to **check** that the balance of the Trading Stock Account is correct. The **cost** of Inventory available according to the stocktake is **compared** with the **Trading Stock Account balance**. An adjustment is made to the Trading Stock Account balance if there is a difference.

- If **Trading Stock Counted** is **more** than the **Trading Stock Account balance** then the difference is recorded as an **Income**. This can occur if there is more Inventory than the books of the business shows.
  The **Trading Stock Surplus Account** is used to record the difference.
- If the **Trading Stock Account balance** is **less** than the **Trading Stock counted** then the difference recorded is an **Expense**. This can occur if Inventory is taken/stolen and not recorded by the bookkeeper.
  The **Trading Stock Deficit Account** is used to record the difference.

BENJI counted that there was R10 000 more Trading Stock than the Trading Stock balance showed. He recorded an adjustment to correct the difference.

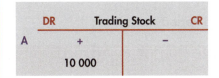
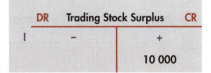

MONDI counted that there was R5 000 less Trading Stock than the Trading Stock balance showed. He recorded an adjustment to correct the difference.

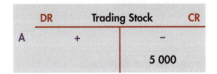

DR	Trading Stock Deficit	CR
E	+	–
	5 000	

ii. **The Trading Account**
The Trading Account is a Temporary Account that is prepared at the end of the Accounting Period to determine the Gross Profit.
The balances of the **Sales Account** and the **Cost of Sales Account** are closed off to the **Trading Account**.

The bookkeeper of **MONT TRADERS** closed off the Cost of Sales And Sales Accounts at the end of the Accounting Period and prepared the Trading Account in the General Ledger.

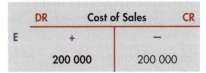
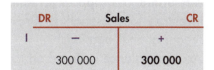

Remember that the Debtors Allowances amount is included in the Sales amount.

DR	Trading Account	CR
	–	+
	200 000	300 000

DR				Trading Account					CR
Date		Details	Fol	Amount	Date		Details	Fol	Amount
2016 Feb.	28	Cost of Sales	GJ	200 000 00	2016 Feb.	28	Sales	GJ	300 000 00
		Profit & Loss Account		100 000 00					
				300 000 00					300 000 00

The Gross Profit of R100 000 (300 000 – 200 000) is closed off to the Profit and Loss Account. 💡

2. THE PERIODIC STOCK SYSTEM

The cost of Inventory available to sell and the cost of Inventory sold is only determined at the end of the Accounting Period. **There is no specific Account that records the cost of Inventory sold.**

a. **Important Accounts used to record transactions during the Accounting Period**

ACCOUNT NAME	DETAILS
Sales (DR − / CR +) — I This is the same as the Sales Account used in the Perpetual Stock System.	**The amount of Income earned from the sale of Inventory** • The Account **increases** on the **Credit** side when **Inventory** is **sold**. • The Account **balance** is **closed off** to the **Trading Account** at the end of the Accounting Period to **determine** the **Gross Profit**. Gross Profit = Net Sales − Cost of Sales
Debtors Allowances (DR + / CR −) — E This is the same as the Debtors Allowances Account used in the Perpetual Stock System.	**The Selling Price of Inventory that is returned to the business** • The Account **increases** on the **Debit** side when **Inventory** sold is **returned** by a customer. • The Account **balance** is **closed off** to the **Sales** Account at the **end** of the Accounting Period to **determine Net Sales** for the Accounting Period. Net Sales = Sales − Debtors Allowances
Purchases (DR + / CR −) — E	**The cost of Inventory purchased during the Accounting Period** • The Account **increases** on the **Debit** side when **Inventory** is **purchased** by the business on credit or with cash. • The Account **decreases** on the **Credit** side when **Inventory purchased is returned** to a **supplier (Creditors Control)**, or the **Owner takes Inventory** for personal use **(Drawings)**, or **Inventory** is **donated** to an organisation **(Donations)**. The Account **balance** is **closed off** to the **Trading Account** at the end of the Accounting Period to **determine** the **Gross Profit**.
Carriage on Purchases (DR + / CR −) — E	**The costs of Carriage on Purchases when Inventory is purchased** • The Account **increases** on the **Debit** side when **Carriage on Purchases** (transport costs) are **included** to purchase **Inventory**. • The Account **balance** is **closed off** to the **Trading Account** at the end of the Accounting Period to **determine** the **Gross Profit**.
Custom Duties (DR + / CR −) — E	**The costs of Customs Duties when Inventory is purchased** • The Account **increases** on the **Debit** side when **Customs Duties** are **included** to purchase **Inventory**. • The Account **balance** is **closed off** to the **Trading Account** at the end of the Accounting Period to **determine** the **Gross Profit**.
Creditors Allowances (DR − / CR +) — I	**The cost of Inventory purchased on credit that is returned by the business** • The Account **increases** on the **Credit** side when **Inventory purchased** on credit is **returned**. • The Account **balance** is **closed off** to the **Purchases Account** at the end of the Accounting Period to **determine Net Purchases**. Net Purchases = Purchases − Creditors Allowances

> The Trading Stock Account that shows the cost of Inventory available to sell is also used with the Periodic Stock System. However, the Account balance is only updated at the end of the Accounting Period when a stocktake is done.

b. **Adjustments at the end of the Accounting Period** See pg 122 for more details on Adjustments.
At the end of an Accounting Period, a business does a physical stocktake to determine the cost of Inventory available and prepares a Trading Account to determine the Gross Profit.

i. **The cost of Inventory available at the end of the Accounting Period is determined by the stocktake and recorded in the books of the business.**
The **Trading Stock** Account is **debited** to show the **cost** of **Inventory available**.
The **Closing Stock** Account is a **Temporary Account** that is **credited** to record the cost of Inventory available according to the stocktake at the end of the Accounting Period.
Notice that when the Periodic Stock System is used, the balance of the Trading Stock Account is only determined at the end of the Accounting Period.

SIMZA LIMITED counted that there was R100 000 worth of Inventory at the end of the Accounting Period.

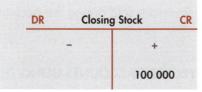

ii. **The Trading Account is a Temporary Account that is prepared at the end of the Accounting Period to determine the Gross Profit.**
The balances of the following Accounts are closed off to the Trading Account:
- Sales Account
- Opening Stock Account (Inventory available at beginning of Accounting Period)
- Closing Stock Account (Inventory available at end of Accounting Period)
- Purchases Account
- Carriage on Purchases Account
- Customs Duties Account

The bookkeeper at **PNT LIMITED** prepared the following Trading Account. *This is often asked in tests.*

DR									Trading Account							CR
Date		Details		Fol		Amount			Date		Details		Fol		Amount	
2016 Feb.	28	Opening Stock		GJ		150 000	00		2016 Feb.	28	Sales		GJ		700 000	00
		Purchases		GJ		500 000	00				Closing Stock		GJ		200 000	00
		Carriage on Purchases		GJ		40 000	00									
		Customs Duties		GJ		10 000	00									
		Profit & Loss Account		GJ		200 000	00									
						900 000	00								900 000	00

The Gross Profit of R200 000 is closed off to the Profit and Loss Account.

There is no Cost of Sales Account when the Periodic Stock System is used.
The following table shows how the Cost of Sales is calculated.

Opening Stock	The balance of the Trading Stock Account at the **beginning** of the Accounting Period
+ Net Purchases	Purchases – Creditors Allowances
+ Carriage on Purchases	Expenses when purchasing Inventory are added to the cost of Inventory
+ Customs Duties	Expenses when purchasing Inventory are added to the cost of Inventory
= Inventory available for sale	The total cost of the Inventory that was available for sale **during** the year
– Closing Stock	The cost of Inventory according to the stocktake at the **end** of the Accounting Period. This is the balance of the Trading Stock Account at the end of the Accounting Period
= Cost of Sales	Cost of Inventory sold **during** the Accounting Period

SHOW HOW THE TRANSACTIONS AFFECT THE ACCOUNTS USING THE PERPETUAL STOCK SYSTEM AND THE PERIODIC STOCK SYSTEM.

1. **Inventory is purchased for R20 000 cash. In addition, R2 000 is paid for Carriage on Purchases and R3 000 for Customs Duties.**

    a. **Perpetual Stock System**

    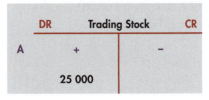 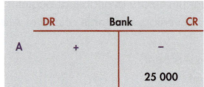

    Carriage on Purchases and Customs Duties are additional costs that sometimes have to be paid when purchasing Inventory. These costs are added to the cost of the Inventory.

    b. **Periodic Stock System**

    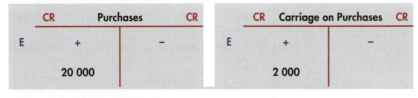

    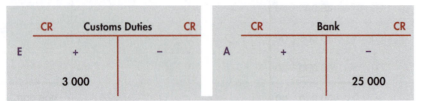

    Notice that Carriage on Purchases and Customs Duties are recorded in separate Accounts.

2. Inventory is sold for R10 000 cash. The Cost Price of the Inventory is R8 000.
   a. Perpetual Stock System

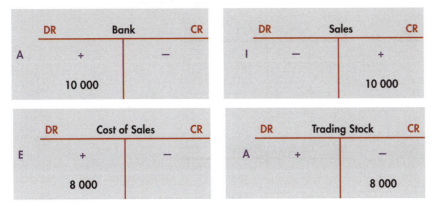

   b. Periodic Stock System

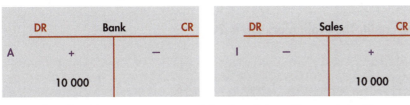

   Notice that there is no entry to record the Cost Price of Inventory sold.

3. The business donates Inventory with a Cost Price of R6 000 to a charity.
   a. Perpetual Stock System

   b. Periodic Stock System

4. Inventory is purchased on credit for R50 000.
   a. Perpetual Stock System

DR	Trading Stock	CR		DR	Creditors Control	CR
A	+	−		L	−	+
	50 000					50 000

   b. Periodic Stock System

DR	Purchases	CR		DR	Creditors Control	CR
E	+	−		L	−	+
	50 000					50 000

5. Inventory purchased on credit by the business for R15 000 is returned to the supplier.
   a. Perpetual Stock System

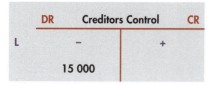

   b. Periodic Stock System

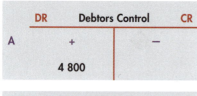 

The Creditors Allowances Account is closed off to the Purchases Account at the end of the Accounting Period.

6. Inventory is sold for R4 800 on credit. The Profit Mark-Up is 20%.
   a. Perpetual Stock System

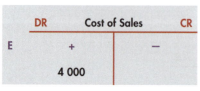 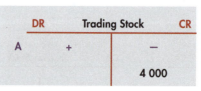

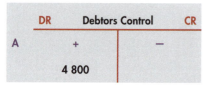 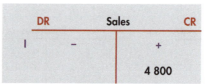

Cost Price = Selling Price × 100 ÷ (100 + mark-up)
Cost Price = 4 800 ÷ (100 + 20) = 4 000   OR   Cost Price = 4 800 × $\frac{100}{120}$ = 4 000

   b. Periodic Stock System

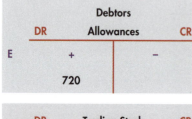 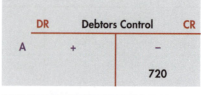

Notice that there is no entry to record the Cost Price of Inventory sold.

7. Inventory sold on credit for R720 is returned by a customer. The Profit Mark-Up was 20%.
   a. Perpetual Stock System

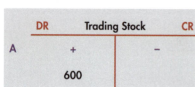 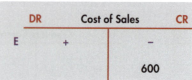

Cost Price = Selling Price × 100 ÷ (100 + mark-up)
Cost Price = 720 × 100 ÷ (100 + 20) = 600

b. **Periodic Stock System**

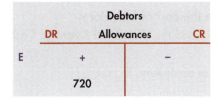 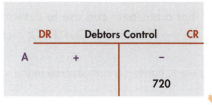

Notice that there is no entry to record the Cost Price of Inventory returned.

8. The Owner of the business takes Inventory with a Cost Price of R2 000 for personal use.
   a. **Perpetual Stock System**

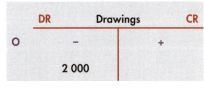 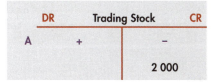

   b. **Periodic Stock System**

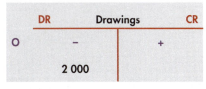 

As you can see, there are sometimes differences when recording transactions using the Periodic or Perpetual Systems. However, the end result should be the same.

Make sure you know how to record each transaction using both systems. In addition, check whether you can record the transactions in the Accounting Equation.
See pg 11 for more information on recording transactions in the Accounting Equation.

B. STOCK VALUATION

There are different types of methods that a business can use to determine the cost of Inventory.
The two most common methods used are the **First In First Out (FIFO)** method and the **Weighted Average Cost (WAC)** method.
Last In First Out (LIFO) is another method used, but this is not covered in the school curriculum.

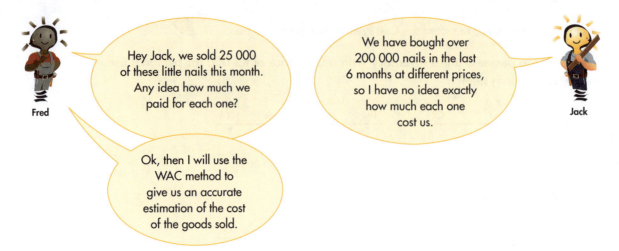

1. FIRST IN FIRST OUT METHOD (FIFO)
The Inventory that the business purchases first is the Inventory that is sold first when using the FIFO method. This method is commonly used for businesses that sell perishable items, or hi-tech items such as cellphones that become dated fairly quickly.

 Perishable items are items that expire. If you are selling milk then it is important to sell the first purchased bottles of milk first, before they expire. However, if you are selling screws then it does not matter in which order you sell the screws.

2. WEIGHTED AVERAGE COST METHOD (WAC)
The cost of the Inventory sold and the cost of the Inventory available for sale is calculated using the average cost of the Inventory.

Weighted average cost per unit = $\dfrac{\text{Total cost of all the units}}{\text{Total number of units}}$

- Cost of Inventory sold (Cost of Sales) = Number of total units sold × Weighted average cost per unit
- Cost of Inventory available = Number of total units available × Weighted average cost per unit

OVERVIEW OF THE TWO DIFFERENT VALUATION METHODS

When all the balls have been sold, these two methods should have approximately the same result.

WASHA sells washing machines. Use the information below to complete the following:
1. Use the **FIFO method** to calculate the value of the closing Stock and the cost of goods sold for the Accounting Period.
2. Use the **Weighted Average Cost method** to calculate the value of the closing Stock and the cost of goods sold for the Accounting Period.

- The table below provides details about the opening balance and Purchases during the year.

DETAILS	NO. OF UNITS	COST PER UNIT	TOTAL
Trading Stock Account balance on 01 March 2016	10	R 2 500	R25 000
Purchases during the Accounting Period: March August September December	15 20 5 10	R2 600 R2 800 R2 700 R3 000	R39 000 R56 000 R13 500 R30 000

- A physical stocktake showed that there were 15 washing machines left on the last day of the Accounting Period.

1. **Using the First In First Out method (FIFO)**
   Total number of units sold = 60 − 15 = 45
   Total units sold = Total units available for sale (Opening Stock + Units Purchased)
   − Total units left over on the last day of the Accounting Period (Closing Stock)

   According to the FIFO method, the first units purchased are the first units sold.
   To calculate the Cost of Sales, we use the values of the first 45 units purchased:
   Cost of Sales = (10 units × R2 500) + (15 units × R2 600) + (20 units × R2 800) = R120 000
   The Cost of Sales when using the FIFO method is R120 000.

   The value of the closing Stock will be the cost of the Inventory that has still not been sold:
   (5 units × R2 700) + (10 units × R3 000) = R43 500
   The cost of the closing Stock when using the FIFO method is R43 500.

2. **Using the Weighted Average Cost method (WAC)**

   Weighted average cost per unit = $\dfrac{\text{Total cost of all the units}}{\text{Total number of units}}$

   $= \dfrac{25\,000 + 39\,000 + 56\,000 + 13\,500 + 30\,000}{\text{Total number of units}}$

   $= \dfrac{\text{R163 500}}{60 \text{ units}}$

   = R2 725 / unit

   Cost of Sales = Number of total units sold × Weighted average cost per unit
   = 45 units × R2 725
   = R 122 625
   The Cost of Sales when using the WAC method is R122 625.

   Cost of closing Stock = Number of total units available × Weighted average cost per unit
   = 15 × R2 725
   = R40 875
   The value of closing Stock when using the WAC method is R40 875.

When using **FIFO**: Cost of Sales (R120 000) + Closing Stock (R43 500) = R163 500
When using **WAC**: Cost of Sales (R122 625) + Closing Stock (R40 875) = R163 500
The total cost (R163 500) of Inventory sold and Inventory available to sell works out to be the same.

FIXED ASSETS
SUMMARY OF CONTENTS

A   **FIXED ASSET ACCOUNTS** **167**

    1. Vehicles Account

    2. Equipment Account

    3. Machinery Account

    4. Furniture Account

    5. Land and Buildings Account

B   **DEPRECIATION** **168**

    1. Recording Depreciation

    2. Carrying Value

    3. Depreciation Calculations

        a. Fixed amount method/Straight line method

            i. Using the lifespan of the Asset **169**

            ii. Using the fixed percentage

        b. Diminishing balance method

C   **DISPOSAL OF A FIXED ASSET** **170**

    Steps to record the sale or trade-in of a Fixed Asset

D   **FIXED ASSET REGISTER** **173**

E   **INTERPRETATION AND REPORTING ON THE MOVEMENT OF FIXED ASSETS** **173**

    1. Lifespan of a Fixed Asset

    2. Age of a Fixed Asset

    3. Replacement rate of a Fixed Asset **174**

    4. Net realisable value of a Fixed Asset

FIXED ASSETS

Fixed Assets are purchased for long-term use (e.g. vehicles and furniture). They are used in the day-to-day operations of a business.

 While working through this section, also look at the Notes to the Financial Statements for Fixed Assets on pg 86.

COST PRICE
According to the Historical Principle, the Cost Price of Fixed Assets must be recorded by the business.
Cost Price = Purchase Price + Direct Costs (transport costs, delivery costs and handling costs to get the Assets to the business)
See pg 152 to learn more about the different Accounting Principles.

A. FIXED ASSET ACCOUNTS

The Cost Price of a Fixed Asset is recorded in one of the five different Fixed Asset Accounts.
Each Account **increases** on the **Debit** side by the Cost Price when the Asset is purchased, and **decreases** on the **Credit** side by the Cost Price when the Asset is sold.

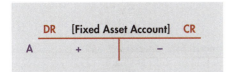

1. **Vehicles Account**
   The Vehicles Account includes all the vehicles that are used to transport Inventory or employees of the business.
   Cars, trucks, vans, etc.

2. **Equipment Account**
   The Equipment Account includes all the equipment that is used to assist with the daily operations of the business.
   Fax machines, printers, computers, phones, scanners, computer modems, etc.

3. **Machinery Account**
   The Machinery Account includes all machines that are used to assist with the production of Inventory.
   Any machine used in a factory to make Inventory
   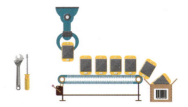

4. **Furniture Account**
   The Furniture Account includes all furniture that is used by employees in the workplace.
   Chairs, desks, cupboards, etc.

5. **Land and Buildings Account**
   The Land and Buildings Account includes all land and buildings that the business owns.
   Buildings, factories, offices, farms, boardrooms, etc.

B. DEPRECIATION

Depreciation is the loss in the value of a Fixed Asset.
Depreciation is recorded for Equipment, Furniture, Machinery and Vehicles at the end of each Accounting Period. These Assets lose value over time.

> Land and Buildings is the only Fixed Asset Account that does not depreciate. Land and buildings usually appreciate in value over time.

1. RECORDING DEPRECIATION
The Depreciation Account and the Accumulated Depreciation Account are affected when Depreciation is recorded.
Depreciation is recorded in the General Journal at the end of the Accounting Period.
- The **Depreciation Account** is an **Expense Account**, so it **increases** on the **Debit** side by the Depreciation recorded.
- The **Accumulated Depreciation Account** is known as a **negative Asset Account** because it decreases the value of an Asset. Accumulated Depreciation is recorded on the **Credit** side. The balance of the Accumulated Depreciation Accounts shows the **total Depreciation** recorded for the Asset.

The following T Accounts show the balances of the Vehicles Account and the Accumulated Depreciation: Vehicles Account in the books of TEBZ TRADERS.

The balance of a Negative Asset is always on the Credit side.

2. CARRYING VALUE   Carrying Value is also called the Book Value.
The value of the Asset in the books of a business is known as the Carrying Value.
Carrying Value of the Asset = Cost Price of the Asset – Accumulated Depreciation of the Asset
Carrying Value of the Asset = Original cost of the Asset – How much value the Asset has lost

The following T Accounts show the balances of the Equipment Account and the Accumulated Depreciation: Equipment Account in the books of JABU TRADERS.
What is the Carrying Value of equipment?

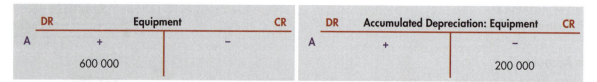

Carrying Value of the Asset = Cost Price of the Asset – Accumulated Depreciation of the Asset
Carrying Value of the Asset = R600 000 – R200 000
Carrying Value of the Asset = R400 000 The Equipment is worth R400 000 in the books of the business.

3. DEPRECIATION CALCULATIONS
There are two different methods used to calculate Depreciation.

a. **Fixed amount method/Straight line method**
   The Depreciation stays the same each year.
   The Depreciation is calculated on the **Cost Price** of the Asset. The **lifespan of the Asset** or a **fixed percentage** can be used to determine the Depreciation amount for each year.
   A **fixed** amount means an amount that stays the **same**.

i. **Using the lifespan of the Asset**
   The Cost Price of the Asset is divided by the lifespan of the Asset to determine the Depreciation amount. The lifespan of an Asset is the number of years for which it is expected to last.
   Yearly Depreciation amount = Cost Price of the Asset ÷ Lifespan of the Asset

   > **MTG TRADERS** owns equipment that costs R20 000. It is expected to last for 5 years. Show the Depreciation amounts for the next five years in the table.
   >
   > **Yearly Depreciation amount = Cost Price of the Asset ÷ Lifespan of the Asset**
   > **Yearly Depreciation = R20 000 ÷ 5 = R4 000 per year**
   >
   > | Year | Depreciation | Accumulated Depreciation
Total Depreciation | Carrying Value at the end of the year |
   > |---|---|---|---|
   > | 1 | R4 000 | R4 000 | 20 000 – 4 000 = R16 000 |
   > | 2 | R4 000 | R8 000 | 20 000 – 8 000 = R12 000 |
   > | 3 | R4 000 | R12 000 | 20 000 – 12 000 = R8 000 |
   > | 4 | R4 000 | R16 000 | 20 000 – 16 000 = R4 000 |
   > | 5 | R3 999 | R19 999 | 20 000 – 19 999 = R1 |
   >
   > **An Asset cannot have a value of R0.** When the Accumulated Depreciation is more than or equal to the Cost Price of the Asset, then we adjust the Depreciation for the year so that the Carrying Value is R1. The Asset is then left in the books at a value of R1. The value that the Asset can be sold for is known as the residual value or scrap value.

ii. **Using the fixed percentage**
   The Cost Price of the Asset is multiplied by a fixed percentage to determine the Depreciation amount.
   Yearly Depreciation amount = Cost Price × Fixed percentage

   > **TT PLASTICS** own a vehicle that costs R80 000 and is depreciated at 20% each year. What is the yearly Depreciation?
   > **Yearly Depreciation = Cost Price × Fixed percentage**
   > **Yearly Depreciation = R80 000 × 20% = R16 000**
   > Each year the vehicle is depreciated by R16 000.
   > **This is the same as dividing the Cost Price by five years: 80 000 ÷ 5 = R16 000 per year.**

b. **Diminishing balance method**
   The Carrying Value of the Asset is multiplied by a fixed percentage to determine the Depreciation amount.
   The yearly Depreciation amount = Carrying Value × Fixed percentage
   Each year the Carrying Value of the Asset decreases, so the amount of Depreciation for the year gets lower. **Diminishing means smaller. In this method, the Depreciation gets smaller each year.**

   > Show the Depreciation of an Asset that costs R20 000 over the first five years.
   > **BT LIMITED** calculates Depreciation at 20% per year according to the diminishing balance method.
   >
   > | Year | Depreciation Calculation | Accumulated Depreciation | Carrying Value at the end of the year |
   > |---|---|---|---|
   > | 1 | 20 000 × 20% = R4 000 | R4 000 | 20 000 – 4 000 = R16 000 |
   > | 2 | 16 000 × 20% = R3 200 | R7 200 | 20 000 – 7 200 = R12 800 |
   > | 3 | 12 800 × 20% = R2 560 | R9 760 | 20 000 – 9 760 = R10 240 |
   > | 4 | 10 240 × 20% = R2 048 | R11 808 | 20 000 – 11 808 = R8 192 |
   > | 5 | 8 192 × 20% = R1 638,40 | R13 446,40 | 20 000 – 13 446,40 = R6 553,60 |

 Depreciation is sometimes not calculated for all twelve months of the year. If an Asset is bought or sold during the year, Depreciation must only be calculated for the number of months in which the business owned the Asset. Depreciation = Depreciation for the year × (No. of months for which the business owned the Asset ÷ 12)

C. DISPOSAL OF A FIXED ASSET

When an Asset is disposed of, all the Accounts that belong to the Asset are closed.
The **Asset Disposal Account** is a **Temporary Account** which is used to **determine** the **Profit or Loss** made on the disposal of the Asset. All the Accounts that belong to the Asset are closed off to the Asset Disposal Account.
Temporary Accounts do not have a plus or minus sign on the Debit or Credit Sides.

STEPS TO RECORD THE SALE OR TRADE-IN OF A FIXED ASSET

1. **Close the Asset Account of the Asset to the Asset Disposal Account.**
   The Debit balance of the Asset Account (**Cost Price**) is **credited** to **close off** the Account to the Asset Disposal Account.

2. **Close the Accumulated Depreciation Account of the Asset to the Asset Disposal Account.**
   The Credit **balance** of the Accumulated Depreciation Account is **debited** to **transfer** the balance to the Asset Disposal Account.

> Make sure that the total Accumulated Depreciation on the date of the sale of the Asset has been calculated.
> Total Accumulated Depreciation = Accumulated Depreciation at the beginning of the Accounting Period in which the Asset is sold + Depreciation up until the date of the sale of the Asset

3. **Record the Sales Price (or Trade-In Value) of the Asset.**
   A business can sell a Fixed Asset for cash or on credit, or trade it in for a new Asset.
   - If the Asset is sold for **cash**, the **Bank Account increases** on the **Debit** side by the Sales Price amount.
   - If the Asset is sold on **credit**, the **Debtors Control Account increases** on the **Debit** side by the Sales Price amount.
   - If the Asset is **traded in**, the **Creditors Control Account decreases** on the **Debit** side by the Sales Price amount. This is to show that the business owes the person less than what was previously owed.

4. **Determine the Profit or Loss made for the Asset.**
   - **If the Credit side is bigger than the Debit side of the Asset Disposal Account then a Profit has been made.**
     The difference (Profit) of the Asset Disposal Account is transferred to the **Profit on Sale of Asset Account**.
   - **If the Debit side is greater than the Credit side of the Asset Disposal Account then a Loss has been made.**
     The difference (Loss) is transferred to the **Loss on Sale of Asset Account**.

See example on next page.

Use the information below to prepare the Vehicles, Accumulated Depreciation and Asset Disposal Accounts in the General Ledger of **EARLY BAKERY** on the last day of the Accounting period, 28 February 2016.

Information
- The following **balances** appeared in the **General Ledger** on 01 March 2015:

Vehicles	R1 200 000
Accumulated Depreciation on Vehicles	R600 000

- A vehicle purchased on 01 March 2013 for R400 000 was **sold** for cash for R280 000 on 31 May 2015.
- **Depreciation** on vehicles is calculated at 10% on cost.
- A **new delivery van** was **purchased** on credit on 30 June 2015 for R600 000.

Calculation for Accumulated Depreciation on the sale of the vehicle
Cost Price = R400 000
Depreciation per year = R400 000 × 10% = R40 000
Accumulated Depreciation on 01 March 2015: R40 000 × 2 years = R80 000
Depreciation for current year: R40 000 × 3 months ÷ 12 = R10 000
Accumulated Depreciation on sold vehicle: R80 000 + R10 000 = R90 000

Calculation for Depreciation for the year
Depreciation needs to be calculated for **all the vehicles on the last day of the Accounting Period**.
Old vehicles: R1 200 000 (cost at beginning of year) − R400 000 (cost of vehicle sold) = R800 000
Depreciation on old vehicles for the year: R800 000 × 10% = R80 000
Depreciation on new vehicle for the year: R600 000 (cost of new vehicle) × 10% × 8 ÷ 12 = R40 000
The new vehicle was purchased on 30 June, so the business has only owned the vehicle for 8 months.
Total Depreciation for the vehicles owned on the last day of the Accounting Period:
R120 000 (R80 000 + R40 000)

See solution on the next page.

General Ledger of EARLY BAKERY

DR — Asset Disposal — **CR**

Date		Details	Fol	Amount		Date		Details	Fol	Amount	
2015 May	31	Vehicles **Cost Price of vehicle**	GJ	400 000	00	2015 May	31	Accumulated Depreciation: Vehicles **Total Depreciation of vehicle**	GJ	90 000	00
								Bank **Cash received for vehicle**	CRJ	280 000	00
								Loss on Sale of Asset	GJ	30 000	00
				400 000	00					400 000	00

The total on the Debit side is higher than the total on the Credit side, so the business has made a Loss. The balance is transferred to the Loss on Sale of Asset Account.

DR — Vehicles — **CR**

Date		Details	Fol	Amount		Date		Details	Fol	Amount	
2015 March	01	Balance **Cost Price of vehicle purchased**	b/d	1 200 000	00	2015 May	31	Asset Disposal **Cost Price of vehicle sold**	GJ	400 000	00
2015 June	30	Creditors Control	CJ/GJ	600 000	00	2016 Feb	28	Balance	c/d	1 400 000	00
				1 800 000	00					1 800 000	00
2016 March	01	Balance	b/d	1 400 000	00						

DR — Accumulated Depreciation: Vehicles — **CR**

Date		Details	Fol	Amount		Date		Details	Fol	Amount	
2015 May	31	Asset Disposal **Total Depreciation for vehicle sold**	GJ	90 000	00	2015 March	01	Balance	b/d	600 000	00
						2015 May	31	Depreciation **Depreciation for vehicle sold**	GJ	10 000	00
2016 Feb	28	Balance	c/d	640 000	00	2016 Feb	28	Depreciation **Depreciation for vehicles owned at end of year**	GJ	120 000	00
				730 000	00					730 000	00
						2016 March	01	Balance	b/d	640 000	00

DR — Depreciation — **CR**

Date		Details	Fol	Amount		Date		Details	Fol	Amount	
2015 May	31	Accumulated Depreciation: Vehicles **Depreciation for vehicle sold**	GJ	10 000	00	2016 Feb.	28	Profit & Loss	GJ	130 000	00
2016 Feb.	28	Accumulated Depreciation: Vehicles **Depreciation for vehicles owned at end of year**	GJ	120 000	00						
				130 000	00					130 000	00

Remember that the balances of all Expense Accounts are transferred to the Profit & Loss Account on the last day of the Accounting Period.

D. FIXED ASSET REGISTER

The Fixed Asset Register is a book that shows the details of every Fixed Asset owned by the business.
All the important information related to the Asset is included:
- **Description** of the Asset
- **Date** of purchase
- **Cost Price** of the Asset
- **Depreciation method** used
- **Depreciation** of the Asset
- If the Asset is sold then the **date of sale**, **Selling Price** and **Profit/Loss** will also be recorded.

FIXED ASSET REGISTER OF PONTEL CC

Description: White Diesel Truck (new)
Date of purchase: 01 March 2014
Purchased from: Northcliff Toyota Dealership
Cost: R650 000 (purchased on credit)
Depreciation: 15% p.a on cost   p.a. = per annum (year)

Date Sold: 01 March 2019
Sold to: M&D Partners
Sold for: R285 000 (cash)

Date	Depreciation	Accumulated Depreciation	Carrying Value
28 Feb 2014	R97 500	R97 500	R552 500
28 Feb 2015	R97 500	R195 000	R455 000
28 Feb 2016	R97 500	R292 500	R357 500
28 Feb 2017	R97 500	R390 000	R260 000
28 Feb 2018	R97 500	R487 500	R162 500
28 Feb 2019	R97 500	R585 000	R65 000

Carrying Value = Cost – Accumulated Depreciation

E. INTERPRETATION AND REPORTING ON THE MOVEMENT OF FIXED ASSETS

The previous sections will also help you to interpret and report on the movement of Fixed Assets.

Fixed Assets must be continuously monitored so that the business can decide if they need to be replaced or repaired. Internal Control measures must be put in place for Fixed Assets. There are a number of different Accounting terms used to interpret and report on the movement of Fixed Assets.

See pg 221 for more information on Internal Control.

1. **LIFESPAN OF A FIXED ASSET**
   The lifespan of a Fixed Asset refers to how long the business expects to keep the Asset.
   Lifespan of a Fixed Asset = Cost Price ÷ Depreciation per year

   > THANDI buys a computer that costs R15 000 and is depreciated at 20% p.a. on cost.
   > What is the lifespan of the computer?
   > Depreciation per year = R15 000 × 20% = R3 000
   > Lifespan of computer = R15 000 ÷ R3 000 = 5 years

2. **AGE OF A FIXED ASSET**
   The age of a Fixed Asset refers to how long the business has had the Fixed Asset.
   Age of a Fixed Asset = Accumulated Depreciation ÷ Depreciation per year

   > For how long has TKY SUPPLIER had its van? The following information is provided on the van:
   > Accumulated Depreciation: R20 000
   > Depreciation per year: R4 000
   > Age of van = R20 000 ÷ R4 000 = 5 years

3. **REPLACEMENT RATE OF A FIXED ASSET**
   The replacement rate of an Asset is what it would cost to replace the current Asset with a new Asset.
   Replacement rate = Cost Price of new Asset – Carrying Value of current Asset

   > **XLT MANUFACTURERS** owns a machine that originally cost R300 000 and that has an Accumulated Depreciation of R100 000. It will cost the business R350 000 to buy a new machine. What is the replacement rate of the current machine?
   > Carrying Value = Cost – Accumulated Depreciation = R300 000 – R100 000 = R200 000
   > Replacement rate = R350 000 – R200 000 = R150 000

4. **NET REALISABLE VALUE OF A FIXED ASSET**
   The Net Realisable Value of an Asset is the amount that a business would receive if they were to sell the Asset, minus the costs incurred to sell the Asset.
   Most businesses use the **Carrying Value** to determine this amount. A business can decide to revalue an Asset if the Carrying Value is not an accurate estimation of what the business could sell the Asset for.
   Net Realisable Value = Selling Price of Asset – Costs incurred to sell the Asset

 This section is often asked in Grade 11 and Grade 12 tests. Make sure you know how to do the adjustments and how to complete the Fixed Asset note when a Fixed Asset is disposed. See pg 97

VALUE-ADDED TAX (VAT)
SUMMARY OF CONTENTS

A   **VAT VENDORS** **176**

    1. Voluntary registration

    2. Compulsory registration

B   **VAT RATES** **176**

    1. Exempt items and services

    2. Zero-rated items and services

C   **HOW VAT WORKS** **176**

D   **VAT CALCULATIONS** **177**

    1. Calculate the VAT amount

    2. Calculate the price excluding VAT

    3. Calculate the price including VAT

E   **ACCOUNTING FOR VAT** **178**

    1. Input Tax

    2. Output Tax

F   **VAT PAYABLE TO SARS** **179**

    1. VAT Input > VAT Output

    2. VAT Output > VAT Input

G   **METHODS USED TO RECORD VAT** **179**

    1. Invoice Basis Method

    2. Receipt Basis Method

H   **VAT ADJUSTMENTS** **180**

    1. Adjustments that decrease the amount of VAT owed to SARS

    2. Adjustments that increase the amount of VAT owed to SARS **181**

VALUE-ADDED TAX (VAT)

VAT (Value-Added Tax) is a type of Tax that is added onto the Sales Price of items and services.
The government earns VAT each time a registered VAT vendor sells an item or a service.

> Governments charge Tax to make the money that they need to run the country. There are many different types of Tax besides VAT e.g. Pay As You Earn (PAYE), Income Tax, Donations Tax, Capital Gains Tax.

A. VAT VENDORS

A **VAT Vendor** is a business that is registered to pay VAT.

All businesses that are registered as VAT vendors add VAT to the Sales Prices of their items and services.
Businesses are not required to add VAT if they are not registered. A business completes a **VAT 201 form** to register as a VAT vendor.

1. VOLUNTARY REGISTRATION
All businesses that have an **income** of more than **R50 000 per annum** can **choose** to **register** for VAT.

2. COMPULSORY REGISTRATION
All businesses that have an **income** of more than **R1 million per annum** are **required** to **register** for VAT.

B. VAT RATES

The VAT rate changed from 14% to 15% on the 1st of April 2018.
Old books and tests will still show 14%.

The current VAT rate of 15% in South Africa is added to most items and services.
The VAT rate is known as the **standard VAT rate**. Registered VAT vendors charge the standard VAT rate on all items and services that do not fall under one of the categories below.
Items or services that include the standard VAT rate are often called **VATable** items or services.

1. EXEMPT ITEMS AND SERVICES
Exempt items and services do not include any VAT.
These items and services will **never** be charged VAT.
Common examples include: education services provided by approved educational institutions; Salaries; Wages; donations; non-fee related financial services such as life insurance; petrol; childcare.

2. ZERO-RATED ITEMS AND SERVICES
Zero-rated items and services have a VAT rate of 0%.
This category consists mostly of **basic foods**. Even though no VAT is currently charged, there is a **possibility** that the Minister of Finance will **increase** the rate to above 0% which means that VAT will then be added.
Common examples include: basic food items such as eggs, brown bread, rice, maize products, milk, fruit, vegetables, lentils and dried beans; paraffin.

The next time you buy something from the shops, check your Receipt to see if the price you paid included VAT.

C. HOW VAT WORKS

People and businesses pay VAT when they purchase items or services from VAT vendors.
The VAT vendor is required to pay SARS the amount of VAT collected from the sale of items or services.
The acronym **SARS** stands for the **South African Revenue Services**. SARS is responsible for collecting all Taxes on behalf of the government.

1. The **standard VAT rate** of **15%** is included in the **Selling Price** of all **items** and **services** that require VAT.
   A business wants to receive R100 for an item or service. The business charges the customer R115.
   R115 (price incl. VAT) = R100 (amount business wants to receive) + R15 (15 % VAT amount owed to SARS).

2. The **VAT vendor owes** the amount of **VAT** collected from the customer to **SARS**.
   The business will keep the R100 and will owe SARS the VAT amount of R15.

D. VAT CALCULATIONS

VAT calculations are used to determine the amount of VAT and the prices of items and services that include or exclude VAT.

1. **CALCULATE THE VAT AMOUNT**
   There are three different formulas that can be used to calculate the amount of VAT.

   i. Multiply the price including VAT by $\frac{15}{115}$

      VAT amount = Price (incl. VAT) $\times \frac{15}{115}$
      What is the VAT amount if an item costs R140 incl. VAT?
      VAT amount = Price (incl. VAT) $\times \frac{15}{115}$ = 140 $\times \frac{15}{115}$ = R18,26

   ii. Subtract the price excluding VAT from the price including VAT
       VAT amount = Price (incl. VAT) – Price (excl. VAT)
       The price of an item incl. VAT is R41,98. If the price excl. VAT is R36,50 what is the VAT amount for the item?
       VAT amount = Price (incl. VAT) – Price (excl. VAT) = 41,98 – 36,50 = R5,48

   iii. Multiply the price excluding VAT by 15%
        VAT amount = Price (excl. VAT) × 15%
        What is the VAT amount if the price of an item excl. VAT is R1 500?
        Price (excl. VAT) × 15% = 1 500 × 15% = R225

2. **CALCULATE THE PRICE EXCLUDING VAT**
   To calculate the price excluding VAT, divide the price including VAT by (1 + 15%), which is the same as dividing it by 1,15.
   Price (excl. VAT) = Price (incl. VAT) ÷ 1,15
   Divide by 100 to change a percentage to a decimal: 15% = 15 ÷ 100 = 0,15

   > **STEVE** calculates the price excluding VAT and the VAT amount for an item that costs R1 380 including VAT.
   > Price (excl. VAT) = Price (incl. VAT) ÷ 1,15
   > Price (excl. VAT) = 1 380 ÷ 1,15
   > Price (excl. VAT) = R1 200
   > VAT amount = Price (excl. Vat) × 15%   or   VAT amount = Price (incl. Vat) – Price (excl. VAT)
   > VAT amount = 1 380 × $\frac{15}{115}$ or   VAT amount = 1 380 – 1 200
   > **VAT amount = R180**   or   **VAT amount = R180**

3. **CALCULATE THE PRICE INCLUDING VAT**
   To calculate the price including VAT, multiply the price excluding VAT by 1,15.
   Price (incl. VAT) = Price (excl. VAT) × 1,15

   > **LETTIE** calculates the price including VAT and the VAT amount for an item that costs R800 excluding VAT.
   > Price (incl. VAT) = 800 × 1,15
   > Price (incl. VAT) = R920
   > VAT amount = Price (excl. VAT) × 15%   or   VAT amount = Price (incl. Vat) – Price (excl. VAT)
   > VAT amount = 800 × 15%   or   VAT amount = 920 – 800
   > **VAT amount = R120**   or   **VAT amount = R120**

E. ACCOUNTING FOR VAT

It is important that a business keeps a record of the amount of VAT collected and the amount of VAT paid.
- VAT is **collected** when items or services are **sold**.
- VAT is **paid** when items or services are **purchased** from VAT vendors.

INPUT TAX AND OUTPUT TAX

[Diagram: Business purchases items or services from VAT Vendors (Business pays VAT) = 1. Input Tax. Business sells items or services to Customers (Business receives VAT) = 2. Output Tax.]

1. Input Tax
The VAT that a business pays is called Input Tax.
All the Input Tax amounts are recorded on the **Debit** side of the **VAT Input Account**.
SARS owes the **business** the amount of VAT that the business pays.

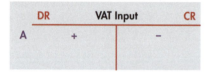

The VAT Input Account is also referred to as the Input Tax Account.

2. Output Tax
The VAT that a business charges for its items or services is called Output Tax.
All the Output Tax amounts are recorded on the **Credit** side of the **VAT Output Account**.
The **business owes SARS** the amount of VAT that the business collects.

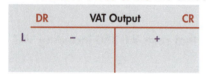

The VAT Ouput Account is also referred to as the Output Tax Account.

What effect will the following two transactions have on the VAT Input and VAT Ouput Accounts of a business?

1. **JENNY** pays cash for Equipment that costs R5 386 (excl. VAT).
2. **SANDILE** receives R4 000 (incl. VAT) for services.

1. VAT amount = Price (excl. VAT) × 15%
   VAT amount = 5 386 × 15% = 808 (rounded off to nearest rand)
   Total paid = 5 386 + 808 = R6 194

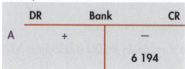

The business pays VAT, so the VAT Input Account will increase by R808.

2. VAT amount = Price (incl. VAT) × $\frac{15}{115}$
   VAT amount = 4 000 × $\frac{15}{115}$ = 522 (rounded off to nearest rand)
   Total received = R4 000 = 3 478 + 522

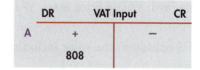

The business collects VAT, so the VAT Output Account will increase by R522.

F. VAT PAYABLE TO SARS

The difference between Input Tax and Output Tax determines how much the business owes SARS, or how much SARS owes the business.
The amount that the business owes SARS, or that SARS owes the business, is calculated in the **VAT Control Account** in the General Ledger.
- The balance of the **VAT Input Account** is closed off to the **Debit** side of the VAT Control Account.
- The balance of the **VAT Output Account** is closed off to the **Credit** side of the VAT Control Account.

1. **VAT Input > VAT Output**   The Debit side is greater than the Credit side in the VAT Control Account.
   The total VAT paid is more than the total VAT collected.
   SARS owes the **business** the **difference** between the **VAT paid** (Input Tax) and the **VAT collected** (Output Tax).
   The VAT Control Account is an **Asset**. The **Debit balance** shows the amount that SARS owes the business.

   > The bookkeeper of **MPANDE CC** closed off the VAT Output Account with a balance of R3 000 and the VAT Input Account with a balance of R9 000 to the VAT Control Account.
   >
   >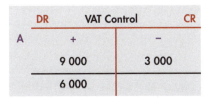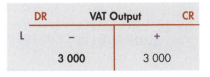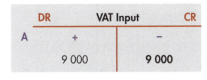
   >
   > The balance of R6 000 is owed to the business by SARS.

2. **VAT Output > VAT Input**   The Credit side is greater than the Debit side in the VAT Control Account.
   The total VAT collected is more than the total VAT paid.
   The **business owes SARS** the **difference** between the **VAT collected** (Output Tax) and the **VAT paid** (Input Tax).
   The VAT Control Account is a **Liability**. The **Credit balance** shows the amount that the business owes SARS.

   > The bookkeeper of **TEBZA LIMITED** closed off the VAT Output Account with a balance of R5 000 and the VAT Input Account with a balance of R3 000 to the VAT Control Account.
   >
   >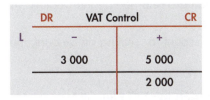
   >
   > The balance of R6 000 is owed to SARS by the business.

G. METHODS USED TO RECORD VAT

 The VAT Control Account can be an Asset or a Liability, depending on the difference between Output Tax and Input Tax.

There are two methods used by businesses to record VAT.

1. **INVOICE BASIS METHOD**
   VAT is recorded when Invoices are received and when Invoices are issued.
   This is the **standard method** that is used by VAT vendors in South Africa.
   VAT is recorded when items and services are purchased or sold on **credit or** for **cash**.

2. **RECEIPT BASIS METHOD**
   VAT is recorded when cash is received and when cash is paid.
   There are **no entries** made for VAT when **items and services are purchased or sold on credit**.
   VAT is only recorded when **cash** is received or paid.

H. VAT ADJUSTMENTS

Businesses may be required to make adjustments for VAT entries that were made using the Invoice Basis method.
Adjustments are required when the recorded amount of VAT to be collected or to be paid, based on the Invoice, is different from the actual amount of VAT collected or paid.
There are no adjustments when the **Receipt Basis method** is used, because VAT is only recorded when cash is received or paid.

1. ADJUSTMENTS THAT DECREASE THE AMOUNT OF VAT OWED TO SARS

When a business sells items on credit, the VAT Output Account increases to reflect the VAT amount that the business **expects to collect**.

LCT LIMITED sold Inventory on credit for R1 500 excl. VAT.
The following T Accounts show the effects of the transaction (the Cost of Sales Account and Trading Stock Account are not shown).

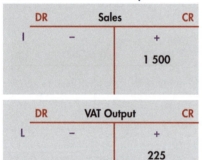
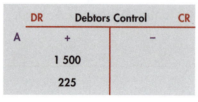

1 500 × 15% = R225

The business expects to collect R175 for VAT when the Account is paid.

The VAT amount that a business **expects to collect** is owed to SARS.
An **adjustment** is required when the business collects **less** VAT than it recorded based on the Invoice.

The actual amount of VAT collected decreases when the following transactions occur:

- **Bad Debts are written off:** When Bad Debts are written off, the business does not collect the VAT amount that was recorded on the Invoice.
- **Items sold on credit are returned by Debtors:** When items sold on credit are returned by the Debtors, the business does not collect the VAT amount that was recorded on the Invoice.
- **Discounts are given to Debtors:** When the business gives a Debtor a discount for settling an amount, the amount collected is less than the VAT amount recorded on the Invoice.

The business decreases the amount of VAT that it owes to SARS by decreasing the VAT Output Account on the Debit side. This decreases the amount of VAT owed to SARS.

A customer returned the Inventory that was sold for R1 500 excl. VAT, to **LCT LIMITED**. The following T Accounts show the effects of the transaction (the Cost of Sales Account and Trading Stock Account are not shown).

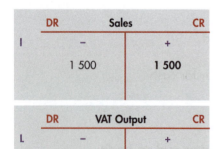

The amount in the VAT Ouput Account is cancelled out, which shows that the business no longer owes SARS this amount.

2. ADJUSTMENTS THAT INCREASE THE AMOUNT OF VAT OWED TO SARS

When a business purchases items on credit, the VAT Input Account increases to reflect the VAT amount that the business **expects to pay**.

ST LIMITED purchased a table on credit for R7 000 excl. VAT. The following T Accounts show the effects of the transaction.

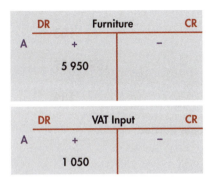

R7 000 × 15% = R1 050

The business expects to pay R1 050 for VAT when the Account is paid.

SARS owes the business the VAT that the business **expects to pay**. An adjustment is required when the business pays **less** VAT than it recorded based on the Invoice.

The actual amount of VAT paid by the business decreases when the following transactions occur:
- **Discounts received from Creditors:** When the business receives a discount from a Creditor when settling an amount, the VAT amount the business pays is **less** than the VAT amount recorded on the Invoice.
- **Items returned to Creditors:** When items purchased on credit are returned to the Creditor, the business does not pay the VAT amount recorded on the Invoice.

To decrease the amount of VAT that SARS owes the business, the business decreases the VAT Input Account on the Credit side.

ST LIMITED returned the table to the supplier. The following T Accounts show the effects of the transaction.

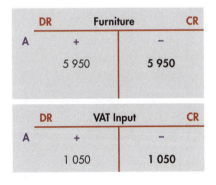

The amount in the VAT Input Account is cancelled out, which shows that the business no longer owes this amount to SARS.

PARTNERSHIPS
SUMMARY OF CONTENTS

A	**OVERVIEW OF THE UNIQUE ACCOUNTS OF A PARTNERSHIP**	183
B	**DETAILS OF THE UNIQUE ACCOUNTS OF A PARTNERSHIP**	184 — 189
	1. Capital Account	184
	2. Current Account, Drawings Account and Accounts to record Income earned by Partners	
	3. Appropriation Account	187

PARTNERSHIPS

A **Partnership** is a business formed by two to twenty people, who are called **Partners**.
The Partners sign a **Partnership Agreement** that outlines the details of the Partnership, including what the Partnership does, what is expected from each Partner and how the Partnership will be managed.
See pg 7 for a comparison of the different forms of ownership of a business.

A. OVERVIEW OF THE UNIQUE ACCOUNTS OF A PARTNERSHIP

The bookkeeping of a Partnership is similar to that of the other types of businesses.
The steps of the Accounting Cycle are the same. However, there are **Accounts** that are **unique** to **Partnerships** and there are also **differences** in how the **Final Accounts** are prepared.
A Partnership has unique Accounts that are used to record transactions that take place between the Partners and the Partnership.

ACCOUNT NAME	DESCRIPTION
Capital: [Partner's Name] (O) DR − / CR +	**The Capital contributions made by each Partner** There is a separate **Capital Account** for each Partner.
Current Account: [Partner's Name] (O) DR − / CR +	**The amount that each Partner owns in the Partnership** There is a separate **Current Account** for each Partner. A Partner can earn a **Salary, bonus, interest on Capital** and a **share** of the **Profit/Loss** made.
Drawings: [Partner's Name] (O) DR − / CR +	**The amounts that the Partner has taken from the Partnership** There is a separate **Drawings Account** for each Partner. Drawings include the Salary paid to the Partner.
Interest on Capital (E) DR + / CR −	**The Interest paid on Capital to the Partners** Partnerships often pay **Interest on Capital** to reward Partners for contributing Capital. The amount of Interest earned by each Partner is recorded on the Debit side of this Account and on the Credit side of the Partner's Current Account, on the last day of the Accounting Cycle.
Salary: [Partner's Name] (E) DR + / CR −	**The Salary earned by each Partner** There is a separate **Salary Account** for each Partner. The Salary earned by each Partner is recorded on the Debit side of this Account and on the Credit side of the Partner's Current Account, on the **last day** of the Accounting Cycle. Any Salary paid to a Partner during the Accounting Period is recorded on the Debit side of the Partner's Drawings Account.
Bonus to Partners (E) DR + / CR −	**The bonuses earned by the Partners** **Bonuses** are recorded at the **end** of the Accounting Period. The bonus earned by each Partner is recorded on the Debit side of this Account and on the Credit side of the Partner's Current Account on the last day of the Accounting Cycle.
Appropriation Account DR Loss / CR Profit	**A Temporary Account that is used to calculate the share of the Net Profit or Loss that is distributed to each Partner at the end of the Accounting Period** The **Profit or Loss** at the end of the Accounting Period is closed off to the Appropriation Account.

Go to pg 93 to see where these Accounts can be found on the Financial Statements and Notes.

B. DETAILS OF THE UNIQUE ACCOUNTS OF A PARTNERSHIP

1. CAPITAL ACCOUNT

The **Capital Account is used to record the Capital that is contributed to the business by each Partner.**

The **percentage** of a Partnership that **each Partner owns** is often **determined** by the **amount** of **Capital** that he or she has contributed. The **Capital Account** increases on the **Credit** side when a Partner contributes Capital.

Doug contributed R20 000 (40%) and Sandy contributed R30 000 (60%) to form a Partnership called **D&S FIRST AID CONSULTANTS**.

DEBIT	CREDIT	ASSETS	OWNER'S EQUITY	LIABILITIES
Bank Account	• Capital Account: Sandy	+ 50 000	+ 30 000	0
	• Capital Account: Doug		+ 20 000	0

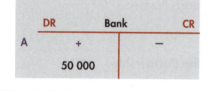
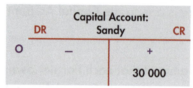
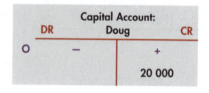

2. CURRENT ACCOUNT, DRAWINGS ACCOUNT AND ACCOUNTS TO RECORD INCOME EARNED BY PARTNERS

The Partners can be paid a Salary, can take items from the business and can earn an Income/Loss from the Partnership.

The **Current Account** is used to record transactions between a Partner and the Partnership.

The balance of a Partner's Current Account shows the difference between the total amount earned by the Partner and the total amount paid to the Partner (**Drawings**).

Make sure you know which transactions increase or decrease the Current Account of a Partner.

Transactions that decrease the Current Account of a Partner

All the transactions that **decrease** the amount earned by a Partner are recorded on the **Debit** side of the Current Account of the Partner.

The **Drawings Account** of each Partner shows the amounts paid to the Partner and the cost of the items taken by the Partner during the Accounting Period. At the end of the Accounting Period, the Drawings Account is **closed off** to the Debit side of the **Current Account** of the Partner.

If the final Profit share is a Loss, the Current Account of each Partner will be Debited.

 The Salaries paid to each Partner are recorded under the Drawings Account of each Partner.
The Salaries of the employees are recorded under the Salaries and Wages Account.

During the Accounting Period, the bookkeeper of **D&S FIRST AID CONSULTANTS** recorded that Sandy was paid a Salary of R120 000 and Doug was paid a Salary of R100 000.

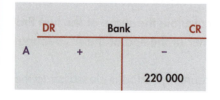

At the end of the Accounting period, the bookkeeper of **D&S FIRST AID CONSULTANTS** closed off the Drawings Accounts of Doug and Sandy.

Sandy's Drawings Account had a balance of R120 000 and Doug's Drawings Account had a balance of R100 000.

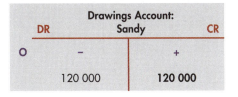
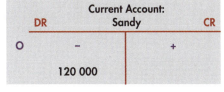

The unbolded amounts are balances from previous transactions.

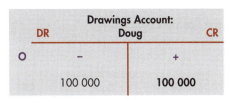
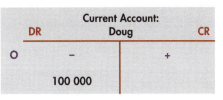

Transactions that increase the Current Account of a Partner

All the transactions that **increase** the amount earned by a Partner are recorded on the **Credit** side of the Partner's Current Account.

At the end of the Accounting Period, the amounts that each Partner earned are recorded.

A Partner can earn **Interest on Capital**, a **Salary**, a **bonus** and a share of the Partnerships' **Profit**.

The Partners of **D&G FIRST AID CONSULTANTS** earned the following Income for the Accounting Period:

DETAILS	SANDY	DOUG
Interest on Capital	3 000	2 000
Salary	150 000	130 000
Bonus	10 000	5 000
Share of Profit	75 000	50 000

1. **Interest on Capital earned by the Partners**

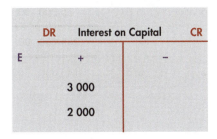
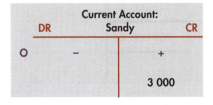
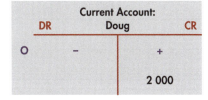

2. **Salaries earned by the Partners**

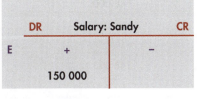
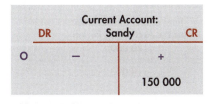
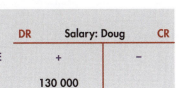

3. **Bonuses earned by the Partners**

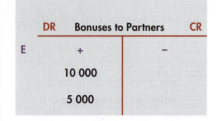
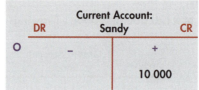

(Current Account: Doug — CR side: 5 000)

4. **Profit earned by the Partners**
   The bookkeeper determined that R125 000 was available to distribute to the Partners (40 : 60).
   See pg 187 for details about the Appropriation Account.

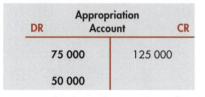
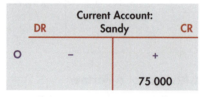
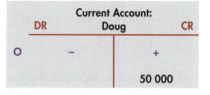

The unbolded amount is a previous balance.

Example of the Current Account of Sandy in the General Ledger of D&G FIRST AID CONSULTANTS

Sandy had an opening balance of R30 000.

DR						Current Account: Sandy			CR
Date		Details	Fol	Amount		Date	Details	Fol	Amount
2017 Dec.	31	Drawings: Sandy	CPJ	120 000 00		2017 Dec. 31	Balance	b/d	30 000 00
							Interest on Capital	GJ	3 000 00
							Salary: Sandy	GJ	150 000 00
							Bonus to Partner	GJ	10 000 00
		Balance	c/d	148 000 00			Appropriation	GJ	75 000 00
				268 000 00					268 000 00
						2018 Jan. 01	Balance	b/d	148 000 00

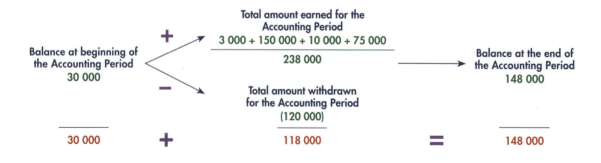

🛈 Make sure you know how to record this information in the Notes to the Financial Statements. See pg 152

3. APPROPRIATION ACCOUNT   The Appropriation Account is often asked in tests.

The Appropriation Account is a **Temporary Account** that is used to calculate the share of the Net Profit or Loss that is distributed to each Partner at the end of the Accounting Period.

DR	Appropriation Account	CR
Amounts earned by the Partners	Net Profit for the Accounting Period	

The **difference** between the **Net Profit** and the total **amounts earned by the Partners** is **distributed** to the **Current Accounts** of the **Partners**.

Steps to prepare the Appropriation Account

1. **Net Profit/Loss for the Accounting Period**
   Total available to distribute
2. **Primary Distribution**
   All the amounts earned by the Partners
3. **Final Distribution**
   Net Profit/Loss – Primary distribution = Amount to distribute to Partners

1. **Transfer the Net Profit/Loss to the Appropriation Account.**
   The Net Profit/Loss for the Accounting Period is transferred to the **Appropriation Account**.
   This amount shows the total Profit or Loss made by the Partnership for the Accounting Period.
   - A **Profit** is recorded on the **Credit** side of the Appropriation Account, to show the increase in the total amount **available** to **distribute** to the Partners.
   - A **Loss** is recorded on the **Debit** side of the Appropriation Account.

   See pg 129 for the steps to determine the Net Profit/Loss for the Accounting Period.

The bookkeeper of **D&S FIRST AID CONSULTANTS** determined that a Profit of R425 000 was made and transferred this amount to the Appropriation Account.

DR	Appropriation Account	CR
		425 000

DR	Profit and Loss	CR
Loss		Profit
425 000		425 000

---

2. **Transfer the amounts earned by the Partners to the Appropriation Account.**
   All the Accounts that are used to record the amounts earned by the Partners are closed off to the **Appropriation Account**. This step is known as the **Primary Distribution**. The balances of the Partners' Interest on Capital, Bonus and Salary Accounts are recorded on the **Debit** side of the **Appropriation Account**.

   See example on next page.

The bookkeeper of **D&S FIRST AID CONSULTANTS** transferred the balances of the following Accounts to the Appropriation Account:
- Salary: Sandy's Account: R150 000
- Salary: Doug's Account: R130 000
- Interest on Capital Account: R5 000
- Bonuses to Partners Account: R15 000

DR	Appropriation Account	CR
150 000		
130 000		
5 000		
15 000		

DR	Salary: Sandy	CR
E +		−
150 000		150 000

DR	Salary: Doug	CR
E +		−
130 000		130 000

DR	Interest on Capital	CR
E +		−
5 000		5 000

DR	Bonuses to Partners	CR
E +		−
15 000		15 000

The unbolded amounts are balances from previous transactions.

3. **Distribute the balance of the Appropriation Account to the Partners' Current Accounts.**
   The difference between the Net Profit/Loss for the Accounting Period and the Primary Distribution is shared between the Partners. This is known as **Final Distribution**. The amount of Profit/Loss distributed to each Partner depends on the agreement the Partners have. There are a number of different possibilities to distribute the amount between the Partners.
   - **Capital Balances**: The amount is shared between the Partners using the ratio of their Capital balances.
   - **Current Account balances**: The amount is shared between the Partners using the ratio of their Current Account balances.
   - **Set ratio**: The amount is shared between the Partners according to a set ratio that is agreed upon when the Partnership is formed.

The bookkeeper of **D&S FIRST AID CONSULTANTS** transferred the difference (R125 000) of the Appropriation Account to the Partners. Sandy received 60% and Doug Received 40%.

DR	Appropriation Account	CR
150 000		425 000
130 000		
5 000		
15 000		
75 000		
50 000		
425 000		425 000

DR	Current Account: Sandy	CR
O −		+
		75 000

DR	Current Account: Doug	CR
O −		+
		50 000

Example of the Appropriation Account in the General Ledger of D&S FIRST AID CONSULTANTS

The bookkeeper calculated that a Profit of R425 000 was made.

DR — Appropriation Account — **CR**

Date		Details	Fol	Amount		Date		Details	Fol	Amount	
2017 Dec.	31	Salary: Sandy	GJ	150 000	00	2017 Dec.	31	Profit and Loss	GJ	425 000	00
		Salary: Doug	GJ	130 000	00						
		Interest on Capital	GJ	5 000	00						
		Bonuses to Partners	GJ	15 000	00						
		Current Account: Sandy	GJ	75 000	00						
		Current Account: Doug	GJ	50 000	00						
				425 000	**00**					**425 000**	**00**

1. **Net Profit/Loss for the Accounting Period**
   Total available to distribute

   R425 000 → R425 000

   R425 000

2. **Primary Distribution**
   All the amounts earned by the Partners

   R150 000
   R130 000
   R5 000
   R15 000
   → R300 000

   R300 000

   —

3. **Final Distribution**
   Net Profit/Loss
   – Primary distribution
   = Amount to distribute

   R75 000 (Sandy)
   R50 000 (Doug)

   R125 000

   =

> ⓘ If the opening/closing balance of the Partner's Current Account is a Debit balance, it must be shown in brackets (negative) in the Current Account Note to the Financial Statements. See pg 99 for the Note to the Financial Statements.

NON-PROFIT COMPANIES
SUMMARY OF CONTENTS

A   **INTRODUCTION TO CLUBS** **191**

      Documents of a Club

B   **OVERVIEW OF THE UNIQUE ACCOUNTS OF A CLUB** **192**

C   **DETAILS OF MEMBERSHIP FEES** **193**

      Different entries recorded for Membership Fees

D   **DETAILS OF FUNCTIONS AND TOURNAMENTS** **194**

      Different entries recorded for Functions and Tournaments

E   **DETAILS OF REFRESHMENTS AND CLUB ITEMS** **196**

      Different entries recorded for Refreshments and Club Items

F   **FINANCIAL STATEMENTS OF A CLUB** **197**

      1.   Statement of Receipts and Payments

      2.   Statement of Income and Expenditure **198**

NON-PROFIT COMPANIES (CLUBS)

Non-Profit Companies are formed by people who have a common purpose to benefit society.
The main aim of a Non-Profit Company is to **improve society**. However, it is still important for a Non-Profit Company to generate enough Income to cover its Expenses.
Non-Profit Companies **do not have** any **Owners**. All **Assets** and any **Surplus** (Profit) belong to the **Non-Profit Company**.
See pg 7 for an overview of the different forms of ownership.

A. INTRODUCTION TO CLUBS

At school, the focus is on the bookkeeping of a Sports Club.

A Sports Club is an example of a Non-Profit Company.
The **Accounting Cycle** is the **same** for a **Club** as it is for the other forms of ownership.

DOCUMENTS OF A CLUB
A Club uses an **Analysis Cash Book** to **record** all its **cash transactions**.
A **General Journal** is used to record all the **other types** of **transactions.** A Club usually does not have as many transactions as a For-Profit business, so it is not necessary to have all the different types of Journals that a For-Profit business has.

A Club prepares a **Statement of Receipts and Payments**, a **Statement of Income and Expenditure** and a **Balance Sheet Statement** at the end of the year.

Read the cartoon below carefully to learn the different terms used for a Club.

DAY 1

Hi everyone, as you know we are all here today to discuss the new Soccer Club we want to start. We believe it will benefit our community. Please see the list below of what we need to prepare:
- **Constitution**
- **Ideas** about how we can make money to cover the Expenses needed to run the Club
- We also need someone to **keep our Accounting records**!

DAY 2

I have prepared the constitution that includes:
- Our Club **name**
- **Aims** and **objectives** of our Club
- **Membership Fees**
- The **officers** (chairman, vice-chairman, secretary and treasurer) of the Club
- How the Club will be **governed**
- Details about the **Annual General Meeting** that will be held on the 30th of June each year

DAY 3

We will need around R1 million each year to run the Club. I have prepared a list of the types of Income we will receive:
- **Entrance fees** when members join
- **Membership Fees** from members each year
- **Donations** from people who want to support the Club
- Soccer **tournaments** where teams need to pay to participate
- Cash from **sponsors**
- **Sales** of soccer **items** with our logos on them
- **Sales** of **refreshments** in our tuck shop
- We can also host **functions** like an annual 'Bring and Braai' if we need more income to cover our Expenses

DAY 4

The books of a Club are similar to the books of my private Sole Trader. However, there is **no Owner**, so all the **Income** belongs to the **Club**. A Club also does not need as many Journals. We will just need a **Cash Book** for all the **cash transactions** and a **General Journal** to record all the **non-cash transactions**. Profit is called a **Surplus** and a Loss is called a **Deficit**. At the end of the Accounting Period, I will prepare the following Financial Statements:
- **Statement of Receipts and Payments**
- **Statement of Income and Expenditure**
- **Balance Sheet Statement**

B. OVERVIEW OF THE UNIQUE ACCOUNTS OF A CLUB

ACCOUNT NAME	DESCRIPTION
Entrance Fees — DR / CR — I / − / +	**Entrance fees** are paid by new members to join a Club.
Membership Fees — DR / CR — I / − / +	Members are required to pay **Membership Fees** to remain a member of the Club. Memberships fees are paid weekly, monthly or yearly to the Club.
Bequests — DR / CR — I / − / +	A **bequest** is cash left to a Club by a member that has passed away. A Club records the cash received in the **Bequest Account**.
Club Items — DR / CR — I / − / +	The difference between the cash received from the sales of items and the cash paid for these items is recorded as Income under the **Club Items Account**. Clubs often sell items branded with the Club's name and logo to earn additional Income.
Club Items on Hand — DR / CR — A / + / −	The costs of the items available are recorded under the **Club Items on Hand Account** at the end of the Accounting Period.
Refreshments — DR / CR — I / − / +	The difference between the cash received from sales of refreshments and the cash paid for the refreshments is recorded as an Income under the **Refreshments Account**. Clubs often sell food and drinks to earn additional Income.
Refreshments on Hand — DR / CR — A / + / −	The costs of the refreshments available are recorded under the **Refreshments on Hand Account** at the end of the Accounting Period.
Membership Fees written off — DR / CR — E / + / −	When members do not pay their Membership Fees, their **Membership Fees are written off** and their memberships are cancelled. The Membership Fees not received are recorded as an Expense.
Affiliation Fees — DR / CR — E / + / −	All Clubs pay **Affiliation Fees** to their province or country, in order to be recognised as a Club.
Honorarium — DR / CR — E / + / −	The amount paid to the treasurer or secretary of the Club is recorded under the **Honorarium Account**. This is a type of 'gift' that the Club pays to certain members for the work they do for the Club.
Crockery — DR / CR — A / + / −	Bowls, plates, cups, glasses and other similar items are known as **crockery**. The costs of these items are recorded under the **Crockery Account**.
Crockery Written Off — DR / CR — E / + / −	Any crockery items that break are recorded as Expenses under the **Crockery Written Off Account**.

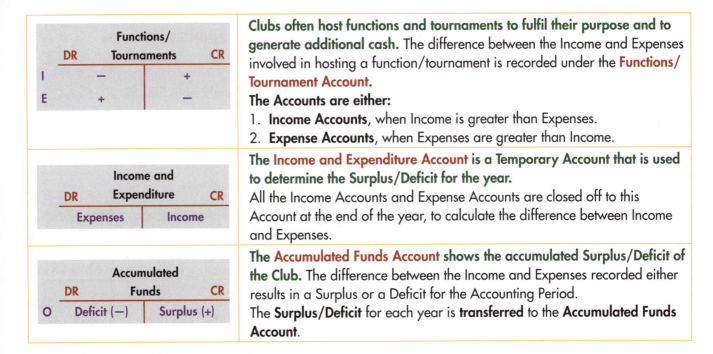

	Functions/	
DR	Tournaments	CR
I	−	+
E	+	−

Clubs often host functions and tournaments to fulfil their purpose and to generate additional cash. The difference between the Income and Expenses involved in hosting a function/tournament is recorded under the **Functions/Tournament Account**.

The Accounts are either:
1. **Income Accounts**, when Income is greater than Expenses.
2. **Expense Accounts**, when Expenses are greater than Income.

	Income and	
DR	Expenditure	CR
Expenses		Income

The **Income and Expenditure Account** is a Temporary Account that is used to determine the Surplus/Deficit for the year.
All the Income Accounts and Expense Accounts are closed off to this Account at the end of the year, to calculate the difference between Income and Expenses.

	Accumulated	
DR	Funds	CR
O	Deficit (−)	Surplus (+)

The **Accumulated Funds Account** shows the accumulated Surplus/Deficit of the Club. The difference between the Income and Expenses recorded either results in a Surplus or a Deficit for the Accounting Period.
The **Surplus/Deficit** for each year is **transferred** to the **Accumulated Funds Account**.

C. DETAILS OF MEMBERSHIP FEES

Membership Fees are the main source of Income for Clubs.
The Membership Fees Account is an **Income Account**, so it **increases** on the **Credit** side and **decreases** on the **Debit** side.

BT SOCCER CLUB received R60 000 cash for Membership Fees.

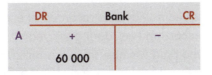

DR	Membership Fees	CR
I	−	+
		60 000

DR	Bank	CR
A	+	−
	60 000	

DIFFERENT ENTRIES RECORDED FOR MEMBERSHIP FEES

1. **At the beginning** of the Accounting Period, the year-end adjustments from the previous Accounting Period are reversed. These amounts appear on the Balance Sheet at the end of the previous Accounting Period.
   - The Membership Fees Account **decreases** on the **Debit** side by the amount of **Accrued Income** recorded in the previous Accounting Period.
   - The Membership Fees Account **increases** on the **Credit** side by the amount of **Income Received in Advance** recorded in the previous Accounting Period.

2. **During** the Accounting Period, all transactions that affect the Membership Fees Account are recorded.
   - The Membership Fees Account **decreases** on the **Debit** side by the amount of cash received for Membership Fees for the **next Accounting Period (Income Received in Advance)**.
   - The Membership Fees Account **increases** on the **Credit** side by the amount of cash received (**Bank**) for Membership Fees during the Accounting Period.

3. **At the end** of the Accounting Period, adjustments are made to the Account.
   - The Membership Fees Account **decreases** on the **Debit** side by the amount that members are **unable to pay** for their **fees (Membership Fees written off)**.
   - The Membership Fees Account **increases** on the **Credit** side by the amount of **Membership Fees earned** for the Accounting Period but **not yet paid (Accrued Income)**.

4. **At the end** of the Accounting Period, the balance of the Membership Fees Account is transferred to the Income and Expenditure Account.
   The **difference** between the **total** on the **Debit** side and the **total** on the **Credit** side gives the **total Membership Fees earned** during the Accounting Period.

Draw up the Membership Fees Account in the General Ledger of **MAZOE RUNNING CLUB** for the Accounting Period that ended on 31 December 2016.

- The **Membership Fees** are R1 200 per member per year.
- On the 31st of December 2015, eight members had **not yet paid** their Membership Fees for 2015 and fifteen members had already paid their Membership Fees for 2016.
- During the Accounting Period, the Club **received** R108 000 for Membership Fees. This amount included the payments from five members who **still owed** their Membership Fees for 2014 and from twelve members who paid their Membership Fees for 2017 in **advance**.
- During the **Annual General Meeting** at the end of the year, members agreed to write off any Membership Fees that were still outstanding for 2015.
- 18 members **still owed** Membership Fees on the last day of 2016.

> This Account is often asked in tests. Make sure you learn the layout.

DR — Membership Fees — **N1 CR**

Date		Details	Fol	Amount		Date		Details	Fol	Amount	
2016 Jan.	01	Accrued Income	GJ	9 600	00	2016 Jan.	01	Income Received in Advance	GJ	18 000	00
2016 Dec.	31	Income Received in Advance	GJ	14 400	00	2016 Dec.	31	Bank	GJ	108 000	00
		Income and Expenditure	GJ	127 200	00			Membership Fees Written off	GJ	3 600	00
								Accrued Income	GJ	21 600	00
				151 200	00					151 200	00

Calculations

- **9 600** = 8 × 1 200: Accrued Income recorded at end of 2015
- **18 000** = 15 × 1 200: Income Received in Advance recorded at end of 2015
- **108 000**: All cash received for Membership Fees during the year
- **14 400** = 12 × 1 200: Members who paid Membership Fees for 2017 (in advance)
- **3 600** = 3 × 1 200: Eight members owed fees at the end of 2015. Five of these members paid their fees during 2016. At the end of 2016, three members still owed fees for 2015
- **21 600** = 18 × 1 200: Total amount still owed by members who had not yet paid

D. DETAILS OF FUNCTIONS AND TOURNAMENTS

The Functions Account is prepared in the same way as the Tournaments Account.

The **difference** between **Income received** from the **sale** of tickets for the function/tournament and the **Expenses paid** for the function/tournament is **recorded** as an **Income** if a **Surplus** is made, and as an **Expense** if a **Deficit** is made. Notice that you can only determine whether the Functions/Tournament Account is an Income or Expense Account at the end of the Accounting Period. It is usually an Income Account.

DIFFERENT ENTRIES RECORDED FOR FUNCTIONS AND TOURNAMENTS

1. The **Functions/Tournaments Account** increases on the Credit side by the amount of cash received and it decreases on the Debit side by the amount of Expenses paid.

NN NETBALL CLUB paid R20 000 cash as Expenses for their annual fundraising tournament.

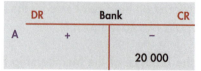

NN NETBALL CLUB received R30 000 cash from the sales of tickets for their annual fundraising tournament.

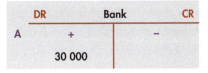

2. **The difference** between the total on the Debit side and the total on the Credit side is transferred to the Income and Expenditure Account. The Income and Expenditure Account is a Temporary Account used to calculate the Surplus or Deficit for the Accounting Period.
   - **If the Credit side is greater than the Debit side, then the difference transferred is an Income.**
     This shows that more cash was received than what was paid for the function/tournament.
     The **difference is** transferred to the **Income and Expenditure Account** as an Income.
   - **If the Debit side is greater than the Credit side, then the difference transferred is an Expense.**
     This shows that more cash was paid than what was received for the function/tournament.
     The **difference** is transferred to the **Income and Expenditure Account** as an Expense.

The bookkeeper of NN NETBALL CLUB transferred the surplus of R10 000 from the Tournaments Account to the Income and Expenditure Account at the end of the Accounting Period.

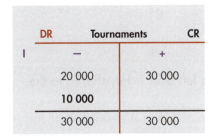
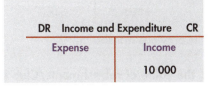

The 20 000 and 30 000 recorded under the Tournaments Account are entries from previous transactions.
The difference of R10 000 is closed off to the Income and Expenditure Account.

BEARS RUGBY CLUB wanted to raise funds to improve the parking area at the Club. They decided to have a dance function. Use the information below to prepare the Functions Account in the General Ledger.
- The Club paid R2 000 to have a DJ at the function.
- Decorations for the hall in which the dance took place cost R4 000.
- The Club paid R3 000 for a cleaning service to clean the hall after the event.
- The Club sold 110 tickets for the event at R120 each.

DR   **Functions**   **CR**

Date	Details	Fol	Amount		Date	Details	Fol	Amount	
2016 Dec.	31 Bank	CPJ	2 000	00	2016 Dec.	31 Bank	CRJ	13 200	00
	Bank	CPJ	4 000	00					
	Bank	CPJ	3 000	00					
	Income and Expenditure	GJ	4 200	00					
			13 200	00				13 200	00

Notice that a Surplus of R4 200 was made.

E. DETAILS OF REFRESHMENTS AND CLUB ITEMS

The Refreshments Account is prepared in the same way as the Club Items Account.
The **difference** between **cash received** from the sale of refreshments/Club items and **Expenses paid** for the refreshments/Club items is recorded as an **Income** if a **Surplus** is made and as an **Expense** if a **Deficit** is made.
The cost of the **left over refreshments/Club items** is recorded as an **Asset**.

Notice that you can only determine whether the Refreshments/Club Items Account is an Income or Expense Account at the end of the Accounting Period. It is usually an Income Account.

DIFFERENT ENTRIES RECORDED FOR REFRESHMENTS AND CLUB ITEMS

1. The **Refreshments/Club Items Account** increases on the Credit side by the amount of cash received and decreases on the Debit side by the amount of Expenses paid.

VEN CHESS CLUB paid R5 000 cash for refreshments.

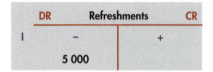

VEN CHESS CLUB received R4 000 for the sale of refreshments.

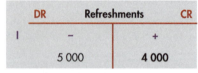

The 5 000s recorded are amounts from the previous transaction.

---

2. At the end of the Accounting Period, the value of refreshments/Club items left over is transferred to the **Refreshments/Club Items on Hand Account**.
   The transaction is recorded on the Debit side of the Refreshments/Club Items on Hand Account and on the Credit side of the Refreshments/Club Items Account.

The bookkeeper of **VEN CHESS CLUB** counted that there was R1 500 worth of refreshments available at the end of the Accounting Period (Closing Stock). This amount was transferred to the Refreshments on Hand Account.

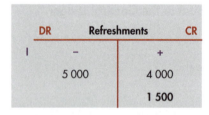

The 5 000 and 4 000 recorded under the Refreshments Account are entries from previous transactions.

---

3. At the end of the Accounting Period, the **difference** between the total on the Debit side and the total on the Credit side of the Refreshments/Club Items Account is transferred to the Income and Expenditure Account. The **Income and Expenditure Account** is a **Temporary Account** used to calculate the Surplus or Deficit for the Accounting Period.
   - If the Credit side is greater than the Debit side then the difference transferred is an **Income**.
     This shows that more cash was received from the sales of the refreshments/Club items than what was paid to buy the refreshments/Club items. The **difference** is transferred to the **Income and Expenditure Account** as an Income.
   - If the Debit side is greater than the Credit side then the difference transferred is an **Expense**.
     This shows that more cash was paid to buy the refreshments/Club items than what was received from the sales of the refreshments/Club items. The **difference** is transferred to the **Income and Expenditure Account** as an Expense.

See example on next page.

The bookkeeper of VEN CHESS CLUB transferred the Surplus of R500 in the Refreshments Account to the Income and Expenditure Account at the end of the Accounting Period.

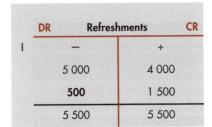

DR	Refreshments		CR
	−		+
	5 000		4 000
	500		1 500
	5 500		5 500

DR	Income and Expenditure		CR
	Expense		Income
			500

The 5 000, 4 000 and 1 500 recorded under the Refreshments Account are entries from previous transactions.

MAZOE RUNNING CLUB sells Club shirts to its members each year. Use the information below to prepare the Club Items Account in the General Ledger at the end of the Accounting Period.
- The Club paid R6 400 cash to purchase a total of 80 shirts with the logo of Mazoe Running Club.
- They sold 55 shirts for R130 each during the Accounting Period. This was received in Cash.
- There were 25 shirts on hand at the end of the Accounting Period.

This Account is often asked in tests. Make sure you learn the layout.

DR   Club Items

Date		Details	Fol	Amount		Date		Details	Fol	Amount	
2016 Jan.	01	Bank	CPJ	6 400	00	2016 Jan.	31	Bank	CRJ	7 150	00
2016 Dec.	31	Income and Expenditure	GJ	2 750	00	2016 Dec.	31	Club items on hand	GJ	2 000	00
				9 150	00					9 150	00

Note that the Closing Stock (25 × 80 = 2 000) is calculated using the Cost Price.
The difference of 2 750 is transferred to the Income and Expenditure Account.

F. FINANCIAL STATEMENTS OF A CLUB

A Club prepares three different Financial Statements at the end of the Accounting Period:
1. Statement of **Receipts and Payments**
2. Statement of **Income and Expenditure**
3. **Balance Sheet** Statement

The details of the Balance Sheet Statement of a Club are not covered in the school curriculum.

See pgs 198 and 199

1. STATEMENT OF RECEIPTS AND PAYMENTS

The Statement of Receipts and Payments shows a summary of the Receipts and payments recorded in the Analysis Cash Book.

The Analysis Cash Book is used to record all the cash received and paid by the Club.

THUNDER SOCCER CLUB
Statement of Receipts and Payments for the year ended 31 December 2016

	Note	Amount
RECEIPTS All the Receipts that affect the Account are added up and the total is recorded.		570 000
Membership Fees		280 000
Entrance Fees		30 000
Donations		50 000
Refreshments		90 000
Tournaments		120 000
PAYMENTS All the payments that affect the Account are added up and the total is recorded.		(388 500)
Affiliation Fees		5 000
Water and Electricity		10 000
Refreshments		60 000
Equipment		120 000
Tournaments		105 000
Maintenance Costs		80 000
Honorarium		8 500
SURPLUS Receipts – Payments		181 500
OPENING BALANCES		22 000
Bank		20 000
Savings Account		2 000
CLOSING BALANCES Surplus/Deficit for the Accounting Period + Opening balance at the beginning of the Accounting Period		203 500
Bank		190 000
Savings Account		13 500

2. STATEMENT OF INCOME AND EXPENDITURE

The Statement of Income and Expenditure of a Club has the same purpose as the Income Statement of a Sole Trader/Partnership. The Statement of Income and Expenditure **lists all** the **Income Accounts** and **Expense Accounts.** The last line shows whether the business has made a **Surplus** or **Deficit** for the Accounting Period. The Surplus or Deficit is **transferred** to the **Accumulated Funds Account**.

Statement of Income and Expenditure is prepared to show the balance of the Income and Expense Accounts and to calculate the Surplus/Deficit for the Accounting Period.

+ Names and balances of all Income Accounts
− Names and balances of all Expense Accounts
= Deficit/Surplus during the Accounting Period
↓
Accumulated Funds Account

The Surplus/Deficit for the Accounting Period is transferred to the Accumulated Funds Account.

SUPER SQUIRRELS HOCKEY CLUB
Income and Expenditure Statement for the year ended 31 December 2017

	Fol	Amount
INCOME List the name and balance of each Income Account at the end of the Accounting Period.		190 000
Membership Fees		120 000
Entrance Fees		15 000
Sponsors		35 000
Profit from Tournament		8 000
Profit from Sale of Refreshments		12 000
EXPENSES List the name and balance of each Expense Account at the end of the Accounting Period.		(114 580)
Water and Electricity		(20 000)
Repairs		(30 000)
Telephone		(6 000)
Honararium: Secretary		(2 500)
Membership Fees Written off		(18 000)
Depreciation		(38 000)
Bank Charges		(80)
SURPLUS (DEFICIT) FOR THE YEAR This amount is transferred to the **Accumulated Funds Account** at the end of the Accounting Period. **Total Income − Total Expenses**		75 420

CLOSED CORPORATIONS
SUMMARY OF CONTENTS

A **DETAILS ABOUT CLOSED CORPORATIONS** **201**

1. Founding Statement
2. Members of a CC
3. Phasing out of CCs
4. Unique Accounts of a CC

B **OVERVIEW OF THE UNIQUE ACCOUNTS OF A CC** **202**

CLOSED CORPORATIONS (CC)

A Closed Corporation (CC) is the recommended form of ownership for a small business that wants Limited Liability without the additional requirements of a Company.
Limited Liability means that the Owners are not personally liable for the Debts of the business.
The setting up of new CCs is no longer allowed.

A. DETAILS ABOUT CLOSED CORPORATIONS

1. FOUNDING STATEMENT
A Founding Statement is the document that is completed to register a CC.
The statement contains all the **important information** about the CC and its Members (Owners).
All Closed Corporations in South Africa need to adhere to the regulations as set out by the **Closed Corporation Act (No. 69 of 1984)**.

2. MEMBERS OF A CC
The Owners of a CC are called Members.
A CC is allowed to have between **one** and **ten Members**. Each Member has a **Certificate of Membership** that shows the percentage of the CC that he or she owns. The Members are responsible for the management of the business but are **not liable** for the **Debt** of the CC. There are unique Accounts that are used to record the transactions that can take place between the Members and the CC. At the end of the Accounting Period, the Members decide how much of the Net Profit to share between the Members and how much of the Net Profit to keep in the business.

3. PHASING OUT OF CCs
It was decided to phase out CCs in South Africa and the registration of new CCs was stopped in 2008.
A small business that wants Limited Liability should now register as a **Private Company**.
CCs that registered before 2008 are still allowed to operate as CCs.
The government has made the requirements easier for a small business to register as a Private Company.

4. UNIQUE ACCOUNTS OF A CC   On the next page there is an overview of all the unique Accounts.
A CC has certain unique Accounts in their books that are used to record transactions with its Members.

Retained Income Account   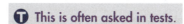 This is often asked in tests.

The balance of the Retained Income Account shows the total amount that is owned by the CC.
The total amount available is calculated at the end of the Accounting Period.
Amount available = Balance at the beginning of the Accounting Period + Net Profit after Tax
The Members decide how much to keep in the CC (Retained Income Account) and how much to distribute to the Members (Distribution to Members Account).

RETAINED INCOME ACCOUNT →

	Balance at beginning of the Accounting Period
+	Net Profit after Tax
=	Total amount available
−	Distribution to Members • **Paid** (Amount already paid to Members) • **Recommended** (Amount still owed to Members)
=	Retained Income Account balance at end of the Accounting Period

B. OVERVIEW OF THE UNIQUE ACCOUNTS OF A CC

ACCOUNT NAME	DESCRIPTION
Remuneration: Accounting Officer DR + / CR − E	**The fees the CC pays the Accountant who does the books of the business** This Account is similar to the Audit Fees Account and the Directors Fees Account.
Salary: [Member Name] DR + / CR − E	**The Salary that is paid to a Member of a CC for his or her work done** There is a separate Account for each Member who is paid a Salary.
Interest on Loan to Members DR − / CR + I	**The Interest paid on a Loan given to a Member** This Account is used when a **Member** who received a Loan from the CC **pays Interest** on the Loan.
Interest on Loan from Members DR + / CR − E	**The Interest on a Loan received from a Member** This Account is used when the **CC pays Interest** on a Loan that was received from a **Member**. This Account is similar to the Interest Expense Account.
Loans to Members DR + / CR − A	**The amount of Loans given to Members** The **Members** of a CC can agree to **lend** cash (from the CC) to one of the Members. The Member must pay the CC back for the Loan.
Loan from Members DR − / CR + L	**The amount of Loans received from Members** A **Member** can decide to **lend** cash **to** the **CC**. The CC will agree to pay back the borrowed amount within a certain time period. This Account is similar to the Loan: Bank XX Account.
Distribution to Members DR + / CR − E	**The CC can decide to pay its Members part of the Net Profit at the end of the Accounting Period** The distribution to Members Account decreases the **Owner's Equity** Account. This Account is similar to the Ordinary Share Dividends Account.
Distribution Payable to Members DR − / CR + L	**The amount that is still owed to the Members** This Account is similar to the Dividends Payable to Shareholders Account/ Shareholders for Dividends Account.
Members Contribution DR − / CR + O	**The amount of Capital contributed to the CC by its Members** This Account is similar to the Ordinary Share Capital Account.
Retained Income DR − / CR + O	**The amount of Profit kept by the CC (Accumulated Profits)**

 Loan **to** Member is an **Asset** Account and therefore the **Interest** on Loan **to** Members is an **Income** Account.
Loan **from** Member is a **Liability** Account and therefore the **Interest** on Loan **from** Members is an **Expense** Account.

COMPANIES
SUMMARY OF CONTENTS

A   **OVERVIEW OF THE UNIQUE ACCOUNTS OF A COMPANY** **204**

B   **DETAILS OF THE UNIQUE ACCOUNTS OF A COMPANY** **205**

    1. **Ordinary Share Capital Account**

       a. Important terms

       b. Buying and selling Shares

           i. Two Accounts are affected when Shares are sold for cash

           ii. Three Accounts are affected when Shares that had previously been issued are bought back by the Company

    2. **Retained Income Account** **206**

    3. **Dividends on Ordinary Shares Account and Shareholders for Dividends Account**

       a. Interim Dividends

       b. Final Dividends

    4. **Income Tax Account and SARS (Income Tax) Account** **207**

       a. Income Tax Account

       b. SARS (Income Tax) Account

           i. Total provisional Income Tax payments > Income Tax according to Tax assessment

           ii. Income Tax according to Tax assessment > Total provisional Income Tax payments

       c. Income Tax Transactions

           i. 1st provisional and 2nd provisional Tax payments

           ii. Tax Assessment

           iii. Final Tax payment **208**

    5. **Directors Fees Account** **209**

    6. **Auditors Fees Account** **209**

    7. **Appropriation Account** **209**

COMPANIES

A Company is a legal business entity that is separate from its Owners.
A **Memorandum of Incorporation** (MOI) is completed to register a Company in South Africa.
A registered Company is required to adhere to the rules set out by the new **Companies Act (71 of 2008)**.
See pg 7 for an overview of the different forms of ownership.

> Companies is very important for the Grade 12 exam!

A. OVERVIEW OF THE UNIQUE ACCOUNTS OF A COMPANY

The bookkeeping of a registered Company is similar to that of other businesses.
The steps of the Accounting Cycle are the same. However, there are certain **Accounts** that are **unique** to **Companies** and there are **differences** when preparing the **Final Accounts**.

ACCOUNT NAME	DETAILS
Ordinary Share Capital (O) — DR – / CR +	**The amount received from Ordinary Shares issued by a Company** A Company sells **Shares** to raise **Capital**. Each person who buys a Share is known as a **Shareholder**.
Retained Income (O) — DR – / CR +	**The total amount that the Company has earned** A Company decides how much **Profit** after Income Tax to keep and how much Profit to pay out as **Dividends**. The amount that it keeps is transferred to the **Retained Income Account**.
Dividends on Ordinary Shares (E) — DR + / CR –	**The amount of Dividends that a Company distributes to its Shareholders** The Directors of a Company can decide to **distribute** an amount to the **Shareholders**. This is known as **Dividends**.
Shareholders for Dividends (L) — DR – / CR +	**The amount of Dividends that are owed to the Shareholders** The total Dividends that have been declared but have not yet been paid to the Shareholders are recorded in this Account.
SARS (Income Tax) (A) DR + / CR – (L) DR – / CR +	**The amount that a Company owes SARS, or the amount that SARS owes a Company** • If **SARS owes** the **Company**, then this is an **Asset Account**. • If the **Company owes SARS**, then this is a **Liability Account**.
Income Tax (E) — DR + / CR –	**The Income Tax for the Accounting Period** A **Company** is required to **pay Income Tax** on its Profits because it is a **separate legal entity**.
Directors Fees (E) — DR + / CR –	**The Directors' Fees for the Accounting Period** The Directors are paid a **fee** for their work.
Auditors Fees (E) — DR + / CR –	**The Auditors' Fees for the Accounting Period** The Auditors are paid a **fee** for their work.
Appropriation Account — DR / CR	**A Temporary Account that shows how the Profits of the Company are distributed at the end of the Accounting Period** See pg 209 for details on this Account.

Go to pg 94 to see where these Accounts can be found on the Financial Statements and Notes.

B. DETAILS OF THE UNIQUE ACCOUNTS OF A COMPANY

1. ORDINARY SHARE CAPITAL ACCOUNT
The amount of Capital received from the issue (sale) of Shares is recorded in this Account.
A Company issues (sells) **Shares** to raise **Capital**. Each person who buys a Share is called a **Shareholder**.

 The Ordinary Share Capital Account for a Company is similar to the Capital Accounts of a Sole Trader and a Partnership.

a. IMPORTANT TERMS

TERM	DEFINITION
AUTHORISED SHARES	The **maximum** number of **Shares** that a **Company can issue**
ISSUED SHARES	The **number** of **Shares** that a Company has **issued**. A Company decides on the amount of authorised Shares to **issue**
ISSUE PRICE	The **price** at which the **Shares** are **issued**

b. BUYING AND SELLING SHARES
A Company can issue Shares and buy back Shares that have previously been issued.

i. **Two Accounts are affected when Shares are sold for cash.**
- The **Bank Account** increases on the Debit side.
- The **Ordinary Share Capital Account** increases on the Credit side to record the increase in Capital.

ii. **Three Accounts are affected when Shares that had previously been issued are bought back by the Company.**
- The **Ordinary Share Capital Account** decreases on the Debit side by the value that the Shares were originally sold for, to record the decrease in Capital.
  Number of Shares bought back × Average Share price
- The **Retained Income Account** decreases on the Debit side by the difference between the amount paid to buy back the Shares (cost of Shares) and the average price of the Shares.
  Number of Shares repurchased × (Price paid per Share – Average Share price)
- The **Bank Account** decreases on the Credit side by the amount paid to buy back the Shares.
  Number of Shares repurchased × Price per Share

A. **BEG COMPANY LIMITED** issued 10 000 Shares at an issue price of R25 per Share on 01 March 2017.

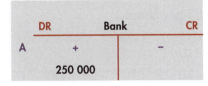 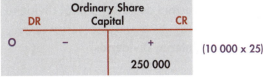
(10 000 × 25)

B. **BEG COMPANY LIMITED** issued 20 000 Shares at an issue price of R30 on 20 March 2017.

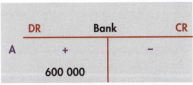 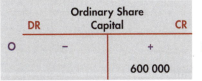
(20 000 × 30)

C. **BEG COMPANY LIMITED** decided to repurchase 12 000 Shares at a price of R35 on 01 May 2017.

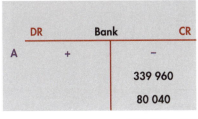

Average price per Share = $\frac{250\,000 + 600\,000}{30\,000}$ = 28,33

2. RETAINED INCOME ACCOUNT
> Make sure you know how to do the Note for Retained Income. See pg 100

The amount that the Company owns is recorded in this Account.
This is a Shareholders' Equity Account, so it **decreases** on the **Debit** side and **increases** on the **Credit** side.
At the end of the Accounting Period, a Company transfers the balance of the Retained Income Account to the **Appropriation Account**. The Appropriation Account is a **Temporary Account** that is used to determine the new balance of the Retained Income Account.
See pg 209 for more information about the Appropriation Account.

3. DIVIDENDS ON ORDINARY SHARES ACCOUNT and SHAREHOLDERS FOR DIVIDENDS ACCOUNT
The amount distributed to the Shareholders is known as Dividends.
The **board of Directors decides** on the amount of **Dividends** to distribute **during** the Accounting Period (**Interim Dividends**) and at the **end** of the Accounting Period (**Final Dividends**).
Shareholders do not automatically get a Dividend. The Directors must first decide how much of the Profit they wish to retain for future growth.

a. INTERIM DIVIDENDS
The Directors can decide to pay the Shareholders a Dividend during the Accounting Period (Interim Dividends). There are two Accounts affected when Dividends are paid:
- The **Dividends on Ordinary Shares Account** decreases on the **Debit** side to record the Dividends.
- The **Bank Account** decreases on the **Credit** side to record the amount of cash paid.

b. FINAL DIVIDENDS
Final Dividends are declared at the end of the Accounting Period.
These Dividends are **not immediately paid**. The Company **makes** an **announcement** about the amount of Dividends they will declare. The Dividends **will be paid** to the Shareholders at the **beginning** of the **new Accounting Period**. There are two Accounts affected when Dividends are declared:
- The **Dividends on Ordinary Shares Account** decreases on the **Debit** side to record the Dividends.
- The **Shareholders for Dividends Account** increases on the **Credit** side to record the amount of Dividends that the Company owes the Shareholders. These Dividends have been declared but not yet paid. This is therefore a Liability Account.

DCM LIMITED has issued a total of 100 000 Ordinary Shares. On the 31 of August 2015, the Directors declared and paid the Shareholders Dividends of R2 per Share. At the end of the Accounting Period on the 28th of February 2016, the Directors declared a final Dividend of R3 per Share.

1. Dividends declared and paid (Interim Dividends)

	DR	Bank	CR		DR	Dividends on Ordinary Shares	CR
A	+		−	E	+		−
			200 000			200 000	

2. Dividends declared (Final Dividends)

	DR	Shareholders for Dividends	CR		DR	Dividends on Ordinary Shares	CR
L	−		+	E	+		−
			300 000			300 000	

4. INCOME TAX ACCOUNT and SARS (INCOME TAX) ACCOUNT
A Company pays Income Tax on its Net Profit for the Accounting Period.

a. INCOME TAX ACCOUNT
The Income Tax Account shows the total Income Tax for the Accounting Period.
It is an **Expense** Account, so it **increases** on the **Debit** side when Income Tax is recorded.

b. SARS (INCOME TAX) ACCOUNT
The SARS (Income Tax) Account shows the total amount that the Company owes SARS, or the total amount that SARS owes the Company.

The **actual** Income Tax that the Company owes (according to the Tax assessment) is compared with the total amount of **provisional** Tax payments made by the Company, to determine whether the Company owes SARS or SARS owes the Company.

i. **Total provisional Income Tax payments > Income Tax according to Tax assessment**
SARS owes the Company because the Company has paid more Income Tax than what was required.
The SARS (Income Tax) Account has a **Debit balance** to show the amount owed to the Company, so it is an **Asset Account**.

ii. **Income Tax according to Tax assessment > Total provisional Income Tax payments**
The Company owes SARS because the Company has paid less Income Tax than what was required.
The SARS (Income Tax) Account has a **Credit balance** to show how much the Company owes SARS, so it is a **Liability Account**.

c. INCOME TAX TRANSACTIONS
The South African Revenue Services (SARS) requires a Company to make **two provisional Tax payments during the year**.
A **final Tax payment** is made after the actual Income Tax for the year has been determined.
The Income Tax **rate** for Companies in South Africa is at present **28%**.
In tests, the Income Tax percentage is often rounded off to 30%.

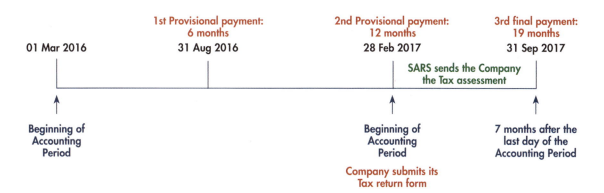

i. **1st provisional and 2nd provisional Tax payments**
Income Tax payments based on the estimated Profits for the Accounting Period are made six months into the Accounting Period and on the last day of the Accounting Period.
The SARS (Income Tax) Account decreases on the **Debit** side to show the amount of Income Tax paid during the Accounting Period.

ii. **Tax Assessment**
The audited Financial Statements are sent to SARS on the last day of the Accounting Period.
SARS sends the Company a final Tax Assessment that shows the actual Income Tax for the Accounting Period. Two Accounts are used to record the actual Income Tax for the Accounting period:
- The **Income Tax Account** increases on the **Debit** side to record the actual Income Tax Expense for the Accounting Period.
- The **SARS (Income Tax) Account** increases on the **Credit** side to record the amount of Income Tax that is owed to SARS.

iii. **Final Tax payment** 🅣 In a test, this payment is usually made on the first day of the Accounting Period.
A **Final Income Tax payment** is made **seven months after the last day** of the **Accounting Period** to **settle the outstanding amount owed.**
SARS pays the Company a refund if the Company has paid more Income Tax than it owed.

A. **OTC LIMITED** paid provisional Tax payments of R800 000 and R600 000 during the Accounting Period.

DR	SARS (Income Tax)	CR		DR	Bank	CR
A	+	−		A	+	−
	800 000					800 000
	600 000					600 000
	1 400 000					1 400 000

B. **OTC LIMITED** received a Tax assessment from SARS that showed that the Company owes R1 200 000 in Income Tax for the Accounting Period.

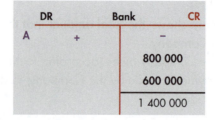

Notice that the Company paid R200 000 more than the actual Income Tax according to the Tax assessment (R1 400 000 instead of R1 200 000). The balance of the SARS (Income Tax) Account is on the Debit side, so SARS owes the Company R200 000 (Asset Account). If the Company had paid less, then they would owe SARS (Liability Account).

Example of a SARS (Income Tax) Account found in the books of BAX LIMTED
Explanations for the amounts are provided below the Account.

DR				SARS (Income Tax)				B1		CR
Date		Details	Fol	Amount		Date		Details	Fol	Amount
2016 March	05	Bank	CPJ	40 000	00	2016 March	01	Balance	b/d	40 000	00
2016 Aug.	31	Bank	CPJ	180 000	00	2017 Feb.	28	Income Tax	GJ	360 000	00
2016 Feb.	28	Bank	CPJ	200 000	00	2017 Feb.	28	Balance	c/d	20 000	00
				420 000	00					420 000	00
2017 March	01	Balance	b/d	20 000	00						

1. **Balance (b/d)** shows the balance brought down from the previous Accounting Period. At the beginning of the Accounting Period, the SARS (Income Tax) Account is a Liability Account because the Company owes SARS R40 000.
   In the next Accounting Period, the SARS (Income Tax) Account is an Asset Account because SARS owes the Company R20 000.

2. The **Bank** entries show all the payments that were made. These decrease the amount owed to SARS.
   a. A **payment** is made to pay the **amount** that is **owed** to **SARS** at the **beginning** of the **Accounting Period.**
   b. The **first provisional payment** is made **during** the Accounting Period. This amount is based on the **expected Profits** for the Accounting period.
   c. The **final provisional payment** is made at the **end** of the Accounting Period. This amount is based on the **expected Profits** for the Accounting period.

3. **Income Tax** shows the **actual amount** of **Income Tax** for the Accounting Period.

5. DIRECTORS FEES ACCOUNT

Directors' fees are paid to the Directors.
The Directors are chosen to **make decisions** on **behalf** of the **Company**.
The **Directors Fees Account** is an **Expense Account**. It **increases** on the **Debit** side when the Directors' Fees are paid.

T&R LIMITED paid R30 000 to their Directors.

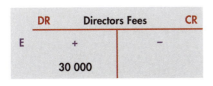
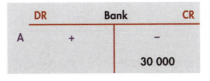

6. AUDITORS FEES ACCOUNT

A Company is required to appoint Independent Auditors to audit the books of the Company.
The Company pays the Auditors a **fee** for their audit. The Auditors provide an **independent opinion** on the **accuracy** of the **Financial Statements**.
The **Auditors Fees Account** is an **Expense Account**. It **increases** on the **Debit** side when the Auditors' Fees are paid.

T&R LIMITED paid R70 000 to their Auditors.

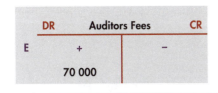
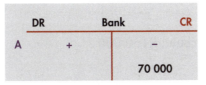

7. APPROPRIATION ACCOUNT

The Appropriation Account is a Temporary Account that is used to show how the accumulated Profit or Loss (Profit or Loss for current period + Balance of Retained Income Account) is distributed.
The accumulated Profit or Loss is distributed between the following Accounts:
- **Income Tax Account:** The amount of Income Tax the Company has to pay on its **Profits** for the Accounting Period
- **Dividends on Ordinary Shares Account:** The amount of **Dividends** the Company pays its Shareholders
- **Retained Income Account:** The **accumulated Profits** are kept by the Company after Income Tax and Dividends for future growth

DIFFERENT ENTRIES TO PREPARE THE APPROPRIATION ACCOUNT

a. **The balance of the Retained Income Account is closed off to the Appropriation Account at the beginning of the Accounting Period.**
The balance of the Retained Income Account shows the **amount owned by the Company** at the beginning of the Accounting Period.

The bookkeeper of **MZA LIMITED** closed off the Retained Income Account with a balance of R100 000 to the Appropriation Account at the end of the Accounting Period.

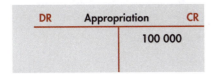

The unbolded 100 000 shows the balance of the Retained Income Account before the transaction.

b. **Net Profit/Loss before Tax is closed off to the Appropriation Account at the end of the Accounting Period.**
The Net Profit/Loss before Tax shows the total **Profit or Loss** made by the Company for the Accounting Period.
See pg 129 for the steps to determine the Net Profit/Loss for the Accounting Period.

The bookkeeper of **MZA LIMITED** closed off the Profit and Loss Account with a Profit of R300 000 to the Appropriation Account at the end of the Accounting Period.

The unbolded 300 000 shows the balance (Profit) of the Account before the transaction.

c. **The balances of the Income Tax Account and Dividends on Ordinary Shares Account are closed off to the Appropriation Account at the end of the Accounting Period.**
The amounts for **Income Tax and Dividends** on Ordinary Shares are closed off to the Debit side of the Appropriation Account.

The bookkeeper of **MZA LIMITED** closed off the following Accounts to the Appropriation Account at the end of the Accounting Period:
- Income Tax Account: R90 000
- Dividends on Ordinary Shares Account: R160 000

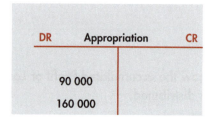 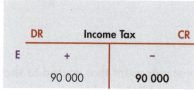 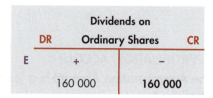

The unbolded amounts show the balances of the Accounts before the transaction.

d. **The balance of the Appropriation Account is transferred to the Retained Income Account at the end of the Accounting Period.**
The difference between the Debit side and the Credit side is transferred to the Retained Income Account.
The amount that is transferred is the new balance of the **Retained Income Account**.
This shows the amount that is **retained** by the Company.

The bookkeeper of **MZA LIMITED** closed off the balance of R150 000 to the Retained Income Account.

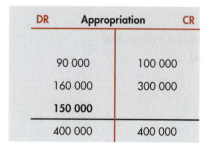 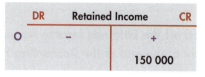

The unbolded amounts show the entries for the Appropriation Account before the transaction.

Example of the Appropriation Account in the General Ledger of MZA LIMITED

DR							Appropriation Account			CR	
		Details	Fol	Amount		Date		Details	Fol	Amount	
2017 Feb.	28	Income Tax	GJ	90 000	00	2017 Feb.	28	Profit and Loss	GJ	300 000	00
2017 Feb.	28	Dividends on Ordinary Shares	GJ	160 000	00	2017 Feb.	28	Retained Income	GJ	100 000	00
2017 Feb.	28	Retained Income	GJ	**150 000**	00						
				400 000	00					400 000	00

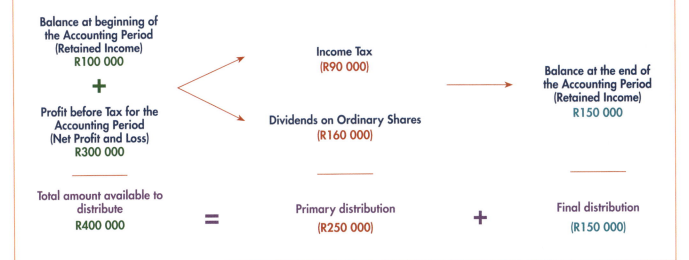

Balance at beginning of the Accounting Period (Retained Income) **R100 000**
+
Profit before Tax for the Accounting Period (Net Profit and Loss) **R300 000**

Total amount available to distribute **R400 000**

=

Income Tax (R90 000)

Dividends on Ordinary Shares (R160 000)

Primary distribution (R250 000)

+

Balance at the end of the Accounting Period (Retained Income) **R150 000**

Final distribution (R150 000)

ANALYSIS OF PUBLISHED FINANCIAL STATEMENTS
SUMMARY OF CONTENTS

| **A** | **DIRECTORS' REPORT** | **213** |
| **B** | **INDEPENDENT AUDITOR'S REPORT** | **214** |

    Format of the Independent Auditor's Report

    1. Introduction

    2. Statement of the Directors' responsibility for the Financial Statements

    3. The Auditor's Opinion

| **C** | **FINANCIAL STATEMENTS** | **215** |
| **D** | **ADDITIONAL INFORMATION** | **215** |

ANALYSIS OF PUBLISHED FINANCIAL STATEMENTS 🔵12

All registered Public Companies are required to publish an Annual Report.
In the school curriculum, a Company always refers to a registered Public Company. 💡

The Annual Report summarises **important information** about the Company.
The Companies Act requires Companies to include the following in their Annual Reports:
A. **Directors' Report**
B. **Independent Auditor's Report**
C. **Financial Statements**
   - Income Statement (Statement of Comprehensive Income)
   - Balance Sheet Statement (Statement of Financial Position)
   - Cash Flow Statement
D. **Additional information relating to Governance and the Company's activities**

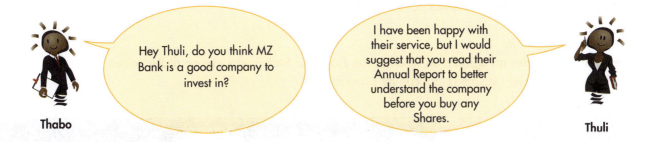

A. DIRECTORS' REPORT

The Board of Directors writes a Directors' Report that is included in the Annual Report.
The Directors' Report provides the Shareholders with information about the Company. Directors are responsible for the management of a Company. The Directors' Report includes:
- **General information** about the Company and the Directors
- A statement from the **Directors** to say that they have **complied** with financial reporting **regulations**
- A statement from the Directors to say that the Financial Statements have been prepared on the basis of Accounting Policies applicable to a **going concern**
- A statement to declare that the **Directors approve** the **Financial Statements**
- Information regarding **Dividends** and **Shares**
- Information about the **Directors' Shareholding** that includes any purchase or sale of Shares by Directors and the number and value of Shares that each Director owns

B. INDEPENDENT AUDITOR'S REPORT

A Company must appoint an independent Auditor to provide an Auditor's Report.
The Auditor's role is to provide a formal opinion on whether or not the Company's Financial Statements fairly represent its Financial Position and Financial Performance. The Auditor compiles an **Independent Auditor's Report**, which provides the public with an **unbiased opinion** on whether the information that has been published by the Company is **reliable** or not.

FORMAT OF THE INDEPENDENT AUDITOR'S REPORT

1. **Introduction**
   The Auditor **addresses** the report to the **Shareholders** of the company and **explains** what has been **included** in the audit.

2. **Statement of the Directors' responsibility for the Financial Statements**
   A statement is inserted on behalf of the **Directors** that shows that the Directors have **complied** with the **requirements** of the **Companies Act** of South Africa.

3. **The Auditor's Opinion**
   The Auditor provides an opinion on whether the Financial Statements are accurate or not.
   There are four different opinions that can be provided.

OPINION	DETAILS
UNQUALIFIED AUDIT OPINION	The Auditors find that the Financial Statements are **accurate**. The Financial Statements **fairly present** the Financial Performance and Financial Position of the Company.
QUALIFIED AUDIT OPINION	The Auditors find that the Financial Statements are **mostly accurate**, with a **few issues**. The Auditors will **list** the **issues** that were found.
ADVERSE AUDIT OPINION	The Auditors find that the Financial Statements are **not accurate**. The Financial Statements **do not fairly present** the Financial Performance and Financial Position of the Company. **This is not covered in the school curriculum.**
DISCLAIMER	The Auditors are **not able to provide an opinion**. This occurs when the Auditors are **not independent**, or they do **not have enough information** to form an opinion.

C. FINANCIAL STATEMENTS

Financial Statements are included in the Annual Report.
The Financial Statements provide details about the Financial Position and the Financial Performance of the Company.

STATEMENT	DETAILS	INTERPRETATION
STATEMENT OF COMPREHENSIVE INCOME (ABRIDGED INCOME STATEMENT) See pg 88 for more information on the Income Statement.	The most important **Income** and **Expense** Accounts	Information about the **Financial Performance** of a Company
STATEMENT OF FINANCIAL POSITION (BALANCE SHEET STATEMENT) See pg 91 for more information on the Balance Sheet Statement.	The **Asset**, **Liability** and **Owner's Equity** Accounts	Information about the **Financial Position** of a Company
STATEMENT OF CASH FLOW (CASH FLOW STATEMENT) See pg 101 for more information on the Cash Flow Statement.	The changes in the **cash** of the business, resulting from **operating**, **investing** and **financing** activities	Information about the **cash changes** and **cash position** of a Company

D. ADDITIONAL INFORMATION

A Corporate Governance Report and Business Review on the Company's activities are also included.
The Corporate Governance Report provides information about how the Company has been managed. It includes a review of the effectiveness of **Internal Control** and **Risk Management** systems.

The Business Review includes:
- A **review** of the Company's performance
- A **description** of the risks and uncertainties of the Company
- **Important events** that have affected the Company during the year
- An **analysis** of the Financial Statements

Other information is also included in the Annual Report, such as the following:
- Statement of **compliance** with **IFRS** (International Financial Reporting Standards)
- Summary of significant **Accounting Policies** used
- **Supporting information** related to items on the **Financial Statements**

MANAGERIAL ACCOUNTING
ETHICS
SUMMARY OF CONTENTS

A BASIC PRINCIPLES OF ETHICS **217**

  1. Leadership
  2. Discipline
  3. Transparency
  4. Accountability
  5. Fairness
  6. Sustainability
  7. Responsible Management **218**

B PROFESSIONAL BODIES **218**

  1. Professional Accounting Bodies in South Africa
  2. Role of a Professional Body
     a. Five Principles
     b. Key roles of SAICA and SAIPA **219**
     c. Disciplinary and punitive measures

C KING REPORT **219**

Key principles on the governance of ethical behaviour in King III

D LEGISLATION GOVERNING COMPANIES **220**

Key principles of the Companies Act

  1. Responsibilities of Directors
  2. Conflicts of Interest
  3. Directors' Performance Evaluation
  4. Directors' Remuneration
  5. Dispute Resolution

ETHICS 10

Business ethics is about understanding what is morally right or wrong in the workplace.
A **Code of Ethics** is a set of rules that explains which behaviours are generally accepted as right or wrong.
Each business has its own Code of Ethics which has been developed according to its needs.
Ethical behaviour is acting in a way that is generally accepted as being right.
The easier decision is not always the right decision.
It is important for both employers and employees of a business to behave ethically to ensure that the business achieves its objectives. There are often difficult decisions to be made when trying to **achieve** the highest possible **Profit** and to **remain ethical** at the same time. A business that behaves ethically will gain a good reputation and will succeed in the long term.

A. BASIC PRINCIPLES OF ETHICS

PRINCIPLE	EXPLANATION	EXAMPLE
Leadership	**Leaders are expected to behave ethically and to set a good example for others to follow.** The leaders of a business should make sure that the **Code of Ethics** is followed at all times.	The leaders at **SUPER SHIRTS LIMITED** make sure that their employees are aware of what is expected of them according to the **Code of Ethics**, and encourage them to make the right decisions and act correctly at all times.
Discipline	**Employees are expected to follow the rules of the business.** All employees and employers are expected to obey the rules set out by the **Code of Ethics** at all times.	**NYC RINGS** takes disciplinary action against any employees who do not follow the rules set out in the **Code of Ethics.**
Transparency	**Businesses should be open about their activities and not hide any information.** **Information** should be **clear** and **available** to the people that have a right to access the information. All **relevant information** should be included **in writing** so that the facts are not misrepresented.	The accountant at **MBV LIMITED** reports all the relevant information of the business as accurately as possible.
Accountability	**Businesses should take responsibility for their decisions.** All employees and employers should be able to **explain** the **actions** and the **decisions** that they make and **take responsibility** for them.	The Directors of **NT LIMITED** understand that they are responsible for the actions of the business and are required to justify their decisions.
Fairness	**Businesses should make all decisions based on facts and not emotions.** The decisions made by a business should **not** be **biased**. **Everyone** should be treated **fairly** at all times.	The manager at **BUSI'S BISCUITS** makes sure that he does not give preference to any of the employees, regardless of colour or creed.
Sustainability	**Businesses should consider economic, social and environmental factors and effects when making decisions.** A business must take into account the effect any decisions they make will have on their **Profits**, the **People** and the **Planet**. This ensures that the business can continue operating in the future – its is a 'Going Concern'. **Triple Bottom Line Reporting** is the name given to the disclosure of information about how the business has had an impact on their **Profits**, the **People** and the **Planet**.	**HOLIDAYS LIMITED** prepares a business plan to assist them with all important decisions. The business plan is used to look at how their decisions will affect: • The Profits of the business • The employees, Shareholders and customers of the business • The planet *This table is continued on the next page.*

| Responsible Management | Management should make decisions that benefit the Company and all related aspects (Profits, People and the Planet). Management should consider all the different **impacts** that their **decisions** might have. | The management at **CANRU LIMITED** looks at all the different factors when deciding whether to open a new store. They aim to make a decision that takes the Company and all related aspects into account (e.g. employment opportunities and servicing the community). |

B. PROFESSIONAL BODIES

A Professional Body is an organisation that is associated with a specific profession.
Professions include Doctors, Advocates, Chartered Accountants, Educators and Social Workers. If a person is a **member of a Professional Body**, it implies that he or she has reached a certain level of competence and excellence.

1. PROFESSIONAL ACCOUNTING BODIES IN SOUTH AFRICA
To work as a professional Accountant in South Africa, one is required to become a member of the relevant Professional Body. Most of the qualifications below are recognised worldwide.

PROFESSIONAL BODIES	PROFESSION
South African Institute of Chartered Accountants (SAICA)	Chartered Accountant CA (SA)
South African Institute of Professional Accountants (SAIPA)	Professional Accountant
Independent Regulatory Board for Auditors (IRBA)	Registered Auditor (RA)
Institute of Certified Bookkeepers (ICB)	Certified Bookkeeper
Chartered Institute of Management Accountants (CIMA)	Management Accountant (ACMA)
Institute of Internal Auditors South Africa (IIA SA)	Internal Auditor (CIA)

The focus is on SAICA and SAIPA in the school curriculum.

2. ROLE OF A PROFESSIONAL BODY
The main role of a Professional Body is to represent, promote and protect the profession they represent.
It is important that a Professional Body has a Code of Professional Conduct. **The Code of Professional Conduct is a set of rules that all members must adhere to.**

c. **Five Principles**
   There are five principles that the Codes of Professional Conduct of SAICA and SAIPA are based on:
   i. **Integrity** – Members must be **honest** and perform their duties to the **best of their ability**.
   ii. **Objectivity** – Members must **not** be **biased**. They must **not** be **influenced** by external factors.
   iii. **Professional Competence and Due Care** – Members must always **act professionally** and ensure that they have the **knowledge** to do what is required of them.
   iv. **Confidentiality** – Members should **not share confidential information** without permission to do so.
   v. **Professional Behaviour** – Members should **obey** the **laws** and **regulations** of their Company and their Professional Bodies.

b. **Key roles of SAICA and SAIPA**
   SAICA and SAIPA have a number of key roles.
   i. **Set standards** – The Professional Body sets requirements to become a member. Members need to complete **specific qualifications and training**.
   ii. **Best practices** – The Professional Body **informs** its members of the **latest best practices**. Members must be kept up to date with the latest information in their field of expertise.
   iii. **Promoting the profession** – The Professional Body plays a key role in **promoting the profession** and making sure that the **public respects** the professionals.
   iv. **Public issues** – The Professional Body **speaks on behalf of** the professionals. They are also required to **address** any **issues** related to their field.
   v. **Code of Professional Conduct** – The Professional Body **writes and updates** the **Code** of Professional Conduct. They also make sure that all members are **following** the **rules** and they take any **necessary action** when members are not following the rules.

c. **Disciplinary and punitive measures**
   Members who do not follow the rules of the Professional Body face disciplinary and punitive measures.
   Members who **breach** the **Code of Professional Conduct** could potentially damage the reputation of the Professional Body. Disciplinary and punitive measures ensure that members are **punished** for not obeying the rules. There are a number of different disciplinary actions that the Professional Body can take against members. The **disciplinary action** will depend on what the member did wrong.
   - If the offence is **not too serious** then the member will be **cautioned or reprimanded**. In some cases, the member could also be required to **pay a fine**. If a similar offence is committed again, the Professional Body could take more serious action.
   - If the offence is **serious** then the member could be **suspended** for a specific amount of time, or **disqualified** from being a member.

C. KING REPORT

The King Report on Governance is a document that sets out policies and principles on Corporate Governance.
Corporate Governance refers to the **rules** and **processes** that are followed to manage a business.
The report is often referred to as **King III** since the latest document is the **third revised edition**.
All registered Public Companies in South Africa are expected to comply with King III.

KEY PRINCIPLES ON THE GOVERNANCE OF ETHICAL BEHAVIOUR IN KING III
King Code III provides a list of principles on ethical behaviour that businesses should follow.
Information is also provided on how businesses should adopt the principles in practice.

PRINCIPLES	EXPLANATION
Ethical Leadership and Corporate Citizenship	The Directors, Boards and Committees should **lead by example** and ensure that the Company follows accepted corporate values. There should be an **ethical culture** at the Company. The effect on **economic, social and environmental resources** should be taken into consideration when making decisions.
Board and Directors	The Board and Directors of a Company must make sure that they **fulfil** their **roles** as set out in King III.
Integrated Reporting	Companies are expected to **disclose information** that includes the impact on the **Profits**, the **People** and the **Planet**.
Risk Governance	The Directors are responsible for **managing** and **controlling** the risks of the Company.
Stakeholder relationships	The Company should **treat** all stakeholders **fairly**. The **communication** with the Shareholders should be **transparent**.

Internal Audit	The Company should have an **effective Internal Audit**. The Internal Audit should **look at** how effective the **Internal Controls** are and all the **risks** that the Company faces. See pg 224 for more information.
Compliance	The Company should **adhere** to all applicable laws, rules, standards and codes.
Independent Auditor	The Company should have an **effective Audit Committee**. The Audit Committee is responsible for appointing an Independent Auditor. The Independent Auditor is required to **provide an opinion** on the accuracy of the Financial Statements. See pg 224 for more information.

D. LEGISLATION GOVERNING COMPANIES

All registered Companies in South Africa are required to adhere to the laws of the The Companies Act (71 of 2008).
The Companies Act provides principles to ensure that Companies meet certain standards.

KEY PRINCIPLES OF THE COMPANIES ACT

1. **Responsibilities of Directors**
   Directors of a Public Company are responsible to act on behalf of the Shareholders.
   The Directors **manage** the **Company**. They are expected to **make decisions** that will **benefit** the **Shareholders** of the Company in the long term.

2. **Conflicts of Interest**
   Directors should make decisions that will benefit the Company and not necessarily themselves personally.
   All Directors are required to **disclose** any **personal financial information** that could affect their decision-making on behalf of the Company. The personal financial information of the Directors is used to make sure that there are **no conflicts of interest**. A conflict of interest occurs when a person makes a decision to benefit himself or herself personally, rather than the Company.

3. **Directors' Performance Evaluation**
   The performance of the Directors should be evaluated each year.
   The evaluations need to be **objective** and should point out any necessary training required by the Directors to improve their decision-making abilities.

4. **Directors' Remuneration**
   The Shareholders of the Company need to approve the amount of remuneration paid to the Directors.
   The details of the Directors' **remuneration** need to be included in the Financial Statements of the Company. The Directors should receive **fair compensation** for their work.

5. **Dispute Resolution**
   A Company should follow the Business Rescue Proceedings set out in the Companies Act when the Company is facing the possibility of going bankrupt.
   The Companies Act provides detailed **information** to **guide** a Company that is in Financial Distress.

INTERNAL CONTROL
SUMMARY OF CONTENTS

A   **TYPES OF CONTROLS** **222**

    1. Preventative Controls

    2. Detective Controls

    3. Corrective Controls

B   **INTERNAL CONTROL COMPONENTS** **222**

    1. Internal Control Environment

    2. Risk Assessment

    3. Monitoring Performance **223**

    4. Information Systems and Communication

    5. Control Activities

C   **INTERNAL AUDIT** **224**

    1. Plan

    2. Audit evidence

    3. Report **225**

INTERNAL CONTROL

Internal Control refers to the system of policies and procedures put into place to prevent theft, fraud, damage and errors in a business.

Internal Control creates an environment that encourages employees to work **ethically** and provides managers with the tools and systems needed to **understand, detect** and **minimise risks**.

> These are usually tested in exams with matching columns.

A. TYPES OF CONTROLS

The controls of a business fall into three different categories.

> 1. PREVENTIVE CONTROLS → 2. DETECTIVE CONTROLS → 3. CORRECTIVE CONTROLS

1. **PREVENTIVE CONTROLS**
   These controls **prevent** unwanted events from happening.
   E.g. Only certain employees are authorised to access the bank accounts at **BGN LIMITED**.

2. **DETECTIVE CONTROLS**
   These controls **find** and **report** unwanted events.
   E.g. **S. MOGEDI** checks that the total amount recorded by the bookkeeper for Cash Purchases in the Cash Payments Journal is the same as the total Cash Purchases recorded by the bank on the Bank Statement.

3. **CORRECTIVE CONTROLS**
   These controls **correct** the effects of an unwanted event.
   E.g. **NC TRADERS** have installed a system in their store room that sprays water and sets off an alarm when a fire is detected.

B. INTERNAL CONTROL COMPONENTS

1. **INTERNAL CONTROL ENVIRONMENT**
   The attitude of a business towards Internal Control.
   The Control Environment **lays the platform** for the Internal Control of a business.
   E.g. The CEO of **MP PLANTS** is satisfied with the control environment at the Company. All the employees are aware of how important it is to follow the rules of the business.

2. **RISK ASSESSMENT**
   Identifies risks and their effects on the business.
   It is important for a business to understand what **different scenarios** could prevent it from achieving its objectives. The business lists different possible scenarios and the **effects** they would have **on** the **business**.
   E.g. **NT LIMITED** imports items from overseas. The Risk Assessment includes the effects that foreign exchange rates could have on its business.

3. **MONITORING PERFORMANCE**
   A business should continuously measure how effective the controls are in achieving its objectives.
   These controls should be **analysed** and **updated** where necessary.

4. **INFORMATION SYSTEMS AND COMMUNICATION**
   Information Systems and Communication are important for Internal Controls to be effective.
   - Effective Information Systems allow a business to continuously **store, analyse, represent and communicate information** in a business; e.g. **Accounting Software** is used to record information.
   - Effective communication allows a business to ensure that everyone is **aware** of the Internal Controls of the business. A **formal line** of **communication** needs to be followed so that employees can communicate important information to the relevant people.

5. **CONTROL ACTIVITIES** ⓫
   Internal Control activities are the policies and procedures of an Internal Control System.
   Controls should be included for **all the activities of a business**, such as receiving and paying cash, buying and selling Stock and acquiring and disposing of Fixed Assets.

ELEMENT	CONTROL
Documentation	**All information should be recorded on documents.** The documents provide a paper trail of the transactions that take place. The bookkeeper records all transactions from a Source Document.
Authorisation	**Authorisation must be given for certain transactions or activities to take place.** There should be at least one person to authorise a transaction for it to take place. The Salaries at the end of each month are authorised by the manager before they are paid.
Internal checks	**There should be regular checks that procedures are being followed.** The checks should pick up any errors or fraud. The manager of the credit department does random checks of transactions to see whether the correct procedures have been followed.
Physical safekeeping	**Assets and Documents should be kept safe in a secure place.** The Documents and Assets should be kept in a place to which only the relevant people have access. Petty Cash should be kept in a locked box or safe.
Division of duties	**The steps to do a certain task should be done by different employees.** There should not be only one employee who completes all the steps for a transaction. Jake purchases stationery on credit and Maria pays for the stationery.
Responsibility	**There should be one person responsible for a specific step.** This person should be held responsible and accountable for making sure that the step has been done correctly. Andile is the only person who has permission to access the Petty Cash kept on the business premises. If any Petty Cash goes missing then he is responsible.

C. INTERNAL AUDIT   Large Companies have an Internal Audit division.

An Internal Auditor reviews the Internal Control Elements, Risk Management and Governance of a business and provides recommendations on how they can be improved.

Internal Auditors need to be independent of the tasks above so that they can provide objective reports on the Internal Controls of a Company. Their roles include reviewing policies, procedures and operations.
They determine whether the business is following the relevant laws and detecting fraud, theft and errors.

> Remember that the purpose of an External Audit is to provide a formal opinion on whether the Financial Statements fairly present the Financial Position and Financial Performance of a business.
> See pg 214 for more information.

STEPS FOR AN INTERNAL AUDIT

1. PLAN → **2. AUDIT EVIDENCE** → **3. REPORT**

- Plan for the Internal Audit
- a. Samples
  b. Methods to gather audit evidence
  c. Testing
- Prepare the Internal Audit Report

1. PLAN
The Internal Audit team plans the Internal Audit each year.
The team needs to understand the **objectives** of the business and focus on relevant information.
Each member of the team has **specific responsibilities**.

2. AUDIT EVIDENCE
Audit Evidence refers to the different information that is collected during the Internal Audit.
The information is used as evidence to make recommendations.

a. **Samples**
   Internal Auditors are not able to check everything in a business, so samples are required.
   The samples should represent all of the information that is being checked.
   There are two different sampling techniques that can be used.

   i. **Statistical sampling**
      Statistics are used to determine the sample.
      Random sampling and systematic sampling are the two common statistical techniques used.

      - **Random sampling**: All items in the population stand an equal chance of being selected. Random numbers are generated to determine which items to use in the sample.
        Sihle's computer generates ten different random numbers. These numbers are used to form the sample.

      - **Systematic sampling**: A random item is selected as the first item. A number (x) is chosen. Count (x) items after the first random item that was selected and then continue systematically adding items to the sample.
        Ronnie randomly selects item number 20. The number 5 is chosen as x.
        The 25th, 30th, 35th, etc. items are systematically selected to form the sample.

   ii. **Non-statistical sampling**
       Judgement is used to determine the sample.
       The Internal Auditors select a sample based on what they believe should form part of the sample.

b. **Methods used to gather Audit Evidence**
   There are a number of different methods used to gather evidence for the Internal Audit.
   It is important that the evidence used is **relevant** and **reliable**.

METHOD	DETAILS
Observation	Observe to see whether employees are working correctly and efficiently. **Watch to see that the employee ordering items on credit follows all the correct steps.**
Analysis	Analyse the information collected and determine if there are any results that are unusual. **The Internal Auditor found that the Gross Profit Margin was a lot lower than in previous years. She decided to look at the possible reasons for this, to determine if there were any mistakes or fraud.**
Inspection	Inspect the physical Accounting Records and the Assets of the business to determine whether the Internal Control procedures are being followed. **The Internal Auditor checks that the Receipts were recorded correctly in the Cash Receipts Journal.**
Enquiry and Confirmation	Discuss what procedures are followed to do certain tasks with the relevant people. People outside the business, such as Creditors, can also be asked to confirm which transactions they have on record with the business. **The Internal Auditor has interviews with the relevant managers to find out how they ensure that everyone in their division is following the correct procedures.**
Recalculation	Recalculate figures to check that the calculations were done correctly. **The Internal Auditor checks that the Debtors Age Analysis has been done correctly by doing the calculations again.**

c. **Testing**
   Two different types of tests are done during the Internal Audit.
   These tests are done to assess the effectiveness of the Internal Controls.
   i. **Compliance Tests (test of controls)**
      These tests determine whether the current Internal Controls in place are effective.
      It is important that the Internal Controls achieve what they have been designed to do.
      All managers must approve payments from Petty Cash by filling out a form.
      The Internal Auditor will check whether managers have filled out a form for the Petty Cash Payments.
   ii. **Substantive Tests (test of financial information)**
      These tests determine whether the financial information is accurate.
      The balances and details of the Financial Statements are checked.
      The Internal Auditors will do a Stock count to check that the balance of the Trading Stock Account reflects the value of the Inventory counted.

3. **REPORT**
   An Internal Audit Report is prepared at the end of the Internal Audit.
   The Internal Report includes the objectives, methods used, significant findings and recommendations of the Internal Audit.

   Chief Audit Executive
   The Chief Audit Executive (CAE) is the most senior person in the Internal Audit Team.
   The CAE presents the Internal Report to the Management and relevant Committees.
   The CAE works closely with the Management to ensure that all of the necessary resources are available for an effective Internal Audit, such as the Financial Statements of the business and the availability of relevant staff.

 Internal Control plays a key role in all successful businesses.

BUDGETING
SUMMARY OF CONTENTS

A IMPORTANT BUDGETING CONCEPTS **227**

    1. Different types of Budgets

        a. Projected Income Statement

        b. Cash Budget

    2. Time period of a Budget

    3. Methods to prepare a Budget

        a. Zero-based budgeting

        b. Incremental budgeting

B CASH BUDGET **228**

    1. Format of the Cash Budget

    2. Collections from Debtors and payments to Creditors **229**

        a. Collections from Debtors

        b. Payments to Creditors

C PROJECTED INCOME STATEMENT **232**

D ANALYSING AND INTERPRETING BUDGETS **233**

    1. Before the budgeted period

    2. During and after the budgeted period

BUDGETING

A budget is a financial plan for the future.
A budget shows what the business **expects** to take place during a **future period**.
Budgets are important tools for **planning** and **Internal Control**.
A budget includes forecasted amounts, projected amounts, predicted amounts, estimated amounts and expected amounts.

A. IMPORTANT BUDGETING CONCEPTS

There are a number of decisions to be made by a business before preparing a budget.

1. DIFFERENT TYPES OF BUDGETS
There are different types of budgets.
Each budget provides the business with **specific information**.
Cash Budget, Projected Income Statement, Capital Budget, Sales Budget, Purchases Budget, Manufacturing Budget

Projected Income Statement and Cash Budget
The **Projected Income Statement** and the **Cash Budget** are two of the most **important** budgets prepared by a business. In the school curriculum, the focus is on these budgets.

a. A **Projected Income Statement** shows the expected **Profit** of a business for a specific period.
   The expected **Income** and **Expenses** are forecasted, in order to calculate the expected **Profit/Loss** for the budgeted period.

b. A **Cash Budget** shows the expected **cash changes** of a business for a specific period.
   The expected **cash** to be **received** and **cash** to be **paid** are forecasted, in order to calculate the **cash Surplus/Deficit** for the budgeted period.

2. TIME PERIOD OF A BUDGET
A budget can be prepared for any length of time.
- A **short-term** Budget is prepared for a time period of **less than a year**.
- A **medium-term** Budget is prepared for a period of around **one year**.
- A **long-term** Budget is prepared for a time period of **a number of years**.

3. METHODS TO PREPARE A BUDGET
There are two different methods that are used to prepare budgets.

a. **Zero-based budgeting**
   The business **does not use past results** to prepare the budget when using zero-based budgeting.
   Each Account in the budget is discussed to decide whether or not it will be required. The estimated Account balances are based on what the business believes will occur during the budgeted period.

b. **Incremental budgeting**
   The business **uses past results** to prepare the budget when using incremental budgeting.
   The results from previous Financial Statements are used to prepare the budget. The business decides by how much the past results are expected to increase or decrease, in order to estimate the Account balances for the budgeted period.

B. CASH BUDGET

A Cash Budget shows the expected cash changes of a business for a future period.
The **cash** that the business **expects** to **receive** and **pay** during the budgeted period is all included in the Cash Budget. The Cash Budget is important for the business to determine the **liquidity** of the business.
Liquidity refers to whether a business has enough cash to pay for everything in the short term.
Remember that a Cash Flow Statement shows the **actual changes in the cash** of a business, at the end of a past period.

1. FORMAT OF THE CASH BUDGET
The Cash Budget has five main sections.

HEADINGS	COMMENTS
Receipts	All the cash the business expects to receive
Payments	All the cash the business expects to pay
Cash Surplus/Deficit	The difference between Receipts and Payments • If Receipts > Payments then the business has a cash Surplus. • If Payments > Receipts then the business has a cash Deficit.
Balance at the beginning of the period	The amount of cash (bank balance) that the business expects to have on the first day of each month
Cash on hand at the end of the period	The expected cash balance on the last day of the month, at the end of the budgeted period **Cash Surplus/Deficit + Balance at the beginning of the period**

TIM'S PAINT
Cash Budget for the period 01 January 2016 to 28 February 2016

	January	February
RECEIPTS All the cash that the business expects to receive is listed below		
Cash Sales from paint Notice that Credit Sales are not included	20 000	25 000
Collections from Debtors pg 229	6 000	5 000
Cash from sale of vehicle If a vehicle is sold on credit then the amount is not included	-	60 000
Total Receipts Total of all the cash the business expects to receive	26 000	90 000
PAYMENTS All the cash that the business expects to pay is listed below.		
Cash Purchases of stock	12 000	15 000
Payments to Creditors pg 229	8 000	9 000
Payment of water and electricity	1 500	1 500
Payment of Telephone Account	500	500
Total payments Total of all the cash the business expects to pay	(22 000)	(26 000)
CASH SURPLUS (DEFICIT) (Total Receipts – Total Payments)	4 000	64 000
CASH BALANCE AT THE BEGINNING OF THE PERIOD Estimated cash balance on the first day of each month	2 000	6 000
CASH BALANCE AT THE END OF THE PERIOD Estimated cash balance on the last day of each month (Cash Surplus (Deficit) + Cash balance at the beginning of the period)	6 000	70 000

2. COLLECTIONS FROM DEBTORS AND PAYMENTS TO CREDITORS

The cash collections from Debtors are important cash **inflows** and the cash payments to Creditors are important cash **outflows** of a business.

A Debtors Collection Schedule and Creditors Payment Schedule is required to complete the Cash Budget.

a. Collections from Debtors

Debtors is the name given to the customers who owe the business cash for Inventory sold on credit. Debtors are expected to pay the amount that they owe the business within a certain time period.

> Remember that the Debtors Control Account balance shows the total amount of cash owed to the business by all the Debtors.

The **Debtors Collection Schedule** is used to **forecast** how much **cash** the business **expects** to **collect** from the **Debtors** during the budgeted period. The amount of cash expected to be collected from Debtors is **recorded** under **Receipts** in the Cash Budget.

Steps to prepare a Debtors Collection Schedule See example on pg 230

i. Determine the expected Credit Sales for the budgeted period.

> (T) In a test, you will be given the past Credit Sales and the details needed to calculate the expected Credit Sales.

ii. Determine how much of the outstanding amounts the business expects to collect each month.

> (T) In a test, you will be given the percentage on which the amounts are based.

b. Payments to Creditors

Creditors is the name given to the suppliers that the business owes cash to, for purchasing items on **credit**. The business is expected to pay the amounts that it owes the Creditors within a certain time period.
The Creditors Control Account balance shows the total amount that the business owes all the Creditors.

The **Creditors Payment Schedule** is used to **forecast** how much the business expects to **pay** the **Creditors** during the budgeted period. The cash expected to be paid to the Creditors is **recorded** under **Payments** in the Cash Budget.

Steps to prepare a Creditors Payment Schedule See example on pg 231

i. Determine the expected Credit Purchases for the budgeted period.

> (T) In a test, you will be given the past Credit Purchases and details to calculate the expected Credit Purchases.

ii. Determine how much of the outstanding amounts the business expects to pay the Creditors each month.
A business often has a Credit Policy that will state when it expects to settle outstanding amounts.

> (T) In a test, you will be given the details of the Credit Policy.

Prepare the **Debtors Collection Schedule** for **TIM'S PAINT** for the months of January, February and March using the given information.

Information about Sales:
- Actual Sales for **December** were R10 000.
- **40% of all Sales are on credit.**
- Sales for **January** are expected to increase by 10% on the December Sales.
- Sales for **February** are expected to increase by 15% on the forecasted January Sales.
- Sales for **March** are expected to increase by R2 000 on the forecasted February Sales.

The Owner, Tim, expects that the Debtors will settle their outstanding amounts as follows:
- 50% will pay before the end of the month in which the Sale takes place (within **30 days**).
- 30% will pay before the end of the first month after the Sale takes place (within **60 days**).
- 15% will pay before the end of the second month after the Sale takes place (within **90 days**).
- 5% will be written off as **Bad Debts** before the end of the second month after the Sale takes place.

Debtors Collection Schedule for the period 01 January 2017 – 31 March 2017

	Sales		Collections		
Month	Total	Credit	January	February	March
December	10 000	4 000	1 200	600	
January	11 000	4 400	2 200	1 320	660
February	12 650	5 060		2 530	1 518
March	14 650	5 860			2 930
	48 300	19 320	3 400	4 450	5 108

The amounts are recorded in the relevant months, under Receipts in the Cash Budget.

Step 1: Forecasted Credit Sales
Jan: 10 000 × 110 ÷ 100 = R11 000 × 40% = **4 400**
Feb: 11 000 × (100 + 15) = R12 650 × 40% = **5 060**
March: R12 650 + R2 000 = R14 650 × 40% = **5 860**

 Notice that the total forecasted Sales are multiplied by 40% (0,4) to find the total Credit Sales. The other 60% (0,6) (Cash Sales) is recorded directly in the Cash Budget under Receipts.

Step 2: Collections from Credit Sales

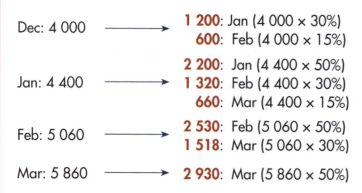

 The cash that will be collected in January, February and March is determined from the forecasted Credit Sales.
- 50% of the amount owed is expected to be collected in the first month of the Sale.
- 30% of the amount owed is expected to be collected in the first month after the Sale.
- 15% of the amount owed is expected to be collected in the second month after the Sale.

© Berlut Books CC

Prepare the Creditors Payment Schedule for TIM'S PAINT for the months of January, February and March using the given information.

- The forecasted amounts for the total **Trading Stock Purchases** are shown in the table below:

January	February	March
5 500	6 325	7 325

- **60% of total Trading Stock purchased is on credit.**
- 80% of Creditors are paid in the **month of the Purchase**. The business receives a **discount of 2%** for all payments made within 30 days.
- 20% of Creditors are paid in the **month following the transaction**.

	Trading Stock Purchases		Payments		
Month	Total	Credit	January	February	March
January	5 500	3 300	2 587	660	–
February	6 325	3 795		2 975	759
March	7 325	4 395			3 446
	19 150	11 490	2 587	3 635	4 205

The amounts are recorded under the relevant months in the Cash Budget.

Step 1: Forecast Trading Stock Credit Purchases:
Jan: R5 500 × 60% = R3 300
Feb: R6 325 × 60% = R3 795
March: R7 325 × 60% = R4 395

Step 2: Payments to Creditors

Jan: 3 300 → **2 587**: Jan (3 300 × 80% × 98%)
660: Feb (3 300 × 20%)

Feb: 3 795 → **2 975**: Feb (3 795 × 80% × 98%)
759: Mar (3 795 × 20%)

Mar: 4 395 → **3 446**: Mar (4 395 × 80% × 98%)

To find a discount of 2% multiply by 98% (100% − 2%)

C. PROJECTED INCOME STATEMENT

A Projected Income Statement shows the expected Profit for a future period.
All the **Income** and **Expenses** are estimated to determine the forecasted Profit or Loss for the period.
See pg 88 for the format of an Income Statement.
The format of the Projected Income Statement is the same as for the Income Statement of the business.
However, in the Projected Income Statement, there are additional columns to show the different months for the budgeted period.

- An **Income Statement** is prepared at the **end** of a specific period.
- A **Projected Income Statement** is prepared **before** a specific period.

FLORA'S FLOWERS
Projected Income Statement for the period 01 January 2016 to 31 March 2016

	January	February	March	Total Projection
Sales This is the forecasted Net Sales amount.	56 000	63 000	70 000	189 000
Cost of Sales This is the forecasted Cost of Sales amount.	(40 000)	(45 000)	(50 000)	(135 000)
Gross Profit Sales – Cost of Sales	16 000	18 000	20 000	54 000
Add: Other Operating Income All the other projected Income Accounts (except for the Interest Income Account) are listed with their estimated balances.	8 200	29 300	8 700	46 200
Rent Income	5 000	5 000	5 500	15 500
Profit on Sale of Asset	-	20 000	-	20 000
Discount Received	3 000	3 500	2 800	9 300
Bad Debts Recovered	200	800	400	1 400
Gross Operating Income Gross Profit + Other Operating Income	24 200	47 300	28 700	100 200
Less: Operating Expenses All the other projected Expense Accounts (except for the Interest Expense Account) are listed with their estimated balances.	(13 500)	(14 500)	(16 300)	(44 300)
Salaries and Wages	7 000	7 000	9 000	23 000
Bad Debts	400	800	1 000	2 200
Repairs	800	-	300	1 100
Water and Electricity	1 500	1 500	1 500	4 500
Stationery	900	300	600	1 800
Advertising	2 000	4 000	3 000	9 000
Depreciation	900	900	900	2 700
Operating Profit/Loss Gross Operating Income – Operating Expense	10 700	32 800	12 400	55 900
Add: Interest Income Projected Interest Income	1 200	1 200	1 500	3 900
Profit/Loss before Interest Expense Operating Profit/Loss + Interest Income	11 900	34 000	13 900	59 800
Less: Interest Expense Projected Interest Expense	(800)	(800)	(800)	(2 400)
Profit/Loss Profit/Loss before Interest Expense – Interest Expense	11 100	33 200	13 100	57 400

 The past Income Statement will be provided in a test, along with any additional information needed to prepare the Projected Income Statement.

D. ANALYSING AND INTERPRETING BUDGETS

Budgets are analysed and interpreted **before, during** and **after** the budgeted period. This is done in all areas of the business.

1. **BEFORE THE BUDGETED PERIOD**
   Budgets are used to plan financially for a future period.
   a. **Projected Income Statement**
      A Projected Income Statement shows the **expected Profit** of the business during the budgeted period.
      - A business uses the projected amounts to **set targets** for employees and for Internal Controls.
      - The expected Sales are used to decide **how many employees** the business requires. A business might need additional staff if it expects Sales to increase substantially.
      - The expected Cost of Sales is used to determine **how much Inventory** a business needs for the period.
   b. **Cash Budget**
      A Cash Budget shows the **expected cash position** of the business during the budgeted period.
      - A business should aim to have a **sufficient** amount of **cash** to pay for everything so that there is no risk of going bankrupt. However, having too much cash is also not ideal. Excess cash can be used for **investments** that provide **returns** to the business.
      - If a business realises that it is not going to have sufficient cash, then the business can decide to look at options to **borrow money** at the **best Interest rates**, or to cut down on its expected costs.
      - If a business realises that it will have a lot more cash than it requires, then the business can decide what the best option is to **invest the cash**.
      - A business looks at the **Creditors Payment Schedule** to determine whether it is a good idea to pay Creditors sooner, to make use of Discounts offered, or to pay Creditors at a later stage.
      - A business looks at the **Debtors Collection Schedule** to determine whether it is a good idea to offer Debtors a discount, in order to encourage them to pay the business sooner.

      > No interest is earned on cash that is kept by a business in a current bank account.
      > If the business invests the cash then interest can be earned.

2. **DURING AND AFTER THE BUDGETED PERIOD**
   Variance Analysis is used to analyse and interpret the differences between the actual amounts and the budgeted amounts. A business investigates the reasons for these differences.
   The differences between the **actual results** and the **budgeted results** are called **variances.**
   - **Projected Income Statement**: The actual Income earned is compared to the budgeted Income, and the actual Expenses that occurred are compared to the budgeted Expenses.
   - **Cash Budget**: The actual cash Receipts are compared to the budgeted cash Receipts and the actual cash payments are compared to the budgeted cash payments.

   Variance Analysis Steps The same steps can be followed for all different types of budgets.
   a. Calculate the difference (in Rands and as a percentage) between the budgeted balance and the actual balance of each Account.
      - **Difference = Actual amount − Budgeted amount**
      - **Percentage increase/decrease = Difference ÷ Actual amount × 100%**
      Comment on whether the actual amount is **more than or less than** the budgeted amount and what the percentage increase or decrease is.

b. **Interpret the results by determining whether the differences are good or bad for the business.**
   - If the **actual Income** is greater than the **budgeted Income** then the **actual results** are better than the business expected.
   - If the **actual Expenses** are greater than the **budgeted Expenses** then the **actual results** are worse than the business expected.
   - Comment on whether the differences are significant or insignificant.
     Budgets are never perfect. If the difference between the budgeted amount and the actual amount is small then the budget has been well done.
c. **Suggest possible reasons for the significant differences and if there is anything the business should do to address the differences.**
   The reasons will depend on what differences were found. There are a number of different reasons which can be used to explain the reason for the budgeted amounts being significantly different from the actual amounts.

GUGU noticed that she sold 60% fewer ice creams during December than budgeted.
This could possibly be because:
- The **weather** was cooler than in previous years, so people purchased fewer ice creams.
- There were **new competitors** which took away customers.
- The **prices** were a lot **higher** than in previous years, so she did not sell as many ice creams.

If you are asked to analyse where you think the biggest problem lies when comparing actual to budgeted amounts, try to find the item which differed the most and focus your comments on this.
- Always keep in mind that **December** is the **holiday period**, which means that retailers might require **additional sales assistants** during this time. This could make **Salaries/Wages increase** but there should also be **increased Sales**, especially because many people will have received end-of-year bonuses. Also look at whether **advertising costs** were increased – especially during November.
- Always try and answer analysis questions **logically**.

COST ACCOUNTING
SUMMARY OF CONTENTS

A   **THE DIFFERENT TYPES OF COSTS** **236**

    1. Production Costs **237**

        a. Prime Costs

            i. Direct Materials Costs

            ii. Direct Labour Costs

        b. Factory Overhead Costs

            i. Indirect Materials Costs

            ii. Indirect Labour Costs

            iii. Other Factory Costs/Other Overhead Costs

    2. Period Costs **238**

        a. Selling and Distribution Costs

        b. Administration Costs

B   **ANALYSING THE COSTS OF A MANUFACTURING BUSINESS** **238**

    1. Overview of important formulas

        a. Total Costs

        b. Unit Costs

    2. Fixed Costs and Variable Costs **239**

        a. Fixed Costs

        b. Variable Costs

    3. Break-Even Analysis **241**

C   **UNIQUE ACCOUNTS OF A MANUFACTURING BUSINESS** **242**

    1. Accounts used during the Accounting Period

    2. Accounts prepared at the end of the Accounting Period **243**

D   **FINANCIAL STATEMENTS OF A MANUFACTURING BUSINESS** **254**

    Production Cost Statement

    Short-Format Income Statement with Notes **256**

COST ACCOUNTING

The focus in this section is on a Manufacturing Business.

Cost Accounting includes capturing costs, organising costs and reporting costs.
The purpose of Cost Accounting is to gain a **better understanding of the costs of a business.**
Costs are the **Expenses** incurred by a business. A business needs to know the costs involved for each item that it manufactures.
Unlike Trading Businesses which buy products at a low price and sell them for a higher price, **Manufacturing Businesses make products** which they then sell.

A. THE DIFFERENT TYPES OF COSTS

The costs of a Manufacturing Business are separated into Production Costs and Period Costs.
Production Costs are also known as Manufacturing Costs.
The diagram below shows some of the different costs involved in manufacturing a table.

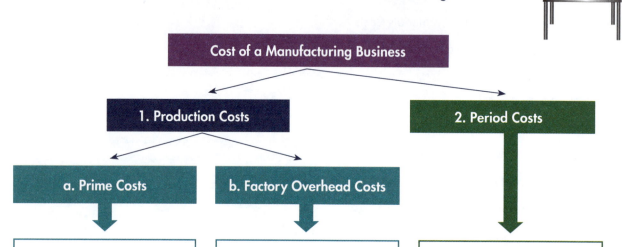

Cost of a Manufacturing Business

1. Production Costs
- a. Prime Costs
- b. Factory Overhead Costs

2. Period Costs

a. Prime Costs

i. **Direct Materials Costs**

wooden table top, steel legs, aluminium edging

+
- Transport Costs
- Storage Costs
- Handling Costs

ii. **Direct Labour Costs**

Salaries and Wages of people who are working with their hands or operating the machines to manufacture the product

b. Factory Overhead Costs

i. **Indirect Materials Costs**

glue, nails, machinery lubricants, cleaning equipment

ii. **Indirect Labour Costs**
- Factory supervisor
- Quality controllers
- Cleaners
- Security guards

iii. **Other Factory Costs**
- Rent
- Water and electricity
- Insurance
- Maintenance
- Depreciation of Machinery
- Safety and Environmental Controls

2. Period Costs

i. **Selling and Distribution Costs**
- Marketing
- Advertising
- Delivery

ii. **Administration Costs**
- Bookkeeper
- Secretary
- Receptionist
- Internal Accountant
- External Accountant
- Rent of office

© Berlut Books CC   236

1. PRODUCTION COSTS

Production Costs are the costs involved in making the items that a Manufacturing Business sells.
Production Costs show the total Expenses incurred to make the items.
Production Costs = Prime Costs + Factory Overhead Costs

a. Prime Costs
Prime Costs are also called Direct Costs. 💡
Prime Costs are the costs that are directly linked to the items that are made.
Prime Costs = Direct Materials Costs + Direct Labour Costs

i. Direct Materials Costs
Direct Materials Costs are the costs for purchasing the raw materials that are used directly to make the items.
These costs have a significant effect on the price of the items that are made. **Transport** costs, **storage** costs and **handling** costs of the Direct Materials are included in the Direct Materials Costs.
The costs of the wooden table top, steel legs and aluminium edging used to make a wooden table are Direct Materials Costs.

ii. Direct Labour Costs
Direct Labour Costs are the costs for employing the workers who make the items.
Only the costs for the employees who **actually make** the **items** are included as Direct Labour Costs.
The Wages and Salaries of the people who are working with their hands or operating the machines to manufacture the product are Direct Labour Costs. This includes UIF, Pension Fund and Medical Aid Fund contributions for the workers.

b. Factory Overhead Costs
Factory Overhead Costs are also called Indirect Costs. 💡
Factory Overhead Costs are the costs that are not directly linked to the items that are made.
The **day-to-day** costs of running the factory are included in the Factory Overhead Costs.
Factory Overhead Costs = Indirect Materials Costs + Indirect Labour Costs + Other Factory Costs

i. Indirect Materials Costs
Indirect Materials Costs are the costs for purchasing the raw materials that are not used directly to make the items.
These **costs** are **low** and do not have a significant effect on the price of the items that are made.
The costs of the glue (an undetermined amount), nails, machinery lubricants and cleaning equipment that are used in the making of a table are Indirect Materials Costs.

> To determine if the cost of a raw material is an Indirect Materials Cost or a Direct Materials Cost, ask the question: Can the raw material be easily identified in the final product? If the answer is no, then it is an Indirect Materials Cost. 💡

ii. Indirect Labour Costs
Indirect Labour Costs are the costs for employing the workers who are not directly involved in making items.
The Wages and Salaries and contributions of the factory supervisor, quality controllers, cleaners and security guards are Indirect Labour Costs.

> To determine whether the cost for a worker falls under Direct Labour Costs or Indirect Labour Costs, ask the question: Is the main role of the worker to make the item? If the answer is no, then the cost for the worker is an Indirect Labour Cost. 💡

iii. Other Factory Costs/Other Overhead Costs
These are the costs for maintaining the machinery and running the factory.
The Factory Costs include Rent, Water and Electricity, Insurance, Depreciation of Machinery, Maintenance and Safety and Environmental Controls.

2. PERIOD COSTS

Period Costs are the costs incurred that are not directly linked to the making of items.
Period Costs = Selling and Distribution Costs + Administration Costs

a. Selling and Distribution Costs
Selling and Distribution Costs are the costs for selling and transporting the items to customers.
The costs for marketing, delivery and advertising

b. Administration Costs
Administration Costs are the costs to complete the administrative tasks of the business.
The costs for the bookkeeper, secretary, receptionist, internal accountant, external accountant and rent of office

 Finance Costs are the costs incurred when a business borrows cash. In the school curriculum, Finance Costs are included as Administration Costs, but in the real world they form a third category under Period Costs.

B. ANALYSING THE COSTS OF A MANUFACTURING BUSINESS

There are different ways to analyse the costs of a business.
The total costs of a business can be broken down into different cost types.
Costs can also be categorised according to how they change when item numbers change.
Break-Even Analysis helps a business to decide how much to sell an item for or how many items to sell, in order to make a **Profit**.

1. OVERVIEW OF IMPORTANT FORMULAS

a. TOTAL COSTS: There are three different ways to calculate total costs

1. Total costs =	Production Costs		+	Period Costs
2. Total costs =	Prime Costs + Factory Overhead Costs		+	Selling and Distribution Costs + Administration Costs
3. Total costs =	Direct Materials Costs + Direct Labour Costs	+ Indirect Materials Costs + Indirect Labour Costs + Other Factory Costs	+	Selling and Distribution Costs + Administration Costs

b. UNIT COSTS: There are different formulas for working out unit costs

NAME OF UNIT COST	FORMULA
Production Costs per unit	Production Costs ÷ Total number of units made
Direct Materials Costs per unit	Direct Materials Costs ÷ Total number of units made
Direct Labour Costs per unit	Direct Labour Costs ÷ Total number of units made
Factory Overheads Costs per unit	Factory Overhead Costs ÷ Total number of units made
Fixed Costs per unit	Fixed Costs ÷ Total number of units made
Variable Costs per unit	Variable Costs ÷ Total number of units made

2. FIXED COSTS AND VARIABLE COSTS

A cost can be classified as either a Fixed Cost or a Variable Cost.

It is important for a Manufacturing Business to know which costs increase and which costs stay the same when the business increases the **number of items made**.

Total Costs = Fixed Costs + Variable Costs

a. Fixed Costs

Fixed Costs stay the same when the number of items made changes.

The total Fixed Costs do not change, no matter how many items are made. If the business stops making items completely, Fixed Costs will still be incurred.

Factory Overhead Costs (e.g. Rent, Depreciation, Water and Electricity, Indirect Materials, Indirect Labour) are Fixed Costs because they do not change when the number of items made increases or decreases.

b. Variable Costs

Variable Costs change when the number of items made changes.

The total Variable Costs increase for each additional item that is made. If the business stops making items completely, then the Variable Costs will not be incurred.

Total Variable Costs = Cost per item × Number of items made

Prime Costs (Direct Materials Costs and Direct Labour Costs) increase when the number of items made increases.

See example on next page.

 Important formulae:
- Fixed Costs = Factory Overhead Costs + Administration Costs
- Variable Costs = Direct Materials Costs + Direct Labour Costs + Selling and Distribution Costs

COOL CHAIRS makes and sells plastic chairs. The Owner, Ronald, has a small factory where he has two workers to assist him to make the chairs. The graph below shows his monthly Fixed Costs and Variable Costs when he makes between 0 and 1 000 chairs.

Graph of Costs

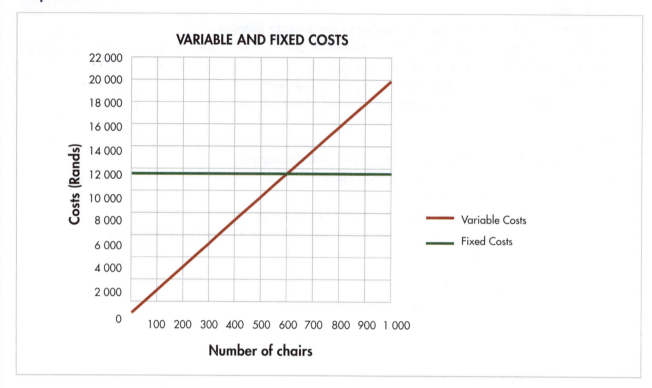

Table of Costs

Number of chairs made	Total Variable Costs	Total Fixed Costs	Total Costs (Variable + Fixed Costs)	Cost per unit ($\frac{\text{Total costs}}{\text{Number of chairs}}$)
0	0	12 000	12 000	N/A
200	4 000	12 000	16 000	80
400	8 000	12 000	20 000	50
600	12 000	12 000	24 000	40
800	16 000	12 000	28 000	35
1 000	20 000	12 000	32 000	32

Understanding Costs

- **The red line** in the graph shows the total **Variable Costs** of the business. **These costs can change.**
  The **Variable Cost per item** is **R20** (Total Variable Costs ÷ Number of chairs made).
  For **each additional chair** that is **made**, the **total Variable Costs increases** by **R20**.
  Variable Costs include **Direct Labour Costs** and **Direct Materials Costs**.

- **The green line** in the graph shows the total **Fixed Costs**. **These costs do not change.**
  The **Fixed Costs stay at R12 000** per month, whether 0 chairs are made or 1 000 chairs are made.
  Fixed Costs include all the **Factory Overhead Costs** such as Rent, Water and Electricity, Indirect Labour Costs (e.g. the Salary of the supervisor of the factory) and Indirect Materials Costs.

Notice that if the number of chairs made increases, then the unit cost per chair decreases. 💡

3. BREAK-EVEN ANALYSIS

Break-Even Analysis is used to find the amount in Rands a business must sell items for and the number of items a business must sell, in order to cover all of their Production Costs.

At the Break-Even Point there is no Profit or Loss made.
- The Break-Even Point in **Rands** shows what the total Sales should be, in order to cover all the Production Costs.
- The Break-Even Point in **units** shows how many items must be sold to cover all the Production Costs.

At the Break-Even Point the total amount received from **Sales** is **equal** to the **Production Costs**.
Total Sales – Total Production Costs = R0

NAME OF UNIT COST	FORMULA
Break-Even Point in Rands	Fixed Costs ÷ Contribution Margin Ratio (see below)
Break-Even Point in units	Contribution Margin ÷ Fixed Costs
Contribution Margin/Contribution per unit	Selling Price per unit – Variable Cost per unit
Contribution Margin Ratio	(Selling Price per unit – Variable Cost per unit) ÷ Selling Price

Make sure you know these formulas.

TED BAKERS makes and sells apple pies. The Owner, Ted, wants to find out how many apple pies he must sell to break even.

Details about Ted's costs
- Ted's total **Fixed Costs** are R22 000 per month.
- He sells **each** apple pie for R30.
- Ted's **Variable Costs** for each apple pie are R10.

Solution
Number of units = Fixed Costs ÷ Contribution Margin
Number of units = 22 000 ÷ (30 – 10)
Number of units = 22 000 ÷ 20
Number of units = 1 100
Ted must sell 1 100 apple pies in a month to break even.

SALLY'S CURTAINS makes and sells curtains. The Owner, Sally, wants to find out how much she must make from Sales to break even each month.

Details about Sally's costs
- Sally's total **Fixed Costs** are R35 000 per month.
- She sells **each** set of curtains for R1 000.
- Sally's **Variable Costs** for each set of curtains are R200.

Solution
Break-Even Point in Rands = Fixed Costs ÷ Contribution Margin Ratio
Break-Even Point in Rands = 35 000 ÷ (1 000 – 200) ÷ 1 000
Break-Even Point in Rands = 35 000 ÷ 0,8
Break-Even Point in Rands = R43 750
Sally must sell curtains to the value of R43 750 per month to break even.

C. UNIQUE ACCOUNTS OF A MANUFACTURING BUSINESS

There are certain General Ledger Accounts that are unique to a Manufacturing Business.

1. ACCOUNTS USED DURING THE ACCOUNTING PERIOD

A Manufacturing Business has unique **Asset Accounts**, which are used to record the costs of the Assets purchased to make items and to record the Expenses incurred to make items.

ACCOUNT NAME	DETAILS
Raw Materials Stock (A) DR + / CR −	**The cost of the Raw (Direct) Materials purchased to make items** • The Account **increases** on the **Debit** side when the raw materials are purchased. • The Account **decreases** on the **Credit** side when the raw materials are sent to the factory to make the items.
Consumable Stores Stock (A) DR + / CR −	**The cost of the Consumable Stock (Indirect Materials) purchased to make items** • The Account **increases** on the **Debit** side when Indirect Materials are purchased. • The Account **decreases** on the **Credit** side when the Indirect Materials are sent to the factory to make the items.
Raw Materials Issued (E) DR + / CR −	**The cost of the Direct (raw) Materials that have been issued to the factory to make the items** • The Account **increases** on the **Debit** side when the raw materials are sent to the production process. • The Account is closed off to the **Direct Materials Cost Account** at the end of the Accounting Period.
Indirect Materials (E) DR + / CR −	**The cost of the Indirect Materials that have been issued to the factory to make the items** • The Account **increases** on the **Debit** side when Indirect Materials Costs are sent to the production process. • The Account is closed off to the **Factory Overhead Cost Account** at the end of the Accounting Period.
[Name of Expense Account] (E) DR + / CR −	A Manufacturing Business has additional Expense Accounts such as the Factory Wages Account, Factory Electricity Account, Factory Rent Account, Depreciation on Factory Equipment Account, etc. These are **Expense Accounts** that are used to record the **costs** incurred to make items. • The Accounts **increase** on the **Debit** side to record the costs incurred. • The Accounts are closed off to the relevant **Cost Accounts** at the end of the Accounting Period.

2. ACCOUNTS PREPARED AT THE END OF THE ACCOUNTING PERIOD

A Manufacturing Business prepares a unique set of Accounts at the end of the Accounting Period.
Five Cost Accounts are prepared to show the **different costs** for the Manufacturing Business during the Accounting Period. The **balances** of all the **Expense** Accounts are **closed off** to the relevant Cost Accounts.
Two Asset Accounts are prepared to show the total costs incurred for the **items** that are in the **process** of **being made** and the total costs incurred for the **completed items**.

ACCOUNT NAME	DETAILS
Direct (Raw) Materials Cost — DR (E +) / CR (−)	**The total cost of the Direct (Raw) Materials used to make items** • The Account **increases** on the **Debit** side by the total cost of the Direct Materials used to make the items. • The Account is closed off to the **Work-In-Progress Account**.
Direct Labour Cost — DR (E +) / CR (−)	**The total cost of the labour used to make items** • The Account **increases** on the **Debit** side by the cost of the Direct Labour used to make the items. • The Account is closed off to the **Work-In-Progress Account**.
Factory Overhead Cost — DR (E +) / CR (−)	**The total cost of the factory overheads needed to make items** • The Account **increases** on the **Debit** side by all the Expenses recorded that fall under Factory Overhead Costs. • The Account is closed off to the **Work-In-Progress Account**.
Administration Cost — DR (E +) / CR (−)	**The total cost of all the Administration Expenses for the Accounting Period** • The Account **increases** on the **Debit** side by all the Expenses recorded that fall under Administration Costs. • The Account is closed off to the **Profit and Loss Account**.
Selling and Distribution Cost — DR (E +) / CR (−)	**The total cost of all the Selling and Distribution Expenses for the Accounting Period** • The Account **increases** on the **Debit** side by all the Expenses recorded that fall under Selling and Distribution Costs. • The Account is closed off to the **Profit and Loss Account**.
Work-in-Progress Stock — DR (A +) / CR (−)	**The costs of the items that are in the process of being made (Work-in-Progress)** • The Account **increases** on the **Debit** side by all the Expenses that were incurred to make the items (**Production Costs**). • The costs of the completed items are transferred to the **Finished Goods Stock Account**.
Finished Goods Stock — DR (A +) / CR (−)	**The sum of all the costs of the completed items (Finished Goods)** • The Account **increases** on the **Debit** side by the total costs incurred for the completed items. • The Account **decreases** on the **Credit** side when the items are sold.

The following example uses T Accounts to show the effects of the transactions recorded by the bookkeeper of **MD MANUFACTURERS**.

Note that any amounts under the T Accounts that are not in bold are previous balances.

a. **MD MANUFACTURERS** purchases R50 000 worth of Direct Materials on credit.

DR	Raw Material Stock	CR		DR	Creditors Control	CR
A	+	–		L	–	+
	50 000					50 000

b. R40 000 worth of Direct Materials are sent to the factory to be used to make items.

DR	Raw Materials Issued	CR		DR	Raw Material Stock	CR
E	+	–		A	+	–
	40 000				50 000	40 000

The Raw Materials Stock Account had a balance of R50 000, but only R40 000 worth of Raw Materials were sent to the factory during the Accounting Period.

c. **MD MANUFACTURERS** pays R8 000 cash for Indirect Materials.

DR	Consumable Stores Stock	CR		DR	Bank	CR
A	+	–		A	+	–
	8 000					8 000

Consumable Stores refers to Indirect Materials.

d. R5 000 worth of Indirect Materials are sent to the factory to be used to make items.

DR	Indirect Materials	CR		DR	Consumable Stores Stock	CR
E	+	–		A	+	–
	5 000				8 000	5 000

The Raw Materials Stock Account had a balance of R8 000, but only R5 000 worth of Raw Materials were sent to the factory during the Accounting Period.

e. The following Factory Expenses are paid during the Accounting Period:
   - Wages of the employees who make the items: R80 000
   - Wages of the supervisor and cleaners of the factory: R100 000
   - Factory Water and Electricity: R60 000
   - Factory Rent: R120 000

DR	Factory Wages	CR		DR	Factory Water and Electricity	CR
E	+	–		E	+	–
	80 000				60 000	
	100 000					

DR	Factory Rent	CR		DR	Bank	CR
E	+	–		A	+	–
	120 000					360 000

f. Depreciation on Factory Equipment is recorded at R30 000.

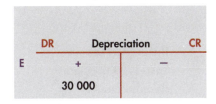

g. The following Selling and Distribution and Administration Expenses are incurred and paid for during the Accounting Period:

Selling and Distribution	Administration
Salaries and Wages: R60 000	Salaries and Wages: R100 000
Advertising: R100 000	Stationery: R5 000
Bad Debts: R5 000	Telephone: R6 000
Rent Expense: R30 000	Rent Expense: R70 000
Commission on Sales: R15 000	

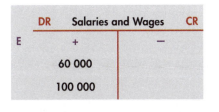

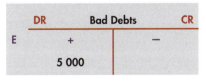

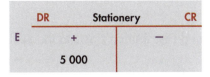

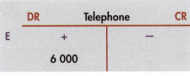

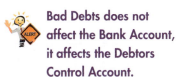

Bad Debts does not affect the Bank Account, it affects the Debtors Control Account.

h. **At the end of the Accounting Period, the bookkeeper closes off the Expenses that fall under Direct Materials to the Direct Materials Cost Accounts.**

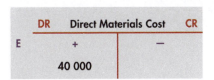

The Raw Materials Issued Account balance of R40 000 is closed off to the **Direct Materials Cost Account.**

i. **The bookkeeper closes off the Expenses that fall under Direct Labour to the Direct Labour Cost Accounts.**

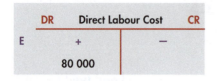

The Indirect Labour Costs (100 000) are closed off to the Factory Overhead Cost Account.

j. **The bookkeeper closes off all the Expenses that fall under Indirect Labour and Indirect Materials to the Factory Overhead Cost Account.**

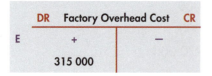

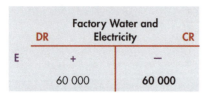
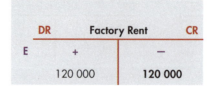

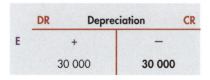

Remember that the amounts that are not in bold are previous balances.

k. **The bookkeeper closes off all the Expenses that fall under Selling and Distribution Costs to the Selling and Distribution Cost Account.**

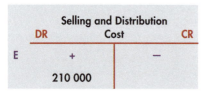
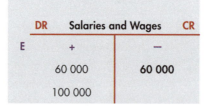

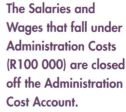 The Salaries and Wages that fall under Administration Costs (R100 000) are closed off the Administration Cost Account.

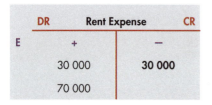

Remember that the amounts that are not in bold are previous balances.

l. The bookkeeper closes off all the Expenses that fall under Administration Costs to the Administration Cost Account.

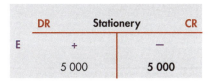

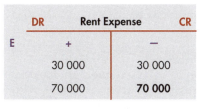

Remember that the amounts that are not in bold are previous balances.

m. The bookkeeper closes off all the Selling and Distribution Accounts and the Administration Account to the Profit and Loss Account, in order to determine the Net Profit/Loss for the Accounting Period.

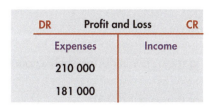
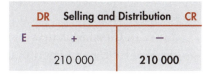

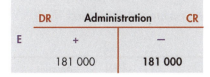

Profit and Loss is a Temporary Account and is therefore not classified as an Asset, Owner's Equity, Liability, Income or Expense Account.

Remember that the amounts that are not in bold are previous balances.

n. The bookkeeper closes off all the Expenses that fall under Production Costs to the Work-in-Progress Account.

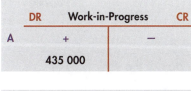

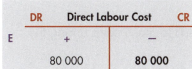

Remember that the amounts that are not in bold are previous balances.

o. **The total costs for all the completed items are closed off to the Finished Goods Stock Account. The total costs for the completed items were R335 000.**
   The balance of the Work-in-Progress Account is R435 000.

DR	Finished Goods Stock	CR		DR	Work-in-Progress	CR
A	+	−		A	+	−
	335 000				435 000	335 000

The Work-in-Progress Account has a new balance of R100 000 (R435 000 − R335 000) at the end of the Accounting Period.

Below are the **General Ledger Accounts** found in the books of **BNT MANUFACTURERS**. Explanations have been provided for the entries recorded.

DR   **RAW MATERIALS STOCK**   **B1**   **CR**

Date		Details	Fol	Amount		Date		Details	Fol	Amount	
2016 Jan.	01	Balance	b/d	50 000	00	2016 Dec.	31	Raw Materials Issued	GJ	400 000	00
2016 Dec.	31	Bank	CPJ	250 000	00						
2016 Dec.	31	Creditors Control	CJ	200 000	00			Balance	c/d	100 000	00
				500 000	00					500 000	00
2017 Jan.	01	Balance	b/d	100 000	00						

🛈 **This is often asked in tests. Learn the format!**

1. **Balance (b/d)**: Balance of the Direct Materials available on the first day of the year (2016)
2. **Bank**: Total Cash Purchases of Direct Materials
3. **Creditors Control**: Total Credit Purchases of Direct Materials
4. **Raw Materials Issued**: Total costs incurred for Direct Materials used to make items during the Accounting Period
5. **Balance (c/d)**: Cost of the Direct Materials available on the last day of the year (2016)
6. **Balance (b/d)**: Balance of the Direct Materials available on the first day of the year (2017)

Any Carriage on Purchases and Customs Duty are included in the amount for materials purchased.

DR   **CONSUMABLE STORES STOCK**   **B2**   **CR**

Date		Details	Fol	Amount		Date		Details	Fol	Amount	
2016 Jan.	01	Balance	b/d	20 000	00	2016 Dec.	31	Indirect Materials Costs	GJ	50 000	00
2016 Dec.	31	Bank	CPJ	30 000	00						
2016 Dec.	31	Creditors Control	CJ	10 000	00			Balance	c/d	10 000	00
				60 000	00					60 000	00
2017 Jan.	01	Balance	b/d	10 000	00						

1. **Balance (b/d)**: Balance of the Indirect Materials available on the first day of the year (2016)
2. **Bank**: Total Cash Purchases of Indirect Materials
3. **Creditors Control**: Total Credit Purchases of Indirect Materials
4. **Indirect Materials Costs**: Total costs incurred for Indirect Materials used to make items during the Accounting Period
5. **Balance (c/d)**: Balance of the Indirect Materials available on the last day of the year (2016)
6. **Balance (b/d)**: Balance of the Indirect Materials available on the first day of the year (2017)

Remember that all Accounts with a **B Folio Reference** are Balance Sheet Accounts (Assets, Owner's Equity and Liabilities). All Accounts with an **N Folio Reference** are Nominal Sheet Accounts (Expenses and Income).

DR				WORK-IN-PROGRESS STOCK				B3		CR
Date		Details	Fol	Amount		Date	Details	Fol	Amount	
2016 Jan.	01	Balance	b/d	100 000	00	2016 Dec. 31	Finished Goods Stock	GJ	700 000	00
2016 Dec.	31	Direct Materials Cost	GJ	400 000	00					
		Direct Labour Cost	GJ	200 000	00					
		Factory Overhead Cost	GJ	300 000	00		Balance	c/d	300 000	00
				1 000 000	00				1 000 000	00
2017 Jan.	01	Balance	b/d	300 000	00					

> **T** This is often asked in tests. Learn the format!

1. **Balance (b/d)**: Costs incurred for the items that are still being made on the first day of the year (2016)
2. **Direct Materials Cost**: Direct Materials Costs incurred during the Accounting Period
3. **Direct Labour Cost**: Direct Labour Costs incurred during the Accounting Period
4. **Factory Overhead Costs**: Factory Overhead Costs incurred during the Accounting Period
5. **Finished Goods Stock**: Total Production Costs for the completed items, transferred to the Finished Goods Stock Account
6. **Balance (c/d)**: Costs incurred for the items that are not finished on the last day of the year (2016)
7. **Balance (b/d)**: Costs incurred for the items that are still being made on the first day of the year (2017)

DR				FINISHED GOODS STOCK				B4		CR
Date		Details	Fol	Amount		Date	Details	Fol	Amount	
2016 Jan.	01	Balance	b/d	100 000	00	2016 Dec. 31	Cost of Sales	GJ	600 000	00
2016 Dec.	31	Work-in-Progress Stock	GJ	700 000	00		Balance	c/d	200 000	00
				800 000	00				800 000	00
2017 Jan.	01	Balance	b/d	200 000	00					

> **T** This is often asked in tests. Learn the format!

1. **Balance (b/d)**: Cost of the items available to sell on the first day of the year (2016)
2. **Work-In-Progress Stock**: Cost of the items that are made during the Accounting Period
3. **Cost of Sales**: Cost of the items that are sold during the Accounting Period
4. **Balance (c/d)**: Cost of the items available to sell on the last day of the year (2016)
5. **Balance (b/d)**: Cost of the items available to sell on the first day of the year (2017)

DR				RAW MATERIALS ISSUED				N1		CR
Date		Details	Fol	Amount		Date	Details	Fol	Amount	
2016 Dec.	31	Raw Material Stock	GJ	400 000	00	2016 Dec. 31	Direct Materials Cost	GJ	400 000	00

1. **Raw Materials Stock**: The cost of the Direct Materials sent to the factory to make items during the Accounting Period
2. **Direct Materials Stock**: The cost of the Direct Materials sent to the factory is closed off to the Direct Materials Cost Account

DR				INDIRECT MATERIALS				N2		CR
Date		Details	Fol	Amount		Date	Details	Fol	Amount	
2016 Dec.	31	Consumable Stores Stock	GJ	25 000	00	2016 Dec.	31 Factory Overhead Cost	GJ	25 000	00

1. **Consumable Stores Stock**: The cost of Indirect Materials sent to the factory to make items during the Accounting Period
2. **Factory Overhead Stock**: The cost of Indirect Materials sent to the factory is closed off to the Factory Overhead Cost Account

DR				FACTORY WAGES				N3		CR
Date		Details	Fol	Amount		Date	Details	Fol	Amount	
2016 Dec.	31	Gross Salaries/Wages	GJ	250 000	00	2016 Dec.	31 Direct Labour Cost	GJ	200 000	00
		Pension Fund Contributions	GJ	17 500	00		Factory Overhead Cost	GJ	100 000	00
		Medical Aid Fund Contributions	GJ	30 000	00					
		UIF Contributions	GJ	2 500	00					
				300 000	00				300 000	00

1. **Gross Salaries/Wages**: The Wages and Salaries of the workers in the factory
2. **Pension Fund Contributions**: The Pension Fund Contributions for the workers in the factory
3. **Medical Aid Fund Contributions**: The Medical Aid Fund Contributions for the workers in the factory
4. **UIF Contributions**: The UIF Contributions for the workers in the factory
5. **Direct Labour Cost**: The Factory Wages and Salaries that fall under Direct Labour Costs are closed off to the Direct Labour Cost Account
6. **Factory Overhead Cost**: The Factory Wages and Salaries that fall under Indirect Labour Costs are closed off to the Factory Overhead Cost Account

DR				FACTORY WATER and ELECTRICITY				N4		CR
Date		Details	Fol	Amount		Date	Details	Fol	Amount	
2016 Dec.	31	Bank	CPJ	60 000	00	2016 Dec.	31 Factory Overhead Cost	GJ	60 000	00
				60 000	00				60 000	00

1. **Bank**: The cost of water and electricity for the factory, paid for during the Accounting Period
2. **Factory Overhead Cost**: The cost of water and electricity for the factory is closed off to the Factory Overhead Account at the end of the Accounting Period

DR				FACTORY RENT				N5		CR
Date		Details	Fol	Amount		Date	Details	Fol	Amount	
2016 Dec.	31	Bank	CPJ	120 000	00	2016 Dec.	01 Factory Overhead Cost	GJ	120 000	00
				120 000	00				120 000	00

1. **Bank**: The cost of rent for the factory, paid for during the Accounting Period
2. **Factory Overhead Cost**: The cost of rent for the factory is closed off to the Factory Overhead Account at the end of the Accounting Period

DR			DEPRECIATION ON FACTORY EQUIPMENT					N6		CR
Date		Details	Fol	Amount		Date	Details	Fol	Amount	
2016 Dec.	31	Accumulated Depreciation on Factory Equipment	GJ	30 000	00	2016 Dec. 31	Factory Overhead Cost	GJ	30 000	00
				30 000	00				30 000	00

1. **Accumulated Depreciation on Factory Equipment**: The Depreciation on factory equipment for the Accounting period
2. **Factory Overhead Cost**: The Depreciation on factory equipment is closed off to the Factory Overhead Account at the end of the Accounting Period

DR			DIRECT MATERIALS (RAW) COSTS					N7		CR
Date		Details	Fol	Amount		Date	Details	Fol	Amount	
2016 Dec.	31	Raw Materials issued	GJ	400 000	00	2016 Dec. 31	Work-in-Progress Stock	GJ	400 000	00
				400 000	00				400 000	00

1. **Raw Materials Issued**: The cost of Direct Materials sent to the factory to make items
2. **Work-in-Progress Stock**: The cost of Direct Materials sent to the factory is closed off to the Work-in-Progress Stock Account at the end of the Accounting Period

DR			DIRECT LABOUR COSTS					N8		CR
Date		Details	Fol	Amount		Date	Details	Fol	Amount	
2016 Dec.	31	Salaries and Wages	GJ	200 000	00	2016 Dec. 31	Work-in-Progress Stock	GJ	200 000	00
				200 000	00				200 000	00

1. **Salaries and Wages**: The cost of Salaries, Wages and Contributions for workers that fall under Direct Labour Costs
2. **Work-in-Progress Stock**: The cost of Direct Labour is closed off to the Work-in-Progress Stock Account at the end of the Accounting Period

DR			FACTORY OVERHEAD COST					N9		CR
Date		Details	Fol	Amount		Date	Details	Fol	Amount	
2016 Dec.	31	Factory Wages	GJ	100 000	00	2016 Dec. 31	Work-in-Progress Stock	GJ	360 000	00
		Factory Water and Electricity	GJ	60 000	00					
		Factory Rent Expense	GJ	120 000	00					
		Depreciation on factory equipment	GJ	30 000	00					
		Indirect Materials Cost	GJ	50 000	00					
				360 000	00				360 000	00

> **This is often asked in tests. Learn the format!**

1. **Factory Wages**: Total cost of Indirect Labour for the Accounting Period
2. **Factory Water and Electricity**: The total cost of factory water and electricity for the Accounting Period
3. **Factory Rent Expense**: The total cost of factory rent for the Accounting Period
4. **Depreciation on Factory Equipment**: The total Depreciation on factory equipment for the Accounting Period
5. **Indirect Materials Costs**: The total Indirect Materials Costs for the Accounting Period
6. **Work-in-Progress-Stock**: The total Factory Overhead Costs are closed off to the Work-In-Progress Stock Account at the end of the Accounting Period
   All Costs that fall under Factory Overheads are closed off to the Debit side of the Factory Overhead Cost Account.

DR					ADMINISTRATION COSTS			N10		CR
Date		Details	Fol	Amount		Date	Details	Fol	Amount	
2016 Dec.	31	Office Salaries and Wages	GJ	160 000	00	2016 Dec. 31	Profit and Loss	GJ	300 000	00
		Stationery	GJ	5 000	00					
		Office Rent Expense	GJ	70 000	00					
		Water and Electricity	GJ	40 000	00					
		Depreciation	GJ	20 000	00					
		Telephone	GJ	5 000	00					
				300 000	00				300 000	00

1. **Wages and Salaries**: Total Wages and Salaries of the employees who do the administrative tasks, for the Accounting Period
2. **Stationery**: The total cost of stationery for the Accounting Period
3. **Rent Expense**: The total cost of office rent for the Accounting Period
4. **Water and Electricity**: Total water and electricity costs of the office for the Accounting Period
5. **Depreciation**: The total Depreciation on equipment and vehicles used by the administration department, for the Accounting Period
6. **Telephone**: The total telephone costs of the administration department for the Accounting Period
7. **Profit and Loss**: The total Administration Costs are closed off to the Profit and Loss Account at the end of the Accounting Period.

All Costs that fall under Administration Costs are closed off to the Debit side of the Administrative Cost Account.

DR					SELLING AND DISTRIBUTION COSTS			N11		CR
Date		Details	Fol	Amount		Date	Details	Fol	Amount	
2016 Dec.	31	Salaries and Wages	GJ	60 000	00	2016 Dec. 31	Profit and Loss	GJ	240 000	00
		Advertising	GJ	100 000	00					
		Bad Debts	GJ	5 000	00					
		Fuel	GJ	10 000	00					
		Depreciation	GJ	50 000	00					
		Commission on Sales	GJ	15 000	00					
				240 000	00				240 000	00

1. **Salaries and Wages**: Total Wages and Salaries of the employees who do the selling and distribution tasks for the Accounting Period
2. **Advertising**: The total cost of advertising for the Accounting Period
3. **Bad Debts**: The total bad debts for the Accounting Period
4. **Fuel**: Total cost of fuel for the vehicles used to transport the items to the customers, for the Accounting Period
5. **Depreciation**: The total Depreciation on vehicles used to transport the items to the customers, for the Accounting Period
6. **Commission**: The total commission paid to the sales employees for the Accounting Period
7. **Profit and Loss**: The total Selling and Distribution Costs are closed off to the Profit and Loss Account at the end of the Accounting Period

> **T** Practise past papers to fully understand and master these various Accounts.

D. FINANCIAL STATEMENTS OF A MANUFACTURING BUSINESS

A Manufacturing Business prepares a Production Cost Statement and Short-Format Income Statement with Notes at the end of the Accounting Period.

Other Financial Statements are also prepared. These are the same as for all types of businesses. See pg 86

PRODUCTION COST STATEMENT

The Production Cost Statement shows the total Production Costs to make the items.

MC MANUFACTURERS
Production Cost Statement for the year ended 31 December 2016

	Note	Amount
DIRECT MATERIALS COST Total of all the Direct Materials Costs; see Note 1 for details.	1	400 000
DIRECT LABOUR COST Total of all the Direct Labour Costs; see Note 2 for details.	2	200 000
PRIME COST Direct Materials Costs + Direct Labour Costs		**600 000**
FACTORY OVERHEAD COST Total of all the Factory Overhead Costs; see Note 3 for details.	3	360 000
TOTAL COST OF PRODUCTION Prime Cost + Factory Overhead Cost		**960 000**
WORK-IN-PROGRESS AT THE BEGINNING OF THE YEAR The costs of all the items that are in the process of being made at the beginning of the Accounting Period (Balance of Work-in-Progress Account at the beginning of the year)		100 000
Total cost of production, including items that are not yet finished Total cost of Production + Work-in-Progress at the beginning of the year		**1 060 000**
LESS: WORK-IN-PROGRESS AT THE END OF THE YEAR Shows the costs of all the items that are still in the process of being made at the end of the Accounting Period (Balance of the Work-in-Progress Account at the end of the year)		(300 000)
PRODUCTION COST OF FINISHED GOODS Production Costs of all the finished items made during the Accounting Period Total cost of Production + Work-in-Progress at the beginning of the period – Work-in-Progress at the end of the period		**760 000**

See Notes to the Production Cost Statement on the next page.

MC MANUFACTURERS
Notes to the Production Cost Statement for the year ended 31 December 2016

1. DIRECT (RAW) MATERIALS COSTS

	Amount
Balance at beginning of year Total Direct Materials available at the beginning of the Accounting Period (Balance of the Direct Materials Account on the first day of the Accounting Period)	50 000
Purchases Total costs of Direct Materials purchased during the Accounting Period **Cash + Credit – Returns**	400 000
Carriage on Purchases Total cost of Carriage on Purchases, for Direct Materials purchased during the Accounting Period	30 000
Customs Duties Total cost of Customs Duties, for Direct Materials purchased during the Accounting Period	20 000
Balance at beginning of year + Purchases + Carriage on Purchases + Customs Duties	500 000
Less: Balance at end of year Subtract the value of all the Direct Materials left at the end of the Accounting Period (Balance of the Direct Materials Account on the last day of the Accounting Period)	(100 000)
Direct (Raw) Materials Costs Total Direct (Raw) Materials Costs	**400 000**

2. DIRECT LABOUR COSTS

	Amount
Direct Wages Total cost of Direct Labour for the Accounting Period	170 000
UIF Contribution Total cost of UIF Contributions for Direct Labour for the Accounting Period	1 700
Medical Aid Contribution Total cost of Medical Aid Contributions for Direct Labour for the Accounting Period	17 000
Pension Fund Contribution Total cost of Pension Fund Contributions for Direct Labour for the Accounting Period	11 300
Direct Labour Costs Total Direct Labour Costs	**200 000**

3. FACTORY OVERHEAD COSTS

	Amount
Factory Indirect Labour Total cost of Indirect Labour for the Accounting Period **Wages + Contributions**	100 000
Factory Indirect Materials Total cost of Indirect Materials for the Accounting Period **Opening Stock + Purchases – Closing Stock**	50 000
Factory Rent Total cost of factory rent for the Accounting Period	120 000
Depreciation on Factory Equipment Total Depreciation on factory equipment for the Accounting Period	30 000
Maintenance on Factory Equipment Total Maintenance Cost on factory equipment for the Accounting Period	5 000
Factory Water and Electricity Total cost of factory water and electricity for the Accounting Period	55 000
Other Indirect Costs List the names of any other Indirect Costs and their amounts; e.g. Insurance	–
Factory Overhead Costs Total Factory Overhead Costs	**360 000**

SHORT-FORMAT INCOME STATEMENT WITH NOTES   See pg 89 for the Income Statement of a Trading Business.

The Short-Format Income Statement is a shortened version of the Income Statement.

MC MANUFACTURERS
Income Statement for the year ended 31 December 2016
Remember that Notes 1–3 are found on the Production Cost Statement.

	Note	Amount
Sales Total of all the Sales for the Accounting Period Sales – Returns		1 200 000
Less: Cost of Sales Total of all costs of the items sold for the Accounting Period Opening Stock: Finished Goods + Work-In-Progress – Closing Stock: Finished Goods		(600 000)
Gross Profit Sales – Cost of Sales		600 000
Selling and Distribution Costs Total of all the Selling and Distribution Costs for the Accounting Period; see Note 4 for details	4	(240 000)
Administration Costs Total of all the Administration Costs for the Accounting Period; see Note 5 for details	5	(300 000)
Net Profit or Loss Gross Profit – Selling and Distribution Costs – Administration Costs		60 000

MC MANUFACTURERS
Notes to the Short Format Income Statement for the year ended 31 December 2016

4. SELLING AND DISTRIBUTION COSTS	Amount
Commission on Sales Commission paid to all sales employees for the Accounting Period	15 000
Advertising Total Advertising Expenses for the Accounting Period	100 000
Bad Debts Total Bad Debts	5 000
Fuel Total fuel costs for the vehicles used to deliver items	10 000
Salaries Salaries of the sales and distribution workers for the Accounting Period	60 000
Depreciation on Vehicles Depreciation on the vehicles used by the sales and transport workers for the Accounting Period	50 000
Total Selling and Distribution Costs	240 000

5. ADMINISTRATION COSTS	Amount
Office Salaries and Wages (including Contributions to Pension Fund, Medical Aid Fund and UIF) Total Salaries and Wages for all the workers who work in the administration division	160 000
Depreciation on Office Equipment Depreciation on the equipment used in the office by the administration employees	20 000
Office Rent Rent Expenses of the office for the Accounting Period	70 000
Water and Electricity Water and Electricity Expenses of the office for the Accounting Period	40 000
Stationery Stationery Expenses of the administration department for the Accounting Period	5 000
Telephone Telephone Expenses of the office for the Accounting Period	5 000
Total Administration Costs	300 000

GLOSSARY
IMPORTANT ACCOUNTING TERMS

TERM	EXPLANATION
Accounting Cycle	The Accounting Cycle is a representation of the different steps that a bookkeeper follows to record all the financial information of a business during the Accounting Period. Pg 20
Accounting Equation	The Accounting Equation shows the relationship between Assets, Liabilities and Owner's Equity. Pg 11
Accounting Period	The Accounting Period is the name given to the time period from when the Accounting Cycle starts to when it ends.
Accrued Expenses	Accrued Expenses are Expenses that have occurred but that have not yet been paid for by the business. Pg 127
Accrued Income	Accrued Income is Income that has been earned by the business but that has not yet been paid for by the customer. Pg 126
Adjustments	Adjustments are recorded at the end of the Accounting Period to correct any mistakes and to update Account balances. Pg 122
Administration Costs	Administration Costs are the costs to complete the administrative tasks of the business. Pg 238
Adverse Audit Opinion	An Adverse Opinion means that the Auditors find that the Financial Statements are not accurate. The Financial Statements do not fairly present the Financial Performance and Financial Position of the Company. Pg 214
Age of a Fixed Asset	The age of a Fixed Asset refers to how long the business has had the Fixed Asset. Pg 173
Analysis Cash Book	A Non-Profit Company uses an Analysis Cash Book to record all cash transactions.
Assets	Asset Accounts show items that have value and are owned by the business. Pg 9
Audit Evidence	Audit Evidence refers to the different information that is collected during an Internal or External Audit.
Authorised Shares	Authorised Shares are the maximum number of Shares that a Company can issue. Pg 205
Bad Debts	Bad Debts are the amounts written off that a business does not expect to receive from a Debtor. Pg 125
Balance Sheet Section	The Balance Sheet Section is the section in the General Ledger that shows the Balance Sheet Accounts (Asset, Liability and Owner's Equity Accounts).
Balance Sheet Statement	The Balance Sheet Statement is a statement that shows the Assets, Liabilities and Owner's Equity of a business. Pg 91
Bookkeeping	Bookkeeping is the process of recording the financial information of a business.
Break-Even Analysis	Break-Even Analysis helps a business to decide how much to sell an item for, or how many items to sell at a certain price, in order to make a Profit. Pg 241
Budget	A budget is a financial plan for the future. Pg 226
Capital	Capital is the amount that an Owner contributes to the business.
Carriage on Purchases	Carriage on Purchases refers to the additional costs to transport Inventory to the business.
Cash	Cash includes physical cash (notes and coins) as well as the money in a bank account.
Cash Budget	A Cash Budget shows the expected cash changes of a business for a specific period. Pg 228
Cash Flow Statement	A Cash Flow Statement shows the cash inflows and outflows of a business. Pg 101
Cash Payments Journal (CPJ)	The CPJ is used to record all transactions where cash is paid. Pg 34
Cash Receipts Journal (CRJ)	The CRJ is used to record all transactions where cash is received. Pg 32
Chief Audit Executive	The Chief Audit Executive (CAE) is the most senior person in the Internal Audit Team.

Closed Corporation	A Closed Corporation (CC) is the recommended form of ownership for a small business that wants Limited Liability without the additional requirements of a Company. Pg 200
Code of Ethics	A Code of Ethics is a set of rules that explains what behaviour is generally accepted as right or wrong. Pg 217
Company	A Company is a legal business entity separate from its Owners. Pg 203
Compliance Tests	Compliance tests determine whether the current Internal Controls in place are effective.
Consumables Stores on Hand	Consumable Stores on Hand includes the cost of Stationery, Packing Material and Consumable Stores purchased, which have not been used by the end of the Accounting Period.
Continuity	Continuity refers to a business that will continue to exist even after an Owner dies.
Contributions	Contributions are amounts that a business pays to an organisation or fund on behalf of an employee. Pg 47
Cost Accounting	Cost Accounting includes capturing costs, organising costs and reporting costs. Pg 235
Cost Price	The Cost Price is the total cost of an item that a business wants to sell. Pg 155
Credit side	The Credit side is the right hand side of an Account. Pg 12
Creditors	Creditors is the name given to the people and organisations that the business owes cash to, for purchasing items or services on credit.
Creditors Allowances Journal (CAJ)	The CAJ is used to record all transactions where: • The business returns an Asset that was purchased on credit • The business receives a discount on the amount owed to a Creditor Pg 44
Creditors Collection Schedule	The Creditors Collection Schedule is used to forecast how much the business expects to pay its Creditors during the budgeted period. Pg 229
Creditors Journal (CJ)	The CJ is used to record transactions where the business makes Purchases on credit. Pg 40
Debit side	The Debit side is the left hand side of an Account. Pg 12
Debtors	Debtors is the name given to the people and organisations that owe the business cash, for Inventory purchased on credit from the business.
Debtors Allowances Journal (DAJ)	The DAJ is used to record all transactions where: • Inventory, sold on credit, is returned to the business • The business gives a Debtor a discount on the amount owed Pg 42
Debtors Collection Schedule	The Debtors Collection Schedule is used to forecast how much cash the business expects to collect from its Debtors during the budgeted period. Pg 229
Debtors Journal (DJ)	The DJ is used to record all transactions where Inventory is sold on credit. Pg 38
Deductions	Deductions are the amounts deducted from the Gross Salary of an employee. Pg 46
Depreciation	Depreciation is the loss in the value of a Fixed Asset over time. Pg 168
Detective Controls	Detective Controls find and report unwanted events. Pg 222
Direct Labour Costs	Direct Labour Costs are the costs for employing the workers who make items. Pg 237
Direct Materials Costs	Direct Materials Costs are the costs for purchasing the raw materials that are used directly to make items. Pg 237
Disclaimer	A Disclaimer means that the Auditors are not able to provide an opinion. This occurs when the Auditors are not independent, or when they do not have enough information to form an opinion. Pg 214
Dividends	Dividends are the amounts distributed to Shareholders. Pg 206
Double-Entry Bookkeeping System	The Double-Entry Bookkeeping System is used by bookkeepers to record financial information. Pg 12
Drawings	Drawings are the amounts that an Owner takes out of the business.

Electronic Fund Transfer (EFT)	When cash is transferred (paid) from one bank account to another bank account online, it is known as an EFT.
Ethics	Ethics is about understanding what is right or wrong. Pg 216
Expense	Expense Accounts show the costs of running the business. Pg 9
Factory Overhead Costs	Factory Overhead Costs are the costs that are not directly linked to the items that are made. Pg 237
Final Accounts	Final Accounts are prepared to determine the Profit or Loss for the Accounting Period. Pg 129
Financial Accounting	The aim of Financial Accounting is to prepare Financial Statements to accurately summarise the financial information of a business. Pg 5
Financial Indicators	Financial Indicators are used to interpret Financial Statements. Pg 106
Financial Statements	Financial Statements summarise all the important financial information of a business. Pg 86
First In First Out (FIFO) Method	The FIFO Method is based on the assumption that the Inventory that the business purchases first is the Inventory that is sold first. Pg 164
Fixed Asset Register	The Fixed Asset Register is a document that shows the details of all Fixed Assets owned by the business. Pg 173
Fixed Assets	Fixed Assets are purchased for long-term use (e.g. vehicles and furniture). They are used in the day-to-day operations of a business. Pg 166
Fixed Costs	Fixed Costs stay the same even when the number of items made changes. Pg 239
Folio Reference	A Folio Reference is a unique code used to refer to something easily in the books of a business. The different Journals, Accounts, Creditors and Debtors are each assigned a Folio Reference. Pg 57
For-Profit Businesses	A For-Profit Business aims to make a Profit. Pg 6
Founding Statement	A Founding Statement is the document that is completed to register a CC. Pg 201
General Journal	All transactions that cannot be recorded in one of the Subsidiary Journals are recorded in the General Journal. Pg 53
General Ledger	The General Ledger is used to record all the effects of the financial activities of a business using Asset, Liability, Owner's Equity, Income and Expense Accounts. Pg 56
Generally Accepted Accounting Principles (GAAP)	GAAP refers to the Accounting Standards used in the United States of America. Pg 152
Gross Salary	The Gross Salary is the Salary of an employee before deductions. Pg 46
IFRS (International Financial Reporting Standards)	IFRS refers to the most common Accounting Standards used across the world. Pg 152
Income	Income Accounts show the amounts the business earns. Pg 9
Income Received in Advance	Income Received in Advance is the amount of cash that has been received by the business for Income that has not yet been earned. Pg 127
Income Statement	The Income Statement shows all the Income and Expenses of a business. Pg 88
Income Tax	Income Tax is the amount of Tax paid by a person or a business. Pg 207
Incremental budgeting	Incremental budgeting is when the business uses past results to prepare the budget. Pg 227
Indirect Labour Costs	Indirect Labour Costs are the costs for employing the workers who are not directly involved in making items. Pg 237
Indirect Materials Costs	Indirect Materials Costs are the costs for purchasing the raw materials that are not used directly to make items. Pg 237
Internal Auditor	An Internal Auditor reviews the Internal Control Elements, Risk Management and Governance of a business and provides recommendations on how they can be improved. Pg 224
Internal Control Environment	Internal Control Environment refers to the attitude of a business towards Internal Control. Pg 222
Inventory	Inventory is the name given to items that are sold by a business. Pg 154

Issue Price	The Issue Price is the price at which Shares are issued (sold). Pg 205
Issued Shares	The Issued Shares are the number of Shares that a Company has issued (sold). Pg 205
Journal	Journals are used to record transactions in a standardised format. They are the books of first entry. Pg 30
Liability	A Liability is an amount owed by the business to someone else.
King Report	The King Report on Governance is a document that sets out policies and principles on Corporate Governance. Pg 219
Legal Entity	A Legal Entity is a person or business that has the right to enter into contracts with other legal entities.
Liability Account	Liability Accounts show amounts the business must pay. Pg 9
Lifespan of a Fixed Asset	The lifespan of a Fixed Asset refers to how long the business expects to keep the Asset.
Managerial Accounting	The aim of Managerial Accounting is to provide useful information that helps a business to plan and make decisions. Pg 5
Manufacturing Business	A Manufacturing Business produces and sells products. Pg 6
Medical Aid Fund	A Medical Aid Fund is a fund that a person can set up to cover medical costs.
Net Realisable Value	The Net Realisable Value of an Asset is the amount that a business would receive if it were to sell the Asset, minus the costs incurred to sell the Asset. Pg 174
Net Salary	Net Salary is the Salary received by an employee after deductions. Pg 47
Net Wage	Net Wage is the Wage received by an employee after deductions. Pg 47
Nominal Accounts Section	The Nominal Section is the section in the General Ledger that shows the Nominal Accounts (Expense and Income Accounts). Pg 57
Non-Profit Company	Non-Profit Companies are businesses formed to benefit society. Pg 190
Owner's Equity	Owner's Equity Accounts show the value of the Assets that belong to the Owner(s) of the business. Pg 9
Partnership	A Partnership is a business formed by two to ten people, who are called Partners. Pg 182
Partnership Agreement	A Partnership Agreement is a document that shows the details of a Partnership. Pg 183
Pension Fund	A Pension Fund is a fund that a person can set up, to save money for when he or she retires.
Period Costs	Period Costs are the costs incurred that are not directly linked to the making of items. Pg 238
Periodic Stock System	When using the Periodic Stock System, the cost of Inventory available to sell and the cost of Inventory sold are only determined at the end of the Accounting Period. Pg 158
Perpetual Inventory System	When using the Perpetual Inventory System, the Trading Stock Account is continuously updated to show the changes in the cost of Inventory available. The Cost of Sales Account is continuously updated to show the cost of Inventory sold. Pg 156
Petty Cash	Petty Cash is the amount of physical cash (coins and notes) kept by the business on the premises. Pg 36
Petty Cash Journal (PCJ)	The PCJ is used to record all transactions where Petty Cash is used by the business to make payments. Pg 36
Post-Adjustment Trial Balance	A Post-Adjustment Trial Balance is prepared after adjusting entries have been made. Pg 85
Post-Closing Trial Balance	A Post-Closing Trial Balance is prepared after closing entries have been made. Pg 85
Pre-Adjustment Trial Balance	A Pre-Adjustment Trial Balance is prepared at the end of the month, before adjusting entries have been made. Pg 85
Prepaid Expenses	Prepaid Expenses are Expenses that have not occurred during the Accounting Period but that have already been paid by the business. Pg 128
Preventative Controls	Preventative Controls prevent unwanted events from happening. Pg 222

Prime Costs	Prime Costs are costs that are directly linked to an item that is made. **Pg 237**
Production Cost Statement	The Production Cost Statement shows the total Production Costs used to make items. **Pg 254**
Production Costs	Production Costs are the costs involved in making the items that a Manufacturing Business sells. **Pg 237**
Professional Body	A Professional Body is an organisation that is associated with a specific profession. **Pg 218**
Projected Income Statement	A Projected Income Statement shows the expected Profit of a business for a specific period. **Pg 232**
Qualified Audit Opinion	A Qualified Audit Opinion means that the Auditors find that the Financial Statements are mostly accurate, with a few issues. The Auditors will list the issues that were found. **Pg 214**
Reconciliations	Reconciliation is the process of finding the differences between two financial Accounts, and correcting these differences so that the records agree with each other. **Pg 135**
Replacement Rate	The replacement rate of an Asset is what it would cost the business to replace the current Asset with a new, similar Asset. **Pg 174**
Reversals	Reversals are recorded to prepare the Accounts for the next Accounting Period. **Pg 132**
Risk Assessment	A Risk Assessment identifies risks and their effects on the business. **Pg 222**
Salaries Journal (SJ)	The Salaries Journal is used to record the Salaries of employees. **Pg 46**
Sales	Sales is the total amount received from selling Inventory. **Pg 155**
Selling and Distribution Costs	Selling and Distribution Costs are the costs for selling and transporting items to customers. **Pg 238**
Selling Price	The Selling Price is the price of an item sold by a business. **Pg 155**
Service Business	A Service Business provides a service for a fee. **Pg 6**
Shareholders	The Owners of a Company are known as Shareholders. **Pg 205**
Skills Development Levy (SDL)	A Skills Development Levy is a fund that has been set up by the government to develop and improve the skills of employees.
Sole Trader	A Sole Trader is a business with one Owner. **Pg 7**
Source Document	A Source Document is the first document used to record a transaction. **Pg 25**
South African Revenue Services (SARS)	SARS is the government department that collects money from Tax Payers.
Subsidiary Journal	Subsidiary Journals are used to record transactions of the same type. **Pg 31**
Subsidiary Ledger	Subsidiary Ledgers are used to record additional details from specific control Accounts in the General Ledger. **Pg 79**
Substantive Tests	Substantive Tests are used to determine whether financial information is accurate. **Pg 225**
T Accounts	T Accounts are drawn to show that the Double-Entry Principle has been correctly used. Entries on the Debit (left) side of Accounts must be equal to entries on the Credit (right) side of Accounts. **Pg 12**
Temporary Account	A Temporary Account is an Account that is formed at the end of an Accounting Period. The Account is only used to determine the difference between two or more Accounts, after which it is closed.
Trading Business	A Trading Business buys products and then sells them. It is also called a Retail Business. **Pg 6**
Trading Stock	Trading Stock is the name given to the items that a business sells. **Pg 155**
Transaction	A transaction is any event that affects the Financial Position (wealth) of a business.
Trial Balance	A Trial Balance is prepared to show an overview of the Account names and their balances on a specific date. **Pg 83**
Unemployment Insurance Fund (UIF)	UIF is a fund that has been set up by the government to assist unemployed people.
Union Fees	Union Fees are fees paid to registered unions.

Unqualified Audit Opinion	The Auditors find that the Financial Statements are accurate. The Financial Statements fairly present the Financial Performance and Financial Position of the Company. **Pg 214**
Variable Costs	Variable Costs are costs that will change when the number of items made changes. **Pg 239**
Variance Analysis	Variance Analysis is used to analyse and interpret the differences between actual amounts and budgeted amounts. **Pg 233**
Wages Journal (WJ)	The Wages Journal is used to record the Wages of employees. **Pg 46**
Weighted Average Cost (WAC) Method	When using the WAC Method, the cost of the Inventory sold and the cost of the Inventory available for sale is calculated using the average cost of the Inventory. **Pg 164**
Zero-based budgeting	Zero-based budgeting is when the business does not use past results to prepare the budget. **Pg 227**

Add in your own examples here.

NOTES

NOTES

NOTES